THE CLAIMS OF
THE FREE CHURCHES

THE CLAIMS

of the

FREE CHURCHES

By

Henry Townsend

M.A., D.D.

PRINCIPAL, BAPTIST COLLEGE,
MANCHESTER

LONDON

HODDER AND STOUGHTON LIMITED

First printed 1949

274.24
T664

115221

Made and Printed in Great Britain for Hodder & Stoughton, Limited, London
by Wyman & Sons Limited, London, Reading and Fakenham

PREFACE

THIS book is not a History of the Free Churches. There are ten Denominations affiliated with the National Free Church Federal Council, and authentic Histories of these Churches already exist. The present volume is the statement of a Claim. The objective study of history which began in the nineteenth century will, in time, disintegrate many subjective theories which have passed for Church history. The Church is burdened and Christianity misrepresented by traditions which would have been ridiculed out of existence long ago in any other field of knowledge than Theology. This book deals with the rise and growth of Free Church principles as they have affected the religious, political and social structures of the British people. The left wing Puritanism of the sixteenth and seventeenth centuries introduced a new tension into the religious life of this country ; a tension peculiar to England, the tendencies of which were worked out in the eighteenth and nineteenth centuries, not only in Britain, but in America and the British Commonwealth of Nations, and which changed the basis of Western civilisation. Such a contribution to religious and political freedom constitutes a Claim on the gratitude of all English-speaking peoples.

I have not written in any official capacity. As a loyal member of the Free Church Federal Council I hope this book will serve its objectives. It will be clear that I seek the self-government of the Church of Christ ; that all authority in the Church should belong to the whole Church and should derive from Him " who loved the Church and bought her with His own blood ".

My friends, Dr. S. M. Berry and the Right Honourable Ernest Brown, C.H., have read a considerable section of the book and I assure them of my gratitude for their help. I am deeply indebted to my colleague, Rev. G. Farr, M.A., B.D., who has read the proofs and made valuable suggestions.

THE BAPTIST COLLEGE,
MANCHESTER.   Hy. Townsend.

CONTENTS

7

CONTENTS

CONTENTS

DEDICATED

TO

ETHEL

whose love and care have
sustained me and inspired
my service for over forty
years.

" If this is what they want, if they are honest, open, candid, as it is seemly for a man to be when he talks with his God, which therefore everyone is if he respects himself and does not so deeply despise himself that he would be insincere in the face of God—well then, if we honestly, candidly, frankly, completely admit to God how it really stands with us men, that the human race in the course of time has taken the liberty of softening and softening Christianity until at last we have contrived to make it exactly the opposite of what it is in the New Testament—and that now, if the thing is possible, we should be so much pleased if this might be Christianity.

" But one thing I will not do, not for anything in the world : I will not, though it were merely with the last quarter of the last joint of my little finger, I will not take part in what is known as official Christianity, which by suppression and by artifice gives the impression of being the Christianity of the New Testament ; and upon my knees I thank my God that He has compassionately prevented me from becoming too far embroiled in it ".

KIERKEGAARD,
Attack on Christendom, p. 39.

INTRODUCTION

RELIGION is the grand experience of the human race : it always has been, it always will be, by reason of its heights and depths and vastness. During a period of over two thousand years we read in the Old Testament of men who were learning " to do justly, and to love mercy, and to walk humbly " with God. But the New Testament surpasses every other book as it relates the dynamic quality of spiritual experience of which Jesus Christ was the source. Men looked into the face of Jesus and saw the fullness of the Grace and the Truth of God. Grace is a New Testament word which too rarely finds a place in modern preaching : it means the unmerited loving-kindness of God who is ever taking the initiative towards men through Christ : and truth in the teaching and activity of Jesus was as unique as grace. To-day, the Church as an Institution, and the priesthood as an official body, are often regarded as controlling grace and defining truth. The New Testament affirms that Jesus was the Gospel, and preached the Gospel, and created the Church ; but we find in later periods that the Church has smothered and even rejected the ideas which gave it birth. We claim, however, that New Testament ideas of God, of Christ and His Grace and Truth, are still normative, final and dynamic for Christian experience. When the Church as the Body of Christ has been loyal to these New Testament ideas she has been creative in her intellectual, spiritual and ethical achievements.

There is deep anguish concerning the condition of the Church in the present world, but there is also strange complacency. There seems little awareness of the tensions within, or underlying the religious situation, or of the exact nature of the tension. I believe it is the kind of tension which runs through much of the history of the Old Testament and through the whole of the New Testament. I cannot deal adequately with the subject of this book and ignore the tensions of Biblical religion, or soft-pedal the religious controversies of the sixteenth to the twentieth centuries in Britain. Recent tendencies in Old Testament

15

scholarship have sought to reconcile the antagonism of priest and prophet within the scope of the covenant relation of God and His people; but the two types of religious experience remain, one priestly and institutional, the other personal and ethical. We cannot lightly dismiss Jeremiah's denial of any divine authority for the sacrificial system after the Exodus: Jer. 7, 22f.

It is, however, the tension of ideas and forces in the New Testament which are chiefly relevant for the purpose of this book. It is possible to read the New Testament and never see the battle-ground over which our Lord fought to the day of the crucifixion. Anglo-Catholic writers think the Church of God began with Abraham: and they link the people of God in the Old Testament with the New Israel in the New Testament, working out un-critically a divine plan which is too rigid and which curiously misses the travail of the ministry of Jesus. Such a view regards God as an Institutionalist who is always concerned with decency and order after the Anglo-Catholic pattern. But what decency was there in the unscrupulous fight of the Jewish Church for its own privileges; or, for that matter, what decency was there in the crucifixion? On the other hand, there are Evangelical Christians who accept a plan of Salvation in the Scriptures, cul-minating in the cross and the resurrection of our Lord, and do not see that the travail of Christ began early in His ministry and continued until the day on the cross when He cried, "It is finished".

The tension in the Gospels is startling. We do not read far before we find Jesus involved in controversy concerning Him-self, His teaching, and His claims. The antagonism between Jesus and His enemies grows deeper as the narrative proceeds. It is vital to any understanding of Jesus and the nature of Christian-ity, to remember that His enemies were the Scribes and Pharisees and priests of the Jewish Church. The Gospel of John is most explicit on this matter; it resolves the controversy into one between Jesus and the Jews, not simply the Jewish leaders. The Fourth Gospel relates long arguments between Jesus and the people—"the Jews said unto Him", "the Jews took up stones to stone Him". Thus the battle was arrayed. No quarter was given. No compromise was attempted. There was a difference of spirit in Jesus as compared with His enemies. He loved His enemies to the end; His enemies hated Him so bitterly, they never rested until they had compassed His death. What lay at the root of this conflict? When He came, why did His own not receive Him?

Jesus revealed a new idea of God and man and their relationship, and the Jews refused to believe Him. And since Jesus was neither docile nor submissive, He pointed out the errors of Judaism and even denounced it as a barrier between God and the human race; it represented God as afar off and alone, dwelling in holiness, unapproachable except through the mediation of the Jewish Church and Law and Priesthood; it was a hard and nationalistic religion, a system which laid burdens upon men such as they could not bear. Judaism worked with a theory of merit which was as scientific as a system could be which dealt with human action. The claim to regulate the approach of God to man, or man to God, was as exclusive as the claim of Romanism in the day of Luther, or at the present time. We are not disputing that there were Jewish saints in our Lord's day. We are drawing attention to the highly organised and official system, based on Tradition, which gave to men a totally mistaken idea of God.

Jesus came preaching the grace of God, the fullness and freedom of God's love to the whole race; He said God was ever taking the initiative towards publicans and sinners, Greeks, Romans and barbarians, because He loved them and yearned to redeem them. As Jesus went amongst the social derelicts of His own race, He made it clear that He was saying and doing the will of His Father. Jesus was the grace of God in speech and action. He made the most uncompromising and absolute claims for Himself; that He had come from God and knew God as no other did; that He had authority to forgive sins; authority over such Jewish institutions as the Sabbath and the Temple; that the destiny of men would finally be decided by relation to Himself. It was a new gospel, a religion of grace instead of merit. For God was no angry Deity, far from sinful men, only relenting His wrath when placated by blood and sacrifice; He was the Father, ever appealing, ever seeking, ever receiving sinners.

Jesus knew early in His ministry that He must reckon with the organised hatred of the Scribes and Pharisees and priests. He knew too well how His gospel of grace would challenge the national and religious exclusiveness of the Jews. Still, He appealed to the lost sheep of the House of Israel. He loved His own people. He wept over the ancient city; but He never thought of asking, " How can I water down the gospel until I find common ground with Jewish Tradition ? " He never asked, " How far can I accommodate the freedom and the fullness of the grace of God to this system of religious merits ? " When He found Himself involved in controversy He held on to the gospel.

The battle opens in the second chapter of Mark. Jesus forgave the sins of the paralytic, and the argument is there for us to read. His opponents debated His claim to forgive sins and accused Him of blasphemy. And unless Jesus did what He claimed to do He was a blasphemer. Either Jesus was right or the Pharisees were right. The Scribes knew at once that if Jesus won on such an issue their priestly and traditional system was doomed. They were alert enough, but the lesson to note is that Jesus refused to negotiate with them ; the reality of the forgiveness of God through Himself was not an open question. On this fact He was uncompromising, nor did it enter His mind to suggest any scheme of union between the gospel and religious legalism.

The situation soon became more serious, for in the third chapter of Mark we read, " the Pharisees went out, and straightway with the Herodians took counsel against Him how they might destroy Him ". The more Jesus taught and the more work He did, the clearer the issue became. The Jewish leaders were awake and determined ; Jesus was awake and gracious. It was to be a fight to a finish. Legalism or grace, sacerdotalism or the gospel ; priestism or personal religion. The controversy continued, until Jesus stood before Pilate, and until they nailed Him to the cross. In one sense we can say that Jesus died on the cross rather than surrender the gospel to tradition, or rather than come to terms with a religious legalism. I am not saying that this explanation exhausts the significance of the cross. I am right, however, in saying that this long, drawn-out battle, recorded in the New Testament, led Christ to Calvary.

What is the significance of this conflict between Jesus and Judaism ? If Judaism was the type of religion well-pleasing to

God, why did Jesus fight to the end for the gospel? Either this struggle of Jesus for the gospel has absolute and decisive value or it means nothing. In other words, did Jesus fight for the gospel and die for it, that His followers might perpetuate the Jewish idea of God, aloof and angry, always needing the mediation of priests, and condoning a system of merits to win His favour? For this is exactly what has happened.

Free Church principles are rooted and grounded in the crisis of New Testament Christianity. If I appear to deal harshly with Institutional Religion it will be that I must present the facts which alone explain the existence and witness of the Free Churches: there is no harshness in my mind nor in my heart. I do not need reminding that good men are serving conscientiously in Institutional Churches. I am deeply conscious, however, for such men, as for myself, sincerity is not enough. Paul was sincere as a Judaist persecutor of the Church: but such sincerity was washed of all its unworthiness on the road to Damascus. May I say that I stand in awe before the majesty of the revelation of the Church of God in the New Testament, as I know good men in the Institutional Churches also do.

CHAPTER I

THE NATURE OF THE CHURCH

IT is usual to contrast the Free Churches of Britain with the State Church and to assume that the attitude toward the State, or to some measure of State control, is the main difference between them. The subject of Church and State in British Christianity has been a critical and divisive issue for over three hundred years. In no other country has the controversy been so long, or so violent, or so creative of spiritual and political progress in the modern world. There was conflict, continuing for centuries, between Pope and Emperor : but it was a struggle to obtain the mastery of the Church over the State, or to safe-guard the independence of the State against Papal claims. There were Protestant, Puritan and Free Church movements, prior to, or contemporary with, the Continental Reformation of the sixteenth century, but important as they were, they did not survive to affect history as did the Free Churches of Britain. The relation of the Church and State in Britain will therefore demand our careful attention : it is essential, however, before we can discuss adequately the antagonisms of Church and State in British history, that we must point out why there was any antagonism at all. Why did such tensions exist ? The answer is that they arose out of different, and what were regarded as irreconcilable, convictions of the Nature of the Church of Christ.

The controversy was many sided, but in the past, when the Churches were involved in political and military conflict, or in the present, when there is a kindlier atmosphere and a new approach toward co-operation or re-union, the Nature of the Church was, and still is, the major stumbling-block. It is, then, of the first importance, that all concerned should under-stand, whether theologians, ecclesiastical statesmen, or the laity of the churches, that the Nature of the Church is the issue upon which all Christians should seek to reach a measure of agreement. It was on this issue that the Church in Britain became divided : it is here that the Churches must find reconciliation and rediscover their unity. Religious sentimentalists in all the Churches fail to understand, that while kindly disposition toward each other is praiseworthy, the ancient divisions of the Church in this land are not going to be healed by emotional platitudes across the fences. The New Testament is written, and we must reckon with its High Churchmanship, rooted as it was in the experience of men, to whom the authority of Christ in His Church was absolute. If this generation of Christian people will set the Nature of the Church first in the order of enquiry, it will be easier to approach such questions as the Ministry and the Sacraments as functions within the whole Church.

I.   ANGLICAN DOCTRINE

The procedure of Elizabeth in effecting " the religious settlement " of the sixteenth century is not in dispute : but no one can possibly defend it as procedure guided by New Testament ideas or studies. Yet the political and religious confusions of the sixteenth century continue to give direction to Anglican statements on the nature of the Church. It will never be possible to agree concerning the true doctrine of the Church until we are all ready to acknowledge the final authority of Scripture. Since " the settlement " by Elizabeth, the ground of authority in religion and politics has shifted. Surely, in these days of biblical and theological study, both the sources of Christian doctrine and the nature of all authority in the Church are to be found in the New Testament and nowhere else. Selecting proof texts from the Old Testament and subjecting them to Rabbinical exegesis cannot be authoritative for modern scholarship.[1]

I cannot refer in detail to the Formularies and Articles of the Anglican Church. But the Commission appointed by the Archbishops in 1922 to consider the nature and grounds of Christian Doctrine in the Church of England, and its Report

[1] Cf. T. W. Manson, *The Church's Ministry*, p. 14.

which was published in 1938, can be regarded as our guide. The nature of the Church is approached through the Old Testament conception of Israel as the people of God : concession is made to the Anglo-Catholic view that the Church begins with Abraham and is continuous with the history of Israel in the Old Testament : other members of the Commission regarded the Church of the New Testament as a new community, constituted by the " new covenant " through the blood of Christ.

In 1886, when the Anglican bishops in America were consulted by other religious leaders on the conditions of re-union, they replied by what is known as the Lambeth Quadrilateral. The Report of the Commission re-affirms the answer of the American bishops : " For the maintenance of the Church's own essential nature as the fellowship of those who have received the Gospel and are called to bear witness to it before those who have not received it, the Church has four institutional safeguards of its own continuity in the activity of that fellowship and of that witness. These are the Scriptures, the Creeds, the Sacraments, and the Ministry ".[1] Of these four safeguards of the Church's continuity, we must examine with care the nature of the Ministry : " The Church on the Day of Pentecost is set before us in the Book of the Acts of the Apostles as a body of believers having within it, as its recognised focus of unity and organ of authority, the Apostolate, which owed its origin to the action of the Lord Himself. . . . The commission to exercise Ministry is bestowed through those who already hold it, but it comes from the Risen, Reigning and Present Lord Himself ". It is here claimed that the New Testament bears witness to the principle of a distinctive ministry as an original and essential element in the Church : and it is further claimed that the Ministry of the Anglican Church is in the succession of the original Apostolate. The Episcopate is the organ essential for the unity and continuity of the Church. It is " pointed out that the Apostles governed the early Christian community as having a commission from the Lord, and that their pastoral authority was not derived from election by the flock, but was inherent in the office to which they were called by Christ. The ministers of the Church in all later generations have possessed a pastoral authority as themselves holding commission from the Lord in

[1] *Christian Doctrine in the Church of England*, p. 112 ff.

succession to the Apostles and the status of ministers in this succession has been guaranteed from one generation to another by a continuously transmitted commission : consequently to preserve continuity in this respect is at all times of great importance ".[1] Whether the Episcopate takes the monarchial form or " may conceivably be changed to a collegiate episcopate " does not affect its authority to bestow grace : " the transition should be effected by the bestowal of commission through those who have received commission to bestow it. We do not doubt that God has accepted and used other Ministries which through breach of continuity in the past are deficient in outward authorisation ; but we are convinced that the Anglican Communion has been right to regard the historic Episcopate as in a special sense the organ of unity and continuity ". Bishop Kirk says that by such transition the ordained man is " ushered into a special and distinctive sphere of grace, possessed of spiritual gifts and powers as well as the right to dispense them to others ; and in no other way could he enter that sphere ".[2] Thus, apostolic succession is by " tactual transmission of grace ". Further, the touch of the bishop on the head of the person for confirmation, his touch of the bread of the sacrament, ushers " the recipient in exactly the same way as in the case of ordination, into a special and distinctive sphere of grace ". Further, such transmission has an " indelible character " and " means in practice that ordination to any grade of the Ministry is a rite which cannot be repeated ; a man who has been ordained has once and for all received the commission whether he exercise it or not ". This means that neither immorality nor apostasy can cancel out the grace which an ordained man has received by the " tactual transmission " of the bishop. To receive the sacrament at the hand of " a corrupt or debased ministry " does not nullify grace.[3]

The Anglican doctrine of the Church can only be understood in relation to this " Essential Ministry ". The Ministry and the Church are inter-dependent. Without the bishop there can be no church : he is the guardian of the Faith and Order of the

[1] p. 120 f.

[2] *The Apostolic Ministry*, p. 15.

[3] Ibid., p. 25. Cf. Manson on the idea of the Remnant and the Ministry, pp. 24, 32 ; also the light thrown on the Ministry of the New Testament from Missionary leadership, p. 33 f.

Church. Non-episcopal ministries may be blessed, but the Anglican priest alone can say to the penitent sinner : " By His authority committed unto me I absolve thee from all thy sins ". These claims to canalise the grace of God are deterministic, rigid, legalistic and hark back to the days of decadent Judaism. The Pharisees worked with a theory of grace which was as exclusive as the claims of Bishop Kirk : they were sure that they controlled the transmission of grace to men. When Jesus forgave the sins of the paralytic they accused Him of blasphemy. Bishop Kirk's contribution to the book on The Aposolic Ministry covers over fifty pages : but his treatment of Scripture is too uncritical and arbitrary ; if the New Testament had been examined as minutely as the Church Fathers, much of his contribution must have been modified. " There is one ' essential ' ministry, the only ministry that is unchallengeably essential. That is the ministry which the Lord Jesus Christ opened in Galilee . . . which He continues to this day in and through the Church, which is His body ".[1]

The Commission found evidence in the New Testament itself which was difficult to reconcile with its rigid views of the Episcopate. For the Apostle Paul was not one of the Twelve, nor can he be fitted into the episcopal theory. When Father Frere was Superior of the Mirfield community and came to address the clergy and ministers of Huddersfield, he was questioned on this matter ; he replied that Paul was an exception. Canon Lacey thinks " it was a dangerous exception ". The Commission says " Paul was called to the Apostolate by a special revelation ". Again, James, the brother of the Lord, who presided over the Church in Jerusalem, was not one of the Twelve. Nor does the position of Barnabas fit easily into a clear-cut scheme. But there is more to the argument than the above statements. I shall deal shortly with the Free Church doctrine of the Church and the Ministry. Here I may suggest that every call of God to the ministry is a special revelation, for the reason that every man's personal relation to God is a special relation. Bishop Kirk does not seem aware that God still calls His Ministers. He thinks non-episcopal ministries are somehow called into existence by the Church, " wholly and exclusively dependent on the Church ". I do not dispute the function of

[1] Manson, p. 21.

the Church in the authorisation of its ministry, for the Free Churches understand their responsibility in this matter. I plead for the recognition of the fact in Scripture that the minister is called by God, and is primarily responsible to God for the fulfilment of his ministry.

If this fact is rejected as " individualist subjectivism " or " godlessness unalloyed ", or " stark individualism ", it is the same stark individualism as the soul's relation to God. Just as no one becomes a Christian by proxy, so no one becomes a minister by proxy. Paul argues in the terms of personal relationship : " He loved *me* and gave Himself for *me* " ; " But the God Who had set me apart from my very birth called me by His grace, and when He chose to reveal His Son to me, that I might preach Him to the Gentiles, instead of consulting with any other human being, instead of going up to Jerusalem to see those who had been apostles before me, I went off at once to Arabia ".[1] The Twelve neither called Paul, nor did they bestow grace upon him for his ministry. It does not seem to have occurred to those who hold the rigid and exclusive views of the Episcopate, that in the Epistle to the Galatians, Paul was resisting an exactly similar claim to that which they make to-day. Paul saw clearly that the attack on his apostolic authority was a blow at the essential nature of the Christian Church ; and he fought the battle to a finish. If his Judaistic enemies had succeeded, they would have reduced Christianity to the level of a Jewish sect ; and would have reduced the Ministry to the level of the Jewish priesthood, with its theory of succession and its exclusive ideas of grace. Paul refuted such religious formalism by the conviction and claim that God had called him.

This hard theory of Apostolic Succession, or the " Essential " Ministry, is a tradition of men. It will be seen as we proceed, how the history of the Episcopate makes havoc of the theory. Not one of the apostles claimed it or taught it. When Peter was rebuked by Paul he never retorted that he had received pre-eminence or authority with which history has invested him. The apostles were humble men, not one of them exalted himself above his brethren. It was their experience, their witness, their message, which concerned them. In the history of the Church

[1] Gal. i, 15.

the Episcopate has disregarded the warning of Jesus, has taken or seized power, and constituted itself into an official caste, and thus ruled the laity. Hebert, in his book, *The Form of the Church*, explains how the tradition took shape : " The Holy Ghost did not desert the Church when the last book of inspired Scripture had been written. He is present continually with the Church, and He is God. Then why should not the whole Catholic system of belief and practice be Divine, *irrespective of any connection with the Jesus of History* ? "[1] To suggest that the history of the Church is the history of the Holy Spirit is an alarming postulate. At the same time Hebert argues that Apostolic Succession derives from Scripture. Any return to Scripture is hopeful, for if Anglo-Catholics will labour at Biblical criticism, textual and historical, and cease to rely on proof texts and allegorical interpretation, there is the possibility of good progress.

There is something of the nature of ecclesiastical magic, or, as Manson says, an " ecclesiological puzzle ", in the use of the notion of the " Essential Ministry ".[2] It is assumed that non-episcopal Churches are illogical, irregular, invalid, and in need of episcopal grace, and the remedy always prescribed is the " essential ordination " ; it is the cure-all : it is the means of restoring the health of the churches and the unity of the broken Body of Christ. But in the history of the Church the heights and depths and vastness of the grace of God in Christ have broken all such ecclesiastical controls. For the Grace of God is a vast unfathomable sea where all our human thoughts and controls are drowned.

" Jesus Christ, Who was so many greater things, was also a poet when he said ' This is my body '. Crass literalism and dogged dogmatism have turned our Poet into a thaumaturgist. . . . Wrong is done by such sacramentalism, not merely to common sense or to science, or even to intellectual honesty, but to the central evangelical thesis—that we are saved not by swallowing consecrated elements, but by the infinite mercy of God our Father revealed to us and bestowed upon us in Jesus Christ ".[3]

[1] p. 15. The italics are mine.
[2] p. 22.
[3] R. Mackintosh : from a letter to the *Manchester Guardian*.

II. FREE CHURCH DOCTRINE

By what approach, and by what methods have Free Church-men arrived at their doctrine of the Nature of the Church? The answer is that they work with all the aids of Biblical criticism, and they follow the historical method of study, convinced that the final authority for the nature of the Church must derive from the Scripture. Neither the Fathers of the Church, nor the rolling stream of tradition, divert Free Church scholars from minute examination of the sources of the New Testament. Any development of doctrine, or organisation, since the close of the New Testament Age, which, of course, there must be, must be tested by New Testament standards. Free Churchmen do not identify, and we reject the claim that the history of the Church, or the history of the Episcopate, is the history of the work of the Holy Spirit.

It is impossible to trace the Confessions, Declarations and Principles of each of the various Free Churches from the sixteenth century onwards concerning the doctrine of the Church. It will suffice if we draw attention to the section of the Constitution of the Free Church Federal Council, which deals with this subject; it is an agreed and therefore an authentic statement.

" We believe that the Catholic or Universal Church is the whole company of the redeemed in heaven and on earth, and we recognise as belonging to this holy fellowship all who are united to God through faith in Christ.

" The Church on earth—which is One through the Apostolic Gospel and through the living union of all its true members with its one Head, even Christ, and which is Holy through the indwelling Holy Spirit Who sanctifies the Body and its members—is ordained to be the visible Body of Christ, to worship God through Him, to promote the fellowship of His people and the ends of His Kingdom, and to go into all the world and proclaim His Gospel for the salvation of men and the brotherhood of all mankind.

Of this visible Church, and every branch thereof, the only Head is the Lord Jesus Christ; and in its faith, order, discipline and duty, it must be free to obey Him alone as it interprets His Holy Will ".

The work of the scholars of the three older " dissenting denominations ", the Presbyterian, Congregational and Baptist Churches, provides a wealth of material from which it would be possible to supplement the above statement. If, however, I refer to Dr. R. Newton Flew's work on *Jesus and His Church*, and indicate his approach, his method and conclusions, it is because Dr. Flew was recently Moderator of the Free Church Federal Council; and because I think his book is as representative of Free Church Doctrine as the work of one scholar can be. As there are ten Free Church denominations in the Federal Council, it will be an advantage to set forth the views of one scholar rather than attempt a synoptic account of the views of many scholars.

Flew does not begin his work by discussing the two occasions when the word " Church " is mentioned in the Gospels, nor by asking the question, " Did Jesus found the Church ? " By the historical method of studying the Gospels he gathers his data, and reaches the conclusion that the teaching and activity of Jesus imply a community, and cannot be understood except in relation to a new kind of community, which Jesus called into existence.

First : Jesus affirmed that God's motive was redemptive and had been revealed in the history of His people Israel. When the nation failed to respond to God the prophets proclaimed that Israel would be saved by the Remnant. Flew refers to Isaiah's study circle of the Remnant (Isa. viii, 16), a new thing in the history of religion. When Jesus began to preach He appealed to the lost sheep of the House of Israel, but when the nation failed to respond there is no doubt that He thought of the disciples whom He had gathered in the terms of the remnant : they were the " little flock ", the nucleus of the new Israel.

Second : The ethical teaching of Jesus assumes and is directed to this nucleus ; it also points forward to the gift of the Spirit. Early in His ministry Jesus " goeth up into the mountain and calleth unto him whom he himself would : and they went unto him. And he appointed twelve, that they might be with him ". " A distinction is made here between an outer and an inner circle of disciples. The Twelve are chosen out of a wider company " (Mark iii, 13 f).[1] It is to this wider company which we must look for the nucleus of the Christian Church. The ethical ideals, the value of personality, the significance of motive as decisive for character, the relations of the disciples to each other and toward the world—this teaching gives a distinctive quality to the new community.

Third : Jesus reveals the meaning of His own Messiahship for the new community. Popular ideas of the Jewish Messiah are directly and indirectly corrected as Jesus states His unique relation with God : He applies to Himself the character and function of the Servant of Isaiah liii. He invests the title Son of Man with original significance, at the same time retaining its eschatological aspect : as Son of Man He has authority on the earth to forgive sins, has authority over such Jewish institutions as the Sabbath : He demands absolute allegiance from His disciples : " When the historical critic has sifted such sayings as these to the uttermost, there remains something strange, startling, irreducible. A new allegiance was entering into the world, disturbing old traditions, transcending the former sweet loyalties of kindred and home, and destined to outlive all other totalitarian claims, whether those of Cæsar in the early centuries, or those of caste and nationality and communism in the twentieth ".[2] This demand for loyalty has its eschatological setting, for whatever His followers suffer they have fellowship with Jesus in this world, and the guarantee of eternal life hereafter. Johnston[3] thinks that in this section on the Messiahship more significance should be given to the necessity of the death of Jesus for the new community. But Flew agrees that it was one of the three decisive moments in the action of Jesus in constituting the Church, when " at the Last Supper He instituted the new covenant with them as representing the new people of God ".

Fourth : The message of Jesus was constitutive of the new

[1] p. 59.
[2] p. 78.
[3] G. Johnston, *Doctrine of the Church in the New Testament*, p. 50.

community and " inevitably marked off those who accepted it from those who did not ". Jesus was the Word of God and revealed the Word as the final authority for the Church. His Gospel was the eternal utterance of God's grace. " The mystery of the kingdom " was revealed to the new community. " If we may look for any one moment wherein the new Israel was constituted, it would be in the act of Jesus at the Last Supper. But even this decisive act should not be regarded in isolation from all that went before and from the Crucifixion, Resurrection, and outflowing of the Spirit that followed after. We may trace various preparatory stages. In His call of the disciples, in His sending them forth to preach, in His acceptance of the confession of Peter and His subsequent unveiling of the ' mystery ' of the suffering Messiah, He had secured a remnant of Israel, entrusted them with a mission and revealed the purpose of God. But hitherto He had not ceased, in the face of repeated rejections, to appeal to Israel as a whole. The last appeal had been made and refused. He turns to His friends ".[1]

Fifth : The mission of the new community is clearly stated in the Gospels. " And He appointed twelve that they might be with Him and that He might send them forth to preach, and to have authority to cast out devils", Mark iii, 14, 15. Luke's tradition of a mission of the seventy or seventy-two has raised critical difficulties and has been explained as a community-legend. But " why should such a tradition arise in the early Church where the Twelve were accorded an acknowledged pre-eminence ? The very preservation of such a tradition in such an environment is an argument for its authenticity. Moreover, the tradition that not only the Twelve, but a larger number, were ' sent out ' by Jesus to preach, would help to account for the application of the term ' apostle ' to a larger number than the Twelve in the early Church".[2] "Those who followed Jesus were ' disciples '. The ' apostles ' were selected out of this larger company, and it is not necessary to assume that even in the lifetime of Jesus the apostles were only twelve in number. The wider meaning given to the term apostle in the early Church is best explained by some justification for it in the earthly life of Jesus Himself".[3] The

[1] p. 105
[2] p. 108
[3] p. 114.

following " three declarations determine the character of an apostle in the early Church, and contain the essential characteristics of the Christian ministry for all time. First, there is the proclamation of the Word ; second, the power given in the New Age for the fulfilment of the tasks laid upon His messengers ; and third, the gathering together of the new community, the people of God. Word, Spirit, Church—these three determine the nature of the ministry. Such creative ministerial work is actually constitutive of the Church. It is now clear that we cannot speak of the apostle as holding an office in the later sense of the word; neither is the apostolate confined to the Twelve ".[1] "The view that Jesus appointed twelve men, and twelve only, to the office of apostles cannot be substantiated by the New Testament evidence. The statements in Luke vi, 13 ('he chose . . . twelve whom also he named apostles') and Acts i, 2, ('the apostles whom he had chosen') do not prove that the author of Luke-Acts believed that the number of apostles is confined to twelve. In Acts xiv, 4, 14, he calls Paul and Barnabas apostles. His use of this word, as of many others, is variable. As against modern theories the conclusion of Bishop Lightfoot still stands. In the account of the foundation of the apostolate, and in the language used in the Gospels of the Twelve, there is no hint that the number was intended to be so limited ".[2] As Hort said of the Last Supper : " The Twelve sat that evening as representatives of the Ecclesia at large : they were disciples more than they were Apostles " and " there is no trace in Scripture of a formal commission for government from Christ Himself".[3] "Recent discussions", says Flew, "have added to our knowledge but have not superseded the work of Lightfoot and Hort " concerning the " sending forth " and the mission of the disciples.[4]

By the same methods of research, Flew shews that the five-fold evidence of the Gospels is confirmed in the other books of the New Testament. It has been claimed that the gift of the Holy Spirit was conferred first on the Apostles and then by the Apostles on others. But the whole Church, all believers, received the gift of the Spirit. The first outward and visible sign of allegiance to

[1] p. 117.
[2] p. 117 f.
[3] p. 27.
[4] p. 118.

Christ was baptism : " So here, in Acts ii, 38, Baptism in the name of Jesus is baptism because Jesus is what He is, the exalted Messiah, and because He has done what He has done, poured forth the promised gift of the Spirit. From the beginning, Christian Baptism means taking Jesus Christ for all that He is. It is therefore a sign both to the supreme allegiance and of admission into the Ecclesia. The minister in Baptism was perhaps an Apostle or one of the Seven, or one who like Ananias is simply described as a disciple. It is curious that neither on the day of Pentecost nor in the success of Philip at Samaria (viii, 12–13) nor after the conversion of Paul, does the tradition explicitly record who administered the rite. In Cæsarea, Peter commanded the Gentiles to be baptized in the name of Jesus Christ. The deduction to be made is that apparently it was competent for any baptized Christian himself to baptize. But one fact is certain from the evidence : the minister in baptism acted as one commissioned by Christ, and guided the convert to fix his gaze on Christ alone. The value of Baptism does not depend on the activity or office of the minister. It is Christ who acts and gives ".[1] From the eleventh chapter of Acts, presbyters (elders), appear side by side with the Apostles and presbyters are appointed in every Church by Paul and Barnabas on their first journey : " The chief passage is in Paul's speech to the Ephesian elders, Acts xx, 27–28. ' I shrank not from declaring to you the whole counsel of God. Take heed unto yourselves, and to all the flock, in the which the Holy Ghost hath made you bishops, to feed the Church of God, which He purchased with His own blood'. From this and the other New Testament passages, we see, first, that the presbyters are all bishops. The first title denotes their office, and the second their function. The function is also described as tending or feeding the flock. Second there are several bishops in each local church, and there is no distinction of rank between them. Third, their appointment is ascribed to the Spirit of God. They may have been commissioned by an Apostle, perhaps by Paul himself, or elected by the Church. But the decisive act is the divine working of the Spirit. There is no distinction between a local ministry and a charismatic ministry ".[2] " In the Pauline writings we find that

[1] p. 116.
[2] p. 197.

all the varied ministries are regarded as the divine gift to the Church, and are regarded as an integral part of its organic life. There is one emphasis in I Cor. xii and Romans xii, and another emphasis in Ephesians iv. In the first case the Church as the Body of Christ is the recipient of the fullness of the divine gift of the Spirit, and within the body various members are given particular functions. In Eph. iv, on the other hand, the ministries of apostle, prophet, evangelist and teacher are given by the glorified Lord to the Church for the building up of the Body of Christ. The emphasis here is on the gift of the ministry to the Church. But the two views are complementary. In I Corinthians and Romans the ministry is not created by the Church but by the Spirit whose divers gifts (charismata) mark out this man and that for special functions. In Ephesians, also, the one Body is the home of the One Spirit, and the gifts are possessed by the Church as a whole ".[1] " We may therefore, hold with confidence to the view that, in the New Testament, order, important as it is to the organic life of the Ecclesia, is never equated with faith. The authority of the New Testament cannot be claimed for the view which would make Word and Sacrament contingent upon the office rather than the office contingent on the Word ".[2]

" O Timotheus ", writes Paul, " keep the securities of the faith intact : avoid the profane jargon and contradictions of what is falsely called ' Knowledge ' (I Tim. vi, 20). Model yourself on the sound instruction you have had from me in the faith and love of Christ Jesus. Keep the great securities of the faith intact, by the aid of the Holy Spirit that dwelleth in us ", 2 Tim. i, 13f. The reference is not to the Holy Spirit which dwells only in Timothy but " in us " : " The one method of guarding the sacred deposit or securities from harm and loss is to live a life sensitive to the pulse and impulse of the Holy Spirit within the community of the faithful ; this alone produces in the apostolical succession a vigilant care for what is vital to the faith ".[3] The securities of the Faith are entrusted to the whole community of the redeemed. " And they continued steadfastly in the apostles' doctrine and fellowship, in the breaking of bread and the prayers ". Acts ii, 42.

[1] p. 225 f.
[2] p. 256 f.
[3] Moffatt, *The Thrill of Tradition*, p. 71.

III.   FREE CHURCH DOCTRINE OF THE MINISTRY

Professor Manson asks, " What meaning should be attached to the words ' Apostolic Succession ' ?   To what do the successors of the Apostles succeed ?   We have seen that it is not the special status involved in our Lord's promise to the Twelve. Equally it is not the quality of having been an eye-witness of the foundation facts of the Faith from John's Baptism to the Resurrection.   That quality ceased with the first generation of Christians : it also was not transmissible.   What is left ?   So far as I can see, three things : the need of the world, the call of Christ, and the tradition of His Ministry in the flesh in Galilee and Judaea and in the Church which is His Body throughout the world.   And so far as I can see, it is the Church that succeeds to these things.   The Church is apostolic because she is called by Christ and empowered and instructed by Christ to go and make disciples of the nations ".[1]   Here is a statement of the Free Church doctrine of the Ministry as an organ of the Body of Christ.   Those who claim to have the " Essential Ministry " have made known their view of Free Church ministries : Dr. Kirk does not call them " null and void " but " invalid " ; Hebert says Free Church Ministries " do not mean the same thing " as those episcopally ordained.   The conflict between the claims of Kirk and Hebert and the Free Churches is irreconcilable.

As Moses was called of God and answered, " Here am I ", but doubted his qualification for the mission to Pharoah, and sought assurance of authority for his task ; as Isaiah's vision of the holiness of God came to him in the temple, and he was undone " because I am a man of unclean lips ", as he was cleansed and heard the voice of God, " who will go for us ", and answered, " Here am I send me " ;[2] as Amos was a herdsman and a dresser of sycomore trees and the Lord said to him, " Go, prophesy unto my people Israel " ;[3] as Jeremiah, before he was born was appointed a prophet unto the nations, but when called, answered,

[1] p. 52.
[2] Isa. vi.
[3] Amos vii, 15 ;

35

" Ah, Lord God! behold I cannot speak for I am a child . . .
and as the Lord put forth His hand and touched my mouth and
said unto me, Behold I have put my words into thy mouth" [1]—thus
Free Churchmen believe that God still calls His ministers. As
Jesus went up into a mountain and called " unto Him whom He
Himself would " : as Paul was converted and called to be an
apostle to the nations—so God has called His ministers and still
calls them. In the Old Testament, the initiative is with God ; in
the New Testament, with God in Christ. The call or election
to the ministry is of Grace, and who are men to limit, or imagine
that they can control the grace of God ? No man inherits grace.
No class of officials can originate grace or bestow it on another.
God alone bestows His grace on the sinner, the saint and the
minister. The ministry is a divine calling and a gift. The Holy
Spirit is the gift of the Risen Christ to His Ministers as to His
Church. It is presumptuous for any one to claim that he can
bestow or guarantee the gift of the Holy Spirit to a man in the
ceremony of ordination : no one possesses the Holy Spirit for
the purpose of " tactual transmission ". A man is possessed
by the Spirit, by reason of his repentance and faith and by his
humble response to God. "For by grace have ye been saved ;
and that not of yourselves : it is the gift of God ".[2] And the
same grace which saves a man calls him to the ministry. " By
grace is not here meant either God's general benignity, or His
particular kindness to our failure or pity for our pain. I mean
His undeserved and unbought pardon and redemption of us in
the face of our sin, in the face of the world-sin, under such moral
conditions as are prescribed by His revelation of His holy love in
Jesus Christ and Him crucified. And by the Gospel of this
grace I would especially urge that there is meant not a statement,
nor a doctrine, nor a scheme, on man's side ; nor an offer, a
promise, or a book on God's side. It is an act and a power ; it
is God's act of redemption before it is man's message of it. It
is an eternal, perennial act of God in Christ, repeating itself
within each declaration of it. Only as a Gospel done by God is
it a Gospel spoken by man. It is a revelation only because it was
first of all a reconciliation. It was a work that redeemed us into

---

[1] Jer. i, 9.

[2] Eph. ii, 8 f.

the power of understanding its own word. It is an objective power, an historic act and perennial energy of the holy love of God in Christ decisive for humanity in time and eternity ; and altering for ever the whole relation of the soul to God, as it may be rejected or believed. The gift of God's grace was, and is, His work of Gospel. And it is this act that is prolonged in the word of the preacher, and not merely proclaimed. The great, the fundamental, sacrament is the Sacrament of the Word.

" What I say will not hold good if the chief gift to the world is the Church and its sacraments, instead of the work and its word. Wherever you have the ritual sacraments to the front the preacher is to the rear, if he is there at all. In Catholicism worship is complete without a sermon ; and the education of the minister suffers accordingly. So, conversely, if the preacher is belittled the priest is enhanced. If you put back the pulpit, by the same act you put forward the altar. The whole of Christian history is a struggle between the apostle, i.e. the preacher, and the priest. The first Apostles were neither priests nor bishops. They were preachers, missionaries, heralds of the Cross, and agents of the Gospel. The apostolic succession is the evangelical. It is with the preachers of the Word and not with the priestly operators of the work, or with its episcopal organisers. Our churches are stone pulpits rather than shrines. The sacrament which gives value to all other sacraments is the Sacrament of the Living Word ".[1]

The Free Churches test the call of a man to the ministry before they train him : they seek evidence of his conversion and confession of Christ ; that he has fulfilled all the conditions of church membership, has convinced his fellow church members of the fitness of his character, and the quality of his Christian Service. Each denomination has its own oral and written tests. Most candidates are expected to have proved their call to preach, and must have conducted divine worship in the presence of ministers and representatives of the churches. Before admittance to college, the utmost significance is attached to strength of character, to capacity to study, to the quality of previous Christian work, and especially the gift of preaching. The same demands

---

[1] Forsyth, *Positive Preaching and Modern Mind*, p. 5 ff.

on personal character, on the ability to labour and learn, are made during residence in college. Many candidates have already matriculated or taken the School and Higher School Certificate before entering college. The period of training may cover three to six years. Most Free Church colleges are affiliated with universities where students prepare for Biblical and Theological Certificates, and Arts and Divinity Degrees. College tutors are on various university staffs. Nor are students isolated under ascetic conditions ; in the older universities, in London, Manchester, Bristol, Leeds and Birmingham, they attend lectures, are members of various societies and share the fellowship of students in other Faculties than Theology.

When college training is over, the Methodist Conference ordains the men and sends them forth to their work : Baptist and Congregational students are available to receive a call to a local church, and are ordained there by College representatives or by leading ministers of their respective Unions ; the Presbyterian Church demands high standards of character and training before licensing a man to preach and ordaining him to the pastorate. As Baptist and Congregational churches are self-governing, it may happen that a non-collegiate man receives a call to the pastorate, but care is taken that such men are approved on the grounds of character and service. The Baptist and Congregational Unions have rules of ministerial recognition, periods of probation after training, and lists of approved ministers. The Methodist Church insists on four years of probationary work in the ministry before final acceptance. Thus, in the selection of candidates, during years in college, especially in the early years of the pastorate and through the whole period of a man's ministry, the Church is testing ministerial character and work by the standards of the New Testament ethic.

It will be seen that the Free Churches do not divorce the intellectual and spiritual training of their students. I do not think Anglican writers, or the public, appreciate the care, thoroughness, and labour which are given to the equipment of Free Church Ministers. The colleges are maintained by the churches. An applicant to college may be poor and unable to contribute little or anything to his training ; but if by character, motive and effectual work he can convince the churches and the colleges of his " call of God ", he will rarely lack the opportunity for training.

And all the Free Churches have been richly blessed through the ministries of such men.

A conference was held in 1944 at Oxford of Free Church College Principals, and six Anglican Principals were invited to share our fellowship. A paper read by an Anglican was on the training of the spiritual life of the student. There were striking contrasts between Anglican and Free Church tests of the men who come to be trained. It was said that some men who were received for training in Anglican colleges had to be taught to pray, since they had never learned the secret of private devotion. The training of the spiritual life of these students proceeded on the basis of the Prayer Book with further help from ancient liturgies ; the aim was to prepare such men to conduct public worship. Of course, Free Church Colleges train their students to lead the congregation in worship, but most men who come to us have learned to pray at their mother's knee, and if in adolescence, the habit of prayer has weakened, it has been revived at conversion or confession, and prayer, through faith in Christ and forgiveness, has become a spiritual power in their lives. Moreover, these men have conducted public worship of which prayer is a part. The spiritual training of these men is directed to develop personality in relation to Christ, a discipline by which the resources of their devotional life are continually enriching the church.

A list of Free Church Colleges in Great Britain, and students for the session 1947-8 is appended :—

	Colleges.	Students.
Baptist Colleges - - - -	8	234
Congregational Colleges - - -	10	245
Churches of Christ - - - -	1	8
Methodist Colleges - - - -	7	255
Moravian Colleges - - - -	1	9
Presbyterian (Cambridge) - - -	1	38
Welsh Calvinistic Methodists - -	2	53
TOTAL	30	842

FREE CHURCH STATISTICS, 1945

Denomination	Members	Ministers	Local and Lay Preachers	Sunday School Teachers	Sunday School Scholars and Bible Class Members
Methodist - -	767,465	4,631	29,674	109,237	701,493
Independent Methodist - - -	9,976	380	—	1,959	12,144
Wesleyan Reform Union - -	11,910	20	422	1,846	16,903
Baptist - - -	382,337	2,101	5,046	52,554	377,316
Congregational -	416,442	2,864	3,696	51,584	366,973
Presbyterian -	74,575	392	—	5,299	35,753
Calvinistic Methodist - - -	174,664	856	208	14,761	88,618
Moravian - -	3,165	38	20	321	2,503
Churches of Christ -	12,764	50	360	1,129	8,243
Total - -	1,853,298	11,332	39,426	238,600	1,609,946

N.B.—These figures are given for guidance, but owing to war-time conditions their accuracy cannot be guaranteed.

CHAPTER II

THE LEGACY OF THE CENTURIES:
CONSTANTINE TO CALVIN

THE preceding chapter has dealt with doctrines : there are deeply-rooted differences which have profoundly affected European history, and the most serious is the claim that the bishop is essential to the very existence of the Church. Thus far it has been unnecessary to indicate how these ideas of the Church and the Ministry have been related to the idea of the State : and to this task we must now turn. It is impossible to make sense of Church history in general, or British history in particular, until we understand how the Church, the Ministry and the State have re-acted on each other ; and how the tension between them has affected the structure of our own national institutions since the sixteenth century. The contending forces in Britain were arrayed as follows : the divine right of Kings against the English Parliament, which stood for the rights and liberties of the people ; the divine right of bishops, often paid officials of the State, who incited rulers to civil war to maintain their ecclesiastical privileges and exact conformity to their authority. We must describe Prelacy, a form of absolutism in the government of the Church, in alliance with Kings, and their absolutism in the State. On the other hand, we must consider those who resisted priestly and political tyranny, who pleaded in the Church and in Parliament for freedom of conscience, of speech, and of the exclusion of the magistracy from any interference in matters of religion ; who also suffered torture, imprisonment, loss of goods and exile, and who at last unsheathed the sword as the only means left to them to establish religious and political liberty in the land. It has been the fashion of late to say that all parties in the seventeenth century were equally intolerant, and then proceed to assume that the past should be decently buried and forgotten. Others write the history of

41

England and Wales in the terms of political and economic struggle and omit entirely, or underrate, the dynamic of religious conviction which was creative of our democratic institutions. The mingling and clash of religion and politics have profoundly affected the social structures of Britain. In the past, when the policy of the bishops in the House of Lords was to maintain their privileges at all costs, the Church of England became alienated from the masses ; and when Dissenters, as they were called, were contending against religious, political and economic injustice, they found the bishops were amongst their most relentless opponents.

Professor Norman Sykes and other Anglican writers, make welcome confessions of these grave oppressions, but persecution and exile leave their wounds, and when such wounds have healed the scars may long remain. It is, therefore, due to the present generation to state the claims of the Free Churches on the British-speaking peoples. It is far from my desire to open old wounds ; but for a generation which has forgotten, or never known the price paid for its liberties, it is desirable to state facts which have been neglected, often in the interests of religious appeasement. Moreover, when the liberties of the individual are being curtailed for economic ends, it will be well, especially for the laity of the churches, to be reminded how religious and political freedom were won ; how at last Free Churchmen taught toleration, self-government and democracy to the British people.

I

Before passing to the seventeenth century in England, the problem of Church and State must be set in its historical perspective. Unless this is done we shall fail to understand the magnitude of the Free Church achievement. Surely to overthrow a Tradition thirteen centuries old was a momentous triumph. After the fourth century, when the Emperor Constantine gave his patronage to the Church, the problem became much more complicated. Even now, outside the British Commonwealth of Nations and America, Free Churches are comparatively few in number : a fact which explains vital differences between the English-speaking and many other peoples : one which has differentiated the political, ethical, and economical approach of the British to domestic and international affairs.

The early Church soon became conscious of the problem of the civil government and loyalty to Christ. " Render unto Cæsar the things which are Cæsar's ", said Jesus : but he never said as many have assumed, that God had chosen Cæsar to rule the Roman Empire ; neither did He express any views on Cæsar's character or on the Roman Senate. He was careful to warn His disciples against exercising such Gentile rule over each other—a command which ecclesiastical Cæsars have rejected by their use of compulsion and by inquisitorial methods and tortures. When the religious motive of the Jewish rulers led them to use any political expedient at hand to gain their end—the end was the crucifixion of Jesus.

Paul advised the church at Corinth to appoint arbitrators to settle disputes between church members, nor should Christians go to law as plaintiffs in a pagan court. But when Paul was in peril from Jewish opponents he did not hesitate to claim the protection of the Roman magistrates. It is in Romans xiii that the Apostle expounds his theory of the divine origin of political authority ; a theory which wins immediate consent, if, as Paul assumed, the magistrate is the righteous instrument of the Wrath of God against wicked men. But what if the magistrate himself is wicked ? The Old Testament records that God used the rod of Assyria to chastise His people ; that He used Cyrus to liberate Israel from exile—facts which verify God's use of non-Israelite forces in world events. But the traditional interpretation of Romans xiii in the relations of Church and State has led to immeasurable tragedies and bloodshed. The Church has used Paul's words to counsel subjection to the vilest and craftiest tyrants : likewise such tyrants have used his words to fortify their fanaticism for enslaving and slaughtering their subjects. A truer interpretation of the Word of God, and a stronger moral realism, led the Puritans of the seventeenth century to draw their sword and rid Britain of Charles Stuart I.

But the scene shifts in the New Testament itself. The sensuality and brutality of Nero and the persecutions changed the whole attitude of the Church to the State. In the Book of Revelation, Cæsar is the Beast which has made war on the

Lamb. The State is now a harlot, full of blasphemy and pride and drunk with the blood of the martyrs. Against such a Beast the Christians of the first century were physically helpless : they had no weapons other than those which were spiritual : all they could do was to default or be ready any day to wash their robes and make them white in the blood of the Lamb— which they did, and thereby taught the pagan world that Christ was worth dying for.

II

In the fourth century Constantine gave his patronage to the Church, and we must trace briefly the legacy of his policy as a preparation for our study of Free Church principles in England. The savage persecutions of the Emperors had nauseated the age and failed to destroy the Church. It is to the enduring credit of Constantine that he initiated a new policy towards the Church. His motives and the reports of his conversion do not concern us here. But his Edict of Milan is one of the turning points in the history of the world. " The two hostile powers—the Church and Empire—became allies, but the terms of the alliance were not settled, nor has the true solution yet been found. The Arian controversy is in fact the opening scene of the great drama of Church and State, and we are able to recognise how the apparently irreconcilable difference in the aims of the two powers became evident from the first. The essence of all progressive civil government must always be expediency . . . with the Church it is otherwise. Since her mission is to deal with verities rather than possibilities, com- promises, which are proofs of wisdom in a statesman, are in many cases rightly regarded as treason in a churchman. Thus it is that, however harmoniously the ecclesiastical and civil polities may seem to work together, circumstances will inevitably arise to place them in opposition to one another, the triumph of either being seldom unattended by dangerous consequences ; nothing being more contemptible than a temporal ruler whose policy is swayed by a priesthood, save a priesthood which is the tool of a secular government ".[1] When the Church was

[1] Foakes Jackson, *History of the Christian Church to* 461, p. 323 f.

persecuted by the Empire she was pure in motive and in morals :
but under the patronage of Constantine it became the fashion
for the Roman nobility and obsequious pagans to enter the
Church : and pagans they remained within her membership.
The formality of worship, the political intrigues of the Arians
in the royal palace, their immoral scandals, the accusations of
murder against Athanasius and his periods of exile, the leaning
of the court to the strongest party for the time being—for
fifty years the squalid quarrel continued. Then the Emperor
Theodosius in 380 issued an Edict that the Faith taught to the
Romans by the Apostle Peter and held by Damasus of Rome,
and Peter of Alexandria, should be accepted by all nations.
Two years later Theodosius established Christianity by declaring
the Nicene Faith as the creed of the Empire. " From henceforth the idea grew apace that the State was responsible for the
maintenance of the true Faith among its subjects. With this
we pass into a new sphere, and for centuries a theory of government began to prevail, that has not yet been entirely relegated
to oblivion ".[1]

The theory was that Governments must wield the sword of
the State to maintain the orthodoxy of the Catholic Faith, thereby
preserving the peace of the Church and the unity of the Empire.
The result was that personal faith and morals became less important than external conformity. But as both Church and
State were concerned to maintain conformity, it seemed reasonable to advocate compulsion by the State on behalf of the
Church. At any rate, so it seemed to Augustine, who literally
interpreted the words of Jesus in the parable of the Great Supper
—" compel them to come in ". Hence persecution became
justified as the policy of the Church : and the heretic was burnt
at the stake to save his soul from worse and more enduring
flames.

Did the policy succeed ? Neo-Catholic apologists assume
that it did, and they would fain persuade us that the hope of
this broken world lies in a return to the unity of the Middle
Ages ; but they seem unaware that their theory of unity is far
from being confirmed by hard facts. For when the Church
proceeded to demand supremacy over the State the result was
often anarchy. There was no such unity as Maritain and others

[1] ibid., p. 392.

assume. The two swords of the Church and State were maintained in fighting condition, and were often unsheathed in battle. The claim of the Papacy to set up, and to put down, rulers was resisted by Emperors on the ground that they themselves had received their authority from God. For the first ten centuries of the Christian era the claims often made for the Papacy have no basis in history. From the eleventh century onwards the Popes used all the ecclesiastical and political pressure at their disposal to enforce the submission of the State.

When Philip IV of France arrested and charged the Bishop of Pamiers with treason, Boniface VIII retaliated : " God hath set us over the princes of the earth and their kingdoms, to root up, destroy, disperse, scatter, build, plant in His name . . . persuade not yourself therefore that you have no superior and that you are not subject to the head of the Church. He who so thinks is a madman ".[1] In 1302 Boniface issued his famous Bull Unam Sanctam : " We declare, assert and define that it is absolutely necessary to salvation for every human creature to be subject to the Roman pontiff ". Philip knew this Bull was intended to force his submission, but we are told that he threw it into the fire and scathingly answered : " Let your most distinguished Fatuousness be assured that in temporals we are subject to no one . . . your power is verbal, that of the king is real ".[2] Shortly afterwards, crying " Death to Boniface ", Philip's mercenaries broke into the papal palace and arrested the Pope : he was released, led back to Rome and died a few weeks later.

Rulers in other lands opposed the aggressive demands of the Papacy. In England, under Edward I, a creative period in English history, a consciousness of nationhood was growing which provoked widespread resentment against traffic in ecclesiastical livings, and the drainage of money to Rome. The English people became impatient under the burden of priestly despotism and taxation. The rival claims of Popes and Princes, the conciliar movements to reform abuses and subject the Pope to the authority of General Councils, the oppressive exactions of ecclesiatical feudalism (which will receive subsequent

---

[1] Mackinnon, *Origins of the Reformation*, p. 16.
[2] Mackinnon, *History of Modern Liberty*, I, p. 371.

treatment) do not confirm the estimate of the Middle Ages as a period of peace within the Church or between Church and State.

III

" The most puzzling problems of modern European history is not the reason of the breakdown of Liberalism and the rise of totalitarianism—but why the Reformation failed ".[1] D. T. Jenkins says as time went on " the Reformers failed to be true to their own first principle " : they " did not sufficiently emphasise the fact that reformation must be a constant activity in the Church if it is to live " ; whereas the Church " gradually succumbed to the securitas of orthodoxy". I appreciate such insights, and criticism of the Reformers, in his excellent book, but D. T. Jenkins confines his strictures to their faith and theology and does not raise the problem with which we are here concerned. But I do not think the Reformation failed : its success was terrific in an age which knew neither spiritual nor political freedom. And remembering the period, the affirmation of spiritual liberty was something permanently won. To proclaim the New Testament doctrine of Grace and to break up a system in which Europe had believed for centuries was a mighty work.

As a youth Luther says his imagination was deeply impressed by an altar picture of a ship in which sat popes, cardinals and bishops, and as the priests and monks were toiling at the oars they were being directed heavenwards by the Holy Spirit. Around the ship laymen were swimming in the water, some were drowning, others were clinging to ropes thrown out by the priests and monks. But no laymen were in the boat and no ecclesiastics were in the water. To restore the spiritual birthright of the individual and the laity in the Church was the beginning of emancipation : even though Luther did not discern the political implications of spiritual freedom. It was when he encouraged the princes to slaughter peasants and Anabaptists and persecute them for heresy, that he clearly failed to be loyal to his first principles.

The truth is the Reformers inherited the mediæval ideas of

[1] *The Gift of Ministry*, p. 88.

the relation of Church and State : they never understood the political implications of their own Biblical theology. As justification by faith declared the freedom of the individual from priestly mediation in the work of salvation, so the priesthood of all believers, worked out in its final conclusion, declares that the Church is a divine society and is competent to exercise self-government under the guidance of the Holy Spirit : and in such a Church there is no room, and no need, for any supremacy other than that of the Redeemer. If Luther had proceeded to organise the Church as such a self-governing society, he would almost certainly have commenced to change the whole political structure of Germany in the sixteenth century. But Luther was politically timid, nor was he conscious of any inconsistency in handing over the government of the Protestant Church to the German princes—and the twentieth century knows the consequences of such subjection. His views on submission to rulers were those of a mediævalist. " The Christian must suffer violence and wrong, especially from his supreme Lord. For although the Emperor should do injustice and act contrary to his duty and his oath, his authority and the obedience of his subjects are not thereby nullified as long as the empire and the electors recognise him as Emperor and do not depose him ".[1]

In Germany, in June, 1939, as the clouds of war were darkening the European sky, a distinguished German, a New Testament scholar, said to the late Dr. Rushbrooke : " If we had only had in Germany the kind of Free Church movement that you have had in England, our history would have been different ".

IV

In 1534 Geneva rejected Catholicism and declared allegiance to the Reformed Faith. Calvin was invited to the city in 1536 and began to reform its morals, for he said he discovered that libertinism was regarded as no reproach to a confessing Christian. The people refused, however, to accept the hard yoke of his discipline and he departed to Strassburg in 1538. He was recalled in 1541 and planned to build the city as a church. He knew the Reformed Faith could only take root as the community

---

[1] Letter to the Elector, 6th March, 1530.

was taught to think as well as worship, and to this end he trained the ministers of the church. He founded a school and academy for the study of Arts as well as Theology—an achievement which entitles Calvin " to rank among the foremost makers of modern education ". Before his death the number of pupils and students had risen to 1,200 and they came from England, Scotland, Germany, Italy and France. The syllabuses were as exacting as all the discipline which Calvin laid upon himself and expected from others. The churches of the Reformed tradition everywhere have owed much to Calvin's educational policy. The motto over the entrance to the academy was *Post Tenebras Lux*.

As a legislator Calvin was equally constructive ; but it was here that he failed to break away from mediæval ideas of Church and State. The Church in Geneva, while largely self-governing in spiritual matters, was subject to the oversight and final control of the Republic. Ministers were approved or disapproved, discipline was enforced, theological disputes were finally settled by the civil authorities. For Sabbath breaking, absence for a year from the sacrament, heresy, adultery or fornication, judgment was pronounced by the magistrates. Excommunication was the decision of the Church, but the punishment was carried out by the State : " Although it is not perfect ", wrote Calvin, " it is tolerable considering the difficulty of the times ". Persecutions for heresy, the death penalty against Servetus, the cruel suffering inflicted upon the Anabaptists, indicate how Calvin was still in bondage to mediæval traditions : " To allow such false doctrine, which is apostasy from God, is to subvert religion and render certainty impossible. It is, therefore, absolutely necessary for the preservation of true religion and the honour of God to punish such apostasy with the sword. This power has been invested in Kings and Magistrates ".[1]

Considering Calvin's merciless logic, there was strange inconsistency or vagueness in his political theory of the relation of rulers and people. His political ideal was a preference for an aristocracy under the control of the people. It is difficult, however, to reconcile his statements regarding obedience to, or the right to revolt against, rulers. His general argument counsels submission, even to wicked rulers whom God may use to

[1] cf. Opera, VIII, p. 457 f.

punish the nation. But he has several qualifications of his general principle ; that the individual must not rebel ; that the magistrates should curb wicked tyrants ; that obedience must be rendered to God rather than to kings who break God's laws. Notwithstanding such qualifications, Calvin's views seem to indicate the attitude of submission to the State. In a letter to Queen Elizabeth he disapproved of the writings of John Knox, whose attitude to ruling tyrants did not lack clear definition.

V

In this brief but necessary review of the relations of Church and State from Constantine to Calvin we find ecclesiastical ambitions, jealousies and arrogance which are alien to the spirit of the Gospel ; we find a persecuting hierarchy calling upon the State to inflict pains and the death penalty for heresy. It is a cruel story, and the Church has yet to confess and repent before God and man for its ignorance and its crimes. Nor is it a matter for a few individuals here and there. Humble men and women, scholars, courageous thinkers and reformers, whose character and work were a rebuke to ecclesiastical rulers, were slaughtered like sheep and hunted to death because they translated the Scriptures or preached the Gospel to the common people. How was this age-long intolerance broken ? Against these mediæval theories and policies how did the Church gain her freedom and the State learn tolerance ? The answer will be found as we trace the development of Free Church principles in England and Wales.

CHAPTER III

THE ENGLISH REFORMATION

THE relation of Church and State raises new problems at the English Reformation. We have seen the Papacy and the Emperors contending for rights or supremacy against one another. But the problem of Church and State in England is now focused in the claims of the ruling monarchs. This does not mean that old tensions were eliminated, they continued to affect the English situation in new ways. It will be granted that the English Reformation was not the result of biblical or theological learning. In 1534, Henry VIII commanded Parliament to pass a law which centred spiritual as well as political authority in himself; thus he became " the only Supreme Head on earth of the Church of England ". Convocation suggested a qualification of his sovereignty over the Church by the words " as far as the law of Christ permits ", but Henry would accept no such restriction of his powers. He was a strong-headed ruler; he would have his divorce; he would defy the claims of the Pope as Head of the Anglican Church and he would rule the Church in the Pope's stead. It was a strange situation for a divorced person to be the Head of the Church and Defender of the Faith in England. How far removed from the spiritual upheaval of Luther which led to the German reformation, or the reforming zeal of Calvin as he contemplated the majesty and sovereignty of God! Well might the Bishop of Gloucester say : " The King has destroyed the Pope but not popery " ; a statement to be kept in mind as we trace the work of the Reformers under the Tudors and the Stuarts. At the English reformation there was no change in the Catholic Faith of the realm. Henry appointed the bishops; he ruled them and dismissed them unless they served his politico-religious policy. He presided at the trial of heretics : when John Lambert rejected the doctrine of transubstantiation, Henry condemned him to death : " I will be no patron of heretics ".

Elizabeth followed the policy of Henry VIII. By a new act of Supremacy in 1559 she became " the only Supreme Governor " in all spiritual and political causes ; and in these matters Elizabeth leaves us in no doubt that she understood her own business : a royal opportunist, with one eye on England and the other on the Continent : believing in herself and in her divine right to rule the Church as well as the State, she insisted on order and unity in both. Her " religious settlement " was effected by means of the Prayer Book and the oath which acknowledged her authority. She was ruthless in pursuit of politico-religious unity. She selected her own bishops and dismissed them unless they put down heretics and served the ends of the State. Elizabeth regarded compulsory worship as a satisfactory guarantee of the loyalty of her subjects : she was no inquisitor of the private ideas and habits of the people, but unless they went to Church voluntarily they must be compelled to go. The Church was the nation and the nation was the Church ; in her later years, Hooker, " the most distinguished of all Anglican writers " at that time, confirmed the Queen in her view.

The Tudors had their own reasons for unifying their authority in Church and State, but their reasons proved the desirability of religious and political freedom as the only alternative of their policy. Elizabeth was beset with enemies and she knew of plot after plot against her life ; she was aware that Jesuit conspirators were ready to use every possible weapon to destroy her. But she did not recognise her friends nor how to use the spiritual forces which were on her side. For in the reforming parties there was solid loyalty to Protestantism and to herself. It is true that she was compelled to watch conflicting religious forces in the country : the risings in the North and the West were evidence of smouldering discontent. But the success of her long reign has always won the admiration of the English people.

II

The Bishop of Gloucester said that Henry VIII " did not destroy popery " when he became head of the Church of England. If we would understand the tumults of religious debate and strife under the Tudors and the Stuarts we must examine this statement. What were these age-long grievances which had provoked conflicts and wars in the past, which were to disrupt the religious life of the English people for the next century and a half, and plunge the nation into devastating civil wars ? It is curious how many Anglican writers who deal with the Tudor and Stuart periods rarely face these facts and their implications. Yet these questions need to be raised, if for no other reason than to explain or justify the heretics, reformers and martyrs, whose suffering paved the road to religious freedom. For only as these grievances were removed was progress possible.

The truth is, these abuses which persisted in the Church of England must be traced largely to the theory of the priesthood which Cyprian forced upon the Church at Carthage in the middle of the third century—the theory of episcopacy which has already been outlined. History does not lie on this matter and such history is more widely known among the people to-day than in the past. To protest against references to this history, or to hope to bury it beyond resurrection, is not likely to serve the Church of the future. The apologists of the hard and exclusive doctrine of apostolic succession need to remember how their priestly predecessors used their power to enslave the minds and bodies of men. For the sake of the Church which we desire in the future, the modern defenders of the " Essential Ministry " should consider how such theory and practice have led to spiritual and moral abuses which have made havoc of their claims. That the bishop is essential to the existence of the Church ; that he received in ordination authority to rule the Church ; that men must be ordained by a bishop before they are authorised to administer the sacraments ; that the Hierarchy is entrusted with the Defence of the Faith and must muzzle or silence every preacher of whom they disapprove—these claims and practices slowly separated the clergy from the laity, and the gulf became wider as the revolutionary powers of the Hierarchy became organised, and could rely on the coercive methods of the State.

It is not always clearly understood how the " Essential Ministry " shifted the centre of authority in Christian thought, worship, the government of the Church, and ethics—shifted it from the Scriptures to itself. The tragic consequences of this transference of authority, both for the Church and civilisation, are terrible to contemplate. For a thousand years, from the Dark Ages, from the crimes of Pope Alexander VI and the scandals of the Borgias to the apostasy of the State Churches of Europe in the twentieth century ; to the failure of the Orthodox Church to evangelise the Russian masses, and by promoting social and economic justice to make impossible the cruelties of the 1917 Revolution, and the moral atheism of Soviet communism ; to the political opportunism of the Vatican's concordats with Mussolini, Hitler and Franco—these scourges and wars of our own century are related to spiritually decadent churches ruled by the " Essential Ministry " for which Dr. Kirk consistently contends.

This accusation is confirmed by all who have contended for the reform of the Church. Individuals like Marsiglio of Padua, William of Occam, Wicklif and his preachers, Hus and his followers, protesting, suffering and dying to cleanse the church of their day ; Church Councils convened to curb the ambition and wealth of the " Essential Ministry " ; only to be tricked by promises which were never meant to be kept, and defeated in the end, partly by ecclesiastical schemers who never intended to yield place, or power, or privilege. Taking the long view of history, who can mistake the falling night of divine judgment on the churches which have thus betrayed the Gospel ?

The substitution of the authority of the " Essential Ministry " for the authority of the whole church led to the neglect of the Scriptures and preaching. As preaching declined the clergy and laity became more ignorant of the Bible, until it became a forbidden and closed book. And the more mentally indolent the clergy and laity became the more abuses became possible. There were brave Protestant prophets and martyrs under the Tudors, especially during the Marian persecutions, who ascribed the spiritual and moral decadence of their age to this ignorance of the Scriptures. None had a truer understanding of this matter than Latimer whose preaching does not spare the " Essential Ministry." A quotation from one of his sermons will go far to explain why this Protestant preacher was burnt at the stake at Oxford Cross.

" Who is the most diligentest bishop and prelate in all England, that passeth all the rest in doing his office ? I can tell, for I know him who it is—I know him well. But now I think I see you listening and hearkening that I should name him. There is one that passeth all others and is the most diligent prelate and preacher in all England. And will you know who it is ? I will tell you—it is the devil. He is the most diligent preacher of all others. He is never out of his diocese, he is never from his cure ; ye shall never find him unoccupied ; he is ever in his parish ; he keepeth residence at all times ; ye shall never find him out of the way ; call for him when you will, he is ever at home ; he is ever at his plough ; no lording nor loitering can hinder him—you will never find him idle, I warrant you. And his office is to hinder religion, to maintain superstition, to set up idolatry. When the devil is resident and hath his plough going, then away with books and up with candles ; away with Bibles and up with beads ; away with the light of the Gospel and up with the light of candles yea, at noonday. . . . Down with Christ's cross and up with purgatory pickpurse—the Popish purgatory, I mean. . . . Up with man's traditions and his laws, down with God's traditions and His most holy Word ".

III

The rise of Nonconformity in the Tudor period must be examined in its historic setting. It was no light matter to refuse to conform to the " religious settlement " of Elizabeth. The earliest Nonconformist groups were few in number, and they were made to pay dearly for their convictions. Not until the Protestants who believed in episcopacy, and the Puritans who desired the Presbyterian form of church government had failed to achieve reform, did Nonconformity under the Tudors come to the birth. We review the ideas and activities of these three groups.

First : We consider the Protestant and Humanist attempt to reform episcopacy : and we select Colet as representative of this group. The training of the humanists distinguished them from the schoolmen ; as students of the classics they enlightened religious debate from the sources of Greek thought and culture. It never occurred to the humanists to follow Luther's methods or break away from the Church. Colet and More in England and their friend Erasmus on the Continent, attempted reform on Biblical and cultural lines. At the same time the attack of Erasmus on the Church was as decided as that of Luther; except that his method was ridicule rather than direct assault, side thrusts rather than frontal blows. It will be relevant to contrast the methods of Luther and Erasmus as they attempted to reform the abuses of the Church. Such a contrast has significance for our purpose.

While Luther was still a member of the Roman Church he visited Rome; he knelt down, overwhelmed at the sight of the city, " rendered sacred by the blood of the martyrs ". But " had I not seen it with my own eyes I would not have believed it. Neither God nor man nor sin nor shame is regarded ". The wealth and simony of the Cardinals, who had personally appropriated the income of the Church, appalled him. He saw such leaders openly addicted to sensual vice. " At Rome there is such a state of things that baffle description. There is buying and selling, exchanging, cheating, stealing, luxury, debauchery, villainy, and every sort of contempt of God, that Anti-Christ himself could not possibly rule more abominably. . . . Here vows are annulled. Here the monk may buy freedom to quit his order. Here the clergy can purchase the marriage state, the children of harlots obtain legitimacy, dishonour and shame be made respectable and evil repute and crime be knighted and ennobled. . . . Whoever has been to Rome knows, alas, that things are worse than anyone can describe or imagine ". Thus Luther writes of the abuses of the Church in his *Address to the Nobility* of the German nation.

Erasmus, in his *Praise of Folly*, written at Sir Thomas More's house in London, presents his indictment of the Church in the form of a satire. In frivolous dress, Folly is personified and delivers her oration. In every personification of abuses by Erasmus there is a sting. Folly pillories Drunkenness, Ignorance, Self-Love, Flattery, Laziness and Sensuality as persons who dance attendance upon her. She holds up the mirror to the absurdities of magic, superstition, indulgences, charms and beads which are said to ward off sickness and guarantee length of days; she ridicules the arithmetic of the " Essential Ministry " which works out to the day and hour the cost of release from purgatory; she makes fun of the school-men, thin-skinned and hot-tempered theologians, impostors who are clever enough to amass wealth and who can tell exactly how every babe has the taint of original sin. Folly lampoons the hierarchy which one day will be compelled to answer at the bar of God and will hear Jesus say : " Woe unto you Scribes and Pharisees, I know you not ". For that age, the book had a large circulation, nor is it surprising that it was placed on the *Index Expurgatorius*. But Erasmus was too popular to be seized and imprisoned for his satire.

The methods of Luther and Erasmus were diametrically opposed to each other, but they were agreed on the fact of the abuses. Erasmus produced his version of the New Testament in Greek and called the Church back to the Scriptures as the source and standard of Christian life and faith. He stood for freedom of conscience and speech. But he was unwilling to break with the Church. For a time both men were friendly ; they had much in common in calling the Church back to the Scriptures. Later, the two men drifted apart and flung hard words at each other. Luther said Erasmus lacked intensity of conviction and moral courage. Erasmus replied, " where Lutheranism prevails, destruction of letters takes place ". To Erasmus, the doubting and enquiring mind was the way to the truth ; to Luther, doubt was of the devil. In the controversy of the two men on Free Will, Luther wished Erasmus would " cease disputing on a subject for which God had not endowed him ". Thus the significance of this comparison between Luther and Erasmus has application to the situation under the Tudors and even into our own age.

Erasmus represents the humanist in every century ; the man who can ridicule and pillory abuses but is not made of the stuff of the reformer ; one who hates controversy and prefers compromise rather than the agony of a fight to the finish. Luther had his serious limitations, but when he was convinced that the hierarchy would neither repent nor reform, he defied its authority and accepted the consequences. Hence his decision to go to Worms against the advice of his friends : " I will enter Worms if all the devils were in it ". Thinking of himself in a similar situation Erasmus confessed : " I fear I should act the part of Peter over again. I follow the Pope and the Emperor when they decide well, because it is pious to do so ; I bear their bad decisions, because it is safe to do so " ; and " I would certainly rather have Luther corrected than destroyed . . . but I shall not oppose if they roast or boil him ". Under the Tudors, the humanists did not break with the Church ; the Nonconformists could do no other.

IV

Colet in the reign of Henry VIII represents English humanism. " When I sit at the feet of my friend Colet", wrote Erasmus, "it seems to me that I am hearkening to Plato himself ". Colet's reputation for classical learning at Oxford, and his own clear literary style, won him far-reaching influence as a preacher, for he had also given " himself up entirely to the study of Holy Scripture ". Though a layman, he announced to the University a free course of lectures on Paul's Epistles. The response was astonishing. His simple direct sentences were " surer than the arrows of Hercules ". His keenest shafts were directed against the schoolmen who " divided the Scripture into four senses "— the literal sense which teaches the facts, the allegorical which tells men what they are to believe, the tropological what they are to do, the analogical what they are to hope. At the best, he said, the teaching of the schoolmen was " a huge and bewilder-ing mass of dreary and lifeless subtlety " ; " but ", wrote Eras-mus to Colet, " you say what you mean and mean what you say. Your words have birth in your heart, not on your lips. You have the happy art of expressing with ease what others can hardly express with the greatest labour ". Turning from the school-men and the Fathers, Colet thrilled his hearers as he made the Bible a living Book. After several years in Italy, he returned to Oxford, more persuaded than ever that the people needed a knowledge of the Word of God. He saw, however, that the " Essential Ministry " had been so diligent to establish its rule over the Church that preaching had been sadly neglected, and was on a low level. And other evidence confirms Colet. About the middle of the sixteenth century the Archbishop of York declared that in all his province, and at that day it included parts of Lancashire, he did not know twelve ministers who were cap-able of preaching. In many churches there had been no sermon for years. Again, I draw attention to the deplorable results of withholding the proclamation of the Gospel from the laity.

Colet was later made Dean of St. Paul's where his expository preaching stirred the people of London. In a sermon to convocation at St. Paul's we find him attacking the abuses of the church, but he also assailed the Puritans as heretics: "We are grieved nowadays also by heretics, mad men with marvellous foolishness, but the heresies of them are not so pestilent and pernicious to us and the people as the evil and wicked lives of the priests ". His invective was merciless against the priesthood whose abuses were immorality, simony and absenteeism. Colet was so outspoken against abuses in Church and State in a sermon preached before Henry VIII that the king summoned him to an interview. Henry was fearful lest such preaching should seduce the army from loyalty at home and abroad. But Colet assured the king of his loyalty and the incident ended by Henry drinking to Colet's health. Admirable as was Colet's humanism, the " Essential Ministry " and Henry VIII preferred to let abuses alone.

v

During the reign of Elizabeth (1558–1603) there were two groups of Puritan reformers and it is desirable, at the outset to distinguish them. At this period the Presbyterians constituted the much larger group which attempted to reform the Church of England while remaining within its membership. The Separatists were also Puritans, who had concluded that the Church neither intended to be reformed by others nor to reform itself. These Separatists were Nonconformists ; they refused to conform to the worship, belief, or the order of government by bishops, as the Elizabethan Act of Uniformity demanded. Before the close of Elizabeth's reign the Nonconformists had become two distinct churches known as Independent or Congregationalists and Baptists. For the latter, the term Anabaptist was often used, and Baxter mostly refers to Anabaptists somewhat slightingly. For the present, I shall use the term Nonconformist to include Congregationalists and Baptists, who have so much in common, especially the form of church-government —the main distinction being that Baptists do not administer baptism to any but those who believe in Jesus Christ as their Lord and Saviour. Thus, there were Puritans who remained within the Church, and Puritans who came out of the Church ; but all Puritans as the name implies, stood for a purer church, one nearer to New Testament ideals. Scripture illuminated by the Holy Spirit was their final authority.

Puritans were far from being the stupid kill-joys, as they have, and are still, represented to have been. The leaders were University men. In the reign of Elizabeth, Cambridge was referred to as " a nest of Puritans ." They were courageous men. Edward Dering educated at Christ's College, preaching to the Queen in 1570, declared the disappointment which he and others felt at her failure to reform the Church ; he presented a vivid picture of the circumstances which were converting Cambridge men to Puritanism : " The benefices of the Church were being permitted to remain, ' defiled with impropriations, some laden with pensions, some robbed of their commodities'. Patrons sell them, farm them out, give them to boys, to serving men, to their own children, seldom to learned pastors. The present incumbents are often Ruffians, Hawkers and Hunters, Dicers and Carders. They are blind guides and cannot see, dumb dogs and will not bark ". To Elizabeth he speaks boldly : " I tell you this before God . . . amend these horrible abuses, and the Lord is on your right hand, you shall not be removed for ever ".

The controversy between Cartwright, Lady Margaret Professor of Divinity at Cambridge, and Whitgift, the Archbishop of Canterbury, throws further light on the Puritan desire for reform. Cartwright had visited Geneva and been impressed by Calvin's system of ministerial training : he was equally influenced by the educated Genevan laity whose privileges and rights in the government of the Church presented a striking contrast to the laity in England under the Episcopate. The discipline of Geneva, the selection of ministers, the dignified ordering of public worship, rebuked the slovenly habits of the English clergy, and the neglect of adequate pastoral oversight by the bishops. In Lincolnshire there were no more than a hundred and twenty-one preachers against five hundred and ninety livings. Out of ten thousand parishes in the country were eight thousand without " preaching ministers ".

The Puritans sought an end of the ceremonies and priestly robes of Rome in the worship of the Anglican Church ; also a thorough reform of Anglican Church polity, nothing less than the abolition of the " Essential Ministry " and the Church Courts which " were full of abominations " ; also the Presbyterian order of the equality of all ministers as a substitute for the rule of the bishops ; also freedom for the preaching of the Word of God. The Puritans were numerous enough to present two Admonitions to Parliament in 1572 to secure their demands : but the Admonitions were nothing less than an attempt to establish Presbyterianism as the National Church in England. Cartwright defended the Admonitions on the basis of Scripture ; but while Whitgift said that no exact direction of Church polity was to be found in the New Testament he argued for the authority of tradition in defence of Episcopacy ; also that Episcopacy was established by the Law of England and any revolt against such law was sedition. The Queen was angry with the Admonitions and dismissed Cartwright from his professorship ; Field and Wilcox, who supported the Admonitions, were imprisoned in Newgate.

The attitude of the Queen to the request for " prophesyings " or larger freedom for preachers of the gospel is judged by her arbitrary treatment of Grindal, Archbishop of Canterbury (1576–83), Whitgift's predecessor. Grindal desired more and better equipped preachers, for the " public and continual preaching of God's Word is the ordinary mean and instrument of the salvation of mankind ". He assured the Queen that the loyalty of London to herself was due to the continual preaching of God's Word in the city. Grindal disowned the name of Puritan, but his broad sympathies were with the Puritan emphasis on the preaching of the Word. The Queen was adamant. Grindal implored her " not to pronounce so peremptorily on matters of faith and religion as you may do in civil matters, but to remember that in God's cause the will of God, and not the will of any earthly creature, is to take place." For such courageous advice Grindal was suspended from his office. Elizabeth refused permissions for free assemblies of people to hear and discuss the Word of God. The laity must be ruled lest they learn the art of governing themselves.

The Puritan reformers contended for their convictions, but they are subject to the strictures which we passed on Calvin their master—they did not repudiate the weapon of persecution, nor did they exclude the magistrate from interference in matters of religious belief and worship. Their Admonitions aimed at the establishment and endowment of Presbyterianism instead of Episcopacy—a noble attempt to abolish the abuses of the Church while remaining within its membership. But the Nonconformists reasoned that these Puritan reforms fell short of the scriptural ideal of the purity of the Church.

VI

The third group of Reformers under the Tudors were Nonconformists. During the reign of Henry VIII in South-East England there were worshippers who withdrew from the Church of England " having gathered congregations of their own ".[1] Under Elizabeth in 1567 about a hundred people, while worshipping in the Plumbers' Hall, London, were surprised, arrested and kept in prison for upwards of a year. But it was the prophetic leadership of Robert Browne, born about 1550, a graduate of Cambridge, which kindled the reforming passion of the Nonconformist movement. He was succeeded by other leaders, Henry Barrowe, educated at Cambridge, and John Greenwood, a Puritan minister who had been expelled from his living in Norfolk, both slightly younger men than Browne: to these must be added John Penry, the evangelist of Wales; another was Francis Johnson, a persecutor, who was converted to Nonconformity and became pastor of a church in London in 1592. He was arrested and imprisoned in the Clink for five years, but reached Amsterdam in 1597. These men and many other suffered for their faith. It is said that Browne was in thirty-two prisons; and broken in health, he defaulted at last and accepted a living in 1591 at Achurch-cum-Thorpe, near Northampton. Barrowe, Greenwood and Penry, after years of imprisonment, were hanged as seditious heretics in 1593. Archbishop Whitgift relaxed no effort until such leaders were silenced. The Nonconformists rejected outright the prevailing idea and condition of church membership under the Tudors: to reckon church membership in the terms of population or nationality, they said, was utterly unscriptural. It was towards the end of

[1] Dale, *History of Congregationalism*, p. 61.

Elizabeth's reign that Hooker wrote his *Laws of Ecclesiastical Polity* and gave classic definition to such matters as membership, order of worship and the government of the Anglican Church. He appealed to reason and scripture to refute the Puritans and defended Anglicanism against their charges of corruption. But it was his doctrine of church membership which the Nonconformists vigorously assailed. The idea of the Church as including good and evil alike had prevailed for a thousand years. Luther and Calvin had not rejected it. When it was assumed under the Tudors that the nation, by attending worship, was the Church, the Nonconformists would have none of it. Hooker reasoned that where the Christian Church existed in a Christian Commonwealth both Church and State constituted one society fulfilling different functions : " seeing that there is not any man of the Church of England, but the same man is also a member of the Commonwealth, nor any member of the Commonwealth which is not also of the Church of England ". To be an Englishman and attend worship was to be counted a Christian, and a member of the Church. When this theory was applied to the parish, and the inhabitants in the parish were reckoned as members of the Church of Christ, Barrowe attacked the theory as morally indefensible. " All the profane and wicked of the land, Atheists, Papists, Anabaptists, and heretics of all sorts, gluttons, rioters, blasphemers, perjurers, covetous, extortioners, thieves . . . witches, conjurors, etc., and who not that dwelleth within this island, or is within the Queen's dominion . . . all without exception or respect of person are received into and nourished in the bosom of this Church, with the word and sacraments . . . all this people, with all these manners, were in one day, with the blast of Queen Elizabeth's trumpet, of ignorant Papists and gross idolaters, made faithful Christians and true professors "[1].

There is no lack of evidence of the prevalence of these spiritual conditions and of the illiteracy of the clergy. In a " supplication " from the people of Cornwall we read the most serious accusations. " We have ", they say, " about one hundred and sixty churches, the greatest part of which are supplied by men who are guilty of the grossest sins ; some fornicators, some

[1] Dale, ibid., p. 148, quoted from Barrowe's *Brief Discoverie of the False Church*.

adulterers, some felons, bearing the marks in their hands for the said offences, some drunkards, gamesters on the Sabbath Day ".[1]

In 1584 seven members of the Privy Council protested to the Archbishop of Canterbury because he removed Puritan preachers who were zealous and learned, and allowed to remain in their livings such clergy as were " charged or chargeable with great and enormous faults, as drunkenness, filthiness of life, gaming at cards, haunting of ale-houses, and such-like ".[2] The lists supplied to the Archbishop named drunkards, swearers, dicers, adulterers who had been allowed to retain their livings in Essex.

In 1560 Lever writes : " Many of our parishes have no clergymen, and some dioceses are without a bishop. And out of that very number who administer the Sacraments throughout this great country there is hardly one in a hundred who is both able and willing to preach the Word of God : but all persons are obliged to read only what is prescribed in the books ".[3]

We have seen how similar immoral conditions had been denounced by the Puritans, but Elizabeth did nothing to remove such abuses. The Nonconformists, however, were far more revolutionary. In his treatise, *Reformation Without Tarrying for Any*, Browne charged the Puritans with inconsistency since they tarried and compromised, hoping the Queen and the magistrates would initiate the reform they desired. The time had now arrived, said Barrowe, for all " Christians to withdraw and to refuse to support by money the false ministries of the Church ".

The price paid by the Nonconformists who did withdraw is indicated in the petition presented by those in London jails. " We are ready to prove our Church order to be warranted by the Word of God, allowable by her majesty's laws, and no ways prejudicial to her sovereign power ; and to disprove the public hierarchy, worship, and government by such evidence of Scripture as our adversaries shall not be able to withstand, protesting, if we fail herein, not only willingly to sustain such deserving punishment as shall be inflicted on us, but to become conformable for the future. But the prelates of this land have for a long time dealt most injuriously and outrageously with us

---

[1] Quoted by Dale, p. 115.
[2] Ibid., p. 115.
[3] A. Peel, *Essays Congregational and Catholic*, p. 273.

by the great power and high authority they have gotten in their hands and usurped, above all the public courts, judges, laws and charters of this land, persecuting, imprisoning, and detaining at their pleasure our poor bodies, without any trial, release or bail, and hitherto without any cause either for error or crime indirectly objected. Some of us they have kept in close prison four or five years with miserable usage, as Henry Barrowe and John Greenwood, now in the Fleet; others they have cast into Newgate and laden with as many irons as they could bear; others into dangerous and loathsome jails among the most facinorous and vile persons, where it is lamentable to relate how many of these innocents have perished within these five years. . . . Their manner of pursuing and apprehending us is with no less violence and outrage; their pursuivants with their assistants break into our houses at all times of the night, where they break open, ransack, and rifle at their pleasure, under pretence of searching for seditious, unlawful books. The husbands in the dead of night they have plucked out of their beds from their wives, and haled them to prison. . . . That which we crave for us all is the liberty to die openly or live openly in the land of our nativity; if we deserve death, let us not be closely murdered, yea, starved to death with hunger and cold, and stifled in loathsome dungeons ".[1]

In 1593 a new effort was made to compel all persons over sixteen years of age to attend church, to silence those who in print or speech denied Elizabeth's supremacy in the Church, and to suppress any gathering of Puritans and Nonconformists for worship. The penalty was prison: if they refused to conform within three months they must leave England; if they returned without permission they were to be hanged. Many Nonconformists who were released from jail sailed to Holland, where they could worship God according to their convictions born of diligent and conscientious New Testament scholarship. It cannot be stressed too firmly that English Nonconformity was a purely spiritual movement, the work of men of learning whose faith and theology were rooted in Biblical sources.

1. The Church, they affirmed, belongs to Christ alone. He is the Head. In the Church there is no other Supremacy than

[1] Mackinnon, *History of Modern Liberty*, II, p. 358 f.

His. The only authority over, or in, the Church derives from Him Who loved the Church and bought her with His own blood.

2. The Church is the divine society on earth constituted of those who believe in Christ and who confess Him as Lord and Saviour : such believers are " gathered " out of the world ; they acknowledge Christ as the Final Revelation of God, and they test faith, worship, the order of Church government, and ethical ideals, by the standard of the New Testament.

3. Wherever and whenever believers gather together in the name of Christ there is Christ Himself ; and where Christ is there the Church is : such a Church is a priesthood of believers, competent after humbly seeking the mind of Christ according to the Scriptures, and praying for the guidance of the Holy Spirit, to receive believers into fellowship, to order its own forms of worship, to choose its own ministers and to discipline its own members.

4. The ministry is the functioning of the whole membership of the Church : it is a divine vocation, the call and gift of Christ and of no other ; but as functioning within the Church the " call " is confirmed by the whole membership of the local fellowship. Dale's High Churchmanship is revealed in his account of the early Nonconformist doctrine of the " call " of the Church to the Minister : " it was not Browne's view that the powers of Pastors, Teachers and Elders were derived from the people. Pastor, Teacher and Elder have the ' office and message of God ', and the Church has simply to discover to what persons the ' office and message of God ' have been entrusted. It was not the right, said Browne, to choose their own ministers, but the right to judge what ministers God had chosen for them ".[1]

5. Browne advised local churches to constitute themselves into a Synod for mutual help and fellowship.

These Principles committed the early Nonconformists to claim freedom for the Church from State Control. In matters of Faith and government the authority was that of the Church, received from Christ. Even so, these pioneers fell short of full religious toleration. When the true Church had been

[1] Dale, p. 128.

66

instituted, said Browne, magistrates and rulers should keep church members to it and even " put them to death " if they defaulted. Pious princes and rulers, said Browne, should " suppress and root out of their dominions " all false religion and worship. Not yet had these early Nonconformists arrived at a true conception of tolerance. Even so, they laid foundations on which their successors were to complete the work they had so nobly begun.

We have claimed that early Nonconformity was a purely spiritual movement. The nature of the Church, as we have sketched it, is clearly based on the study of Scripture ; and such study illustrates the methods of early Nonconformist scholars and preachers. They knew the biblical and theological work of Calvin, but they went behind Calvin to the original sources of the Faith itself. When Whitgift argued from Tradition in support of Episcopacy, Cartwright replied that the Church had taken wrong turnings in history, and that tradition must bear the test of, and must not contradict, the authority of the Word of God. The early Nonconformists did not make the mistake of interpreting Scripture according to the Fathers ; they judged the Fathers as we judge them—valuable witnesses in their generation—but after all, second-hand witnesses. Anyone who knows the patristic writings is conscious of their inferior quality. " When we pass to the Sub-Apostolic age the spiritual, ethical, intellectual tone of the books ", says Raven, " falls to a lower level ". Back of Calvin and the Fathers and Tradition, the Nonconformists returned to the sources of the Faith once for all delivered to the saints. There they learned how superstition and ecclesiastical policies had distorted the Faith. As they studied the New Testament they found no Hierarchy therein ; no gulf between the priesthood and the laity ; no claims by the apostles such as others have made for them ; no evidence to support the view that monarchial episcopacy was essential to the very existence of the Church. On the other hand, they found that the whole Church was the Body of Christ, and they found throughout the New Testament that the ministry was the gift of Christ to men to proclaim the Gospel and to serve, not to rule over, the Church.

This return to New Testament sources, leaping as it did the centuries, affirms that spiritual " succession " between the

Church to-day and the New Testament is the only vital " succession " that counts. It meant a return to personal religion, to a first-hand experience of repentance and faith and communion with God in Christ. And it is a sufficient answer to any uninformed criticism of early Nonconformity to point out that it was a return to the High Churchmanship of the apostles, prophets and martyrs of the New Testament.

But there is more to be said : early Nonconformity was a movement of the Holy Spirit. These students of the Word of God learned that the Holy Spirit was ever renewing their thought, emotion and initiative. The sickly atmosphere of scholasticism and custom was swept and cleansed as they experienced the freedom and exhilaration of the life of the Spirit. Under the guidance of the Holy Spirit their world was vaster and more spacious than the eccelsiastical world they had known. The Holy Spirit who inspired the writers of the New Testament inspired their own spirit, thus leading them into the truth. The indwelling of the Holy Spirit to the Puritans and Nonconformists was a startling discovery.

Dr. Geoffrey F. Nuttall in his most valuable book, *The Holy Spirit in Puritan Faith and Experience*, shows how Erasmus and Edmund Campion " had sufficient penetration to perceive that in the doctrine of the Holy Spirit lay the fundamental difference between Protestantism and Roman Catholicism, a difference deeper than that over Scripture, for which in fact it was the basis " : he adds, " The Separatism of Browne and Barrowe in this country was bound up with a re-assertion of the doctrine of the Holy Spirit ". It is remarkable that " Aquinas treats the whole subject of revelation without referring to the Spirit ". On the contrary, " Browne believed that the Spirit was all that mattered " and based the " life of the Church solely upon the inward power of the Spirit ". Barrowe's " anticipation of Quaker practice in rejecting the democratic principle of discovering majorities by voting, for the charismatic principle of seeking the unity of the Spirit ' in the sense of the meeting ' is noteworthy in this connection ".[1]

The review[2] by Dean Matthews of Dr. Nuttall's book is

---

[1] p. 4 ff.
[2] *Congregational Quarterly*, January, 1947.

relevant to my claims for the early Nonconformists. Free Churchmen owe the Dean much gratitude for his own lucid contributions to Theology and the Philosophy of Religion. He admits, however, that Dr. Nuttall's " field of which he gives a thoroughly documented survey is a strange one to me and one which, to an Anglican who has had some connection with cathedrals, has always appeared slightly repellant ". The book inspired in the Dean " a respect for some of the Puritan divines ". He agrees that " the spiritual and intellectual energy which was generated in the Puritan movement was intense, but one cannot help feeling that it was less effective for good than it might have been, because of the lack of a sense of the importance of the Body of Christ as the dwelling-place of the Spirit. If the men of the seventeenth century had thought more than they did of keeping " the unity of the Spirit in the bond of peace " it would have been better for them and for us ". Dr. Nuttall " almost persuades me that the Puritans were really tolerant, but I fear that a tolerance which stopped short of Anglicans, Roman Catholics and Quakers was not the genuine article ".

I have quoted Dean Matthews for his appreciation of the work of Dr. Nuttall, a review which is marred, however, by his reference to tolerance. Surely the Dean sees that when Barrowe, Greenwood and Penry were hanged for refusing to conform, when others were imprisoned for years in stinking gaols, when others were exiled—the Anglican Church was guilty of an intolerance and a crime which stains her history. Nonconformity was a movement of the Spirit, but the State refused permission to Nonconformists to speak or preach or gather for worship, and the Bishops supported the State. What were they to do ? Were they to take a vow of silence, or condemn themselves to solitariness, denying themselves the spiritual and social fellowship of kindred souls ? The Anglican Church was no spiritual home for these men. Nuttall says, to grant " the liberty of the Spirit " to others is tolerance, and there is more of this attitude in the reformers than in the Church of the Tudors ; he adds that " the government of the Spirit is toleration "—which we shall consider later. It is enough to point out here that " the government of the Spirit " was something unknown to the Church under the Tudors. The Nonconformists were not subversive theorists as their principles prove. They asked to be let alone to worship God ; when the State and the Church refused to let them alone, but tried to compel them against their convictions, they were courageous, refusing to be silenced, ready to accept martyrdom rather than be traitors to themselves or to God. And these spiritual convictions, so revolutionary in the age of the Tudors, became transmuted into dynamic forces which created religious and political structures which have endured.

CHAPTER IV

EXILES: PILGRIMS: PRINCIPLES

I

THE martyrdom of Barrowe, Greenwood and Penry, the continued severity of persecution, the numbers of the exiles in Holland, must have encouraged Elizabeth and the Bishops to assume that Nonconformity was well-nigh stamped out of existence. But during the closing years of the Queen's reign, Puritanism had been spreading its roots in the rural areas of Gainsborough and Scrooby, where we find incumbents who had left the Church and accepted Nonconformist principles. To this district were attracted remarkably gifted men who had been penalised for their convictions and had separated from the Church of England; such were John Smyth, Thomas Helwys, John Robinson, Murton, Brewster and Bradford—all members of the church at Gainsborough or later at Scrooby. Most of them were university trained and all were convinced Nonconformists. It soon became impossible for these two churches to escape the detection of the authorities. Pickets kept watch on the homes and movements of these people. Some were imprisoned and after much tribulation the Gainsborough Church fled to Amsterdam and the Scrooby Church finally settled at Leyden.

What new factors accounted for these exiles seeking religious freedom in a strange land? In 1603, James I became King. As he journeyed from Scotland a Puritan-Presbyterian deputation met him to present "The Millenary Petition", signed by upwards of eight hundred Puritan ministers; also to discuss the redress of grievances which had been stated in previous Admonitions to Parliament. The answer of James was to call the Hampton Court Conference in 1604 to consider anything in the settlement of the Church which "might deserve a review and amendment". Representatives of the Bishops and the Puritans

71

were present, and James, who regarded himself a theologian, presided. The Puritans stated their requests—ceremonial changes of dress and worship, more freedom in preaching, an opportunity for the clergy to meet every three weeks, and a final appeal on matters under dispute to a synod at which the bishop should preside. James, who had often been in trouble with the Presbyterians in Scotland, took fright at the word Synod ; and in contemptuous manner he accused the Puritans of seeking to introduce " the local Presbytery " into the Church of England. In answer to this charge the Puritans replied that they accepted the King's supremacy of the church. At which remark James turned to the Bishops : " If once you were out and they in your place, I know what would become of my supremacy—No bishop, no king ! " The grievances remained and Dale says the Bishops offered James " profane adulation ". The Archbishop of Canterbury thought James' speech was prompted " by the special assistance of the Holy Ghost. Bancroft, Bishop of London, fell upon his knees, and protested that his heart melted within him for joy, and he acknowledged to Almighty God the singular mercy they had received at His hands in His giving them such a king as since Christ's time, he thought had never been . . . to see a bishop in lawn sleeves kneeling on the floor . . . and to hear the assurance of an Archbishop that he had spoken with the special assistance of the Holy Ghost made him (James) feel that at last he had the power as well as the name of a king, and must have convinced him that episcopacy had the most sacred claims to his protection and support ".[1]

The Puritans received nothing from James but contemptuous manners and speech. " If this is all they have to say, " he remarked, " I shall make them conform or I will harry them out of the land or do worse ." Shortly after the Hampton Court Conference, Bancroft was made Archbishop of Canterbury ; he had been ferocious in his resolve to destroy Puritanism and Nonconformity, and proceeded to organise " measures suggestive of a rat hunt ".[2] The heaviest penalties were exacted upon all who refused to conform to the worship of the Church of England. And the loss of precious civil rights was added to all other suffer-

[1] Dale, p. 183.
[2] F. J. Powicke, *Essays Congregational and Catholic*, p. 282.

ings and humiliation. This was in 1604. By 1608 the Non-conformists of Gainsborough and Scrooby had escaped to Holland.

II

We must now consider these exiles, for spiritual forces were stirring within these men who were destined to make history in England and America. The church in Amsterdam, of which Francis Johnson was pastor, had sent a deputation to James with a request that they might return to England, also setting forth in fourteen clauses their Nonconformist principles. To which approach James does not appear to have made any response. When John Smyth had been but a short time in Amsterdam, he became involved in controversy with Johnson regarding forms and methods of worship, and the government of the church by the elders—a dispute which led to the secession of Smyth and the Gainsborough group, and the formation of a separate church of which Smyth was chosen as minister. Within this church a discussion soon arose on Baptism, for Smyth was now convinced that baptism of believers was the New Testament practice : whereupon the church dissolved its membership and Smyth baptized himself and afterwards the rest of the members. Smyth's baptism was by affusion not by immersion. Controversy soon arose over the procedure of Smyth baptizing himself. And the controversy shook Smyth's confidence in his own baptism. He therefore sought out the Mennonites who practised believers' baptism and was baptized. Over thirty members of the church agreed and bound themselves by covenant to this course of action. Thus was founded in Holland in 1609 the first English Baptist Church. Smyth died in 1612 at the age of forty-five.

When Helwys heard of the sufferings of Nonconformists who had remained in England he regretted the flight of the Gainsborough church to Holland. And before the end of 1612, Helwys and the church of which he had been appointed pastor had returned to England, prepared to face all the trials which they knew awaited them. They made their spiritual home in Spitalfields outside London—the first Baptist Church established on English soil. The same year Helwys wrote his short Declaration of *The Mistery of Iniquity*, a courageous statement of Free Church principles addressed to James I. But the king decided that such an author was too dangerous to be at liberty ; he was arrested, imprisoned, and died before the close of 1616.

The Scrooby group of exiles led by Brewster and John Robinson found the controversial atmosphere of Amsterdam uncongenial and moved to Leyden. Here they became a happy and flourishing community. John Robinson became pastor and an honoured member of the University. Brewster was the elder and became a printer and publisher. But Leyden was no abiding city for these exiles ; they feared " their posterity would in a few generations become Dutch and so lose their interest in the English nation ". They yearned for a permanent home and resolved to seek it in Virginia. The licence to found a colony there was long delayed, and not until 22nd July, 1620, were they able to sail in the *Speedwell* to Southampton ; " and so ", writes Bradford, " they left that goodly and pleasant city which had been their resting place near twelve years. But they knew they were Pilgrims, and looked not much on those things, but lifted up their eyes to the heavens, their dearest country, and quieted their spirits ". At Southampton they joined the *Mayflower* and later set sail from Plymouth. The *Speedwell* was twice compelled to put back to harbour and on September 16th the *Mayflower* sailed alone, arriving on December 21st at Plymouth Rock. Bradford became the governor of the new colony and Brewster the elder of the church. John Robinson remained at Leyden and his farewell message to the Pilgrims is written in the heart of the Churches of the Congregational Order.

" We are now ere long to part asunder, and the Lord knoweth whether ever he should see our faces again, but whether the Lord had appointed it or not, he charged us before God and His blessed angels, to follow him no further than he followed Christ. And if God should reveal anything to us by any other instrument of His, to be as ready to receive it, as ever we were to receive any truth by his ministry ; for he was very confident the Lord had more truth and light to break forth out of His holy Word ".

III

The Nonconformists had divided into Congregationalists and Baptists and the division has continued to this day. It will be useful still to refer to these churches as Nonconformist. But it is now possible to state Free Church principles which were being defined more clearly than under the Tudors. Nonconformity had been growing, it was becoming organised, it was no longer the isolated effort of the individual. We pointed out how Browne and Barrowe would use the magistrate and the ruler " to keep church members to it and suppress and root out all false religion ". The Pilgrims did not establish full religious and political freedom in the colony of New Plymouth. But John Smyth, Thomas Helwys and Leonard Busher, all Baptist pioneers, declared the high principle of religious tolerance.

John Smyth was educated at Cambridge and elected a Fellow of Christ College in 1579. He was ordained by the Bishop of Lincoln and held a Lectureship in the city. As a Puritan he was soon in trouble with the authorities, left the Church of England, and later became a member of the church at Gainsborough. In his search for truth he did not shrink from controversy, although the tenderness of his nature is obvious from his later writings. He drew up a comprehensive Confession of Faith extending to a hundred clauses, in one of which he affirmed : " that the magistrate is not by virtue of his office to meddle with religion, or matters of conscience, to force and compel men to this or that form of religion or doctrine : but to leave religion free to every man's conscience ". It is claimed that John Smyth was the first Englishman to enunciate this principle of complete religious freedom.

Thomas Helwys was a Nottinghamshire man who received his legal training at Gray's Inn. We have pointed out that he returned to England in 1612 with the church of which he was pastor. It was in the same year that he published *A Short Declaration of the Mistery of Iniquity*. The Treatise is dedicated to King James, and indicates the nature of the Iniquity against which Helwys writes with passion. The burden of his argument is that James is but an earthly king and has no authority to meddle in the matter of a man's religion. The king should recognise that religion is a matter between a man and his God. James has not received authority from God to persecute heretics.

Of Leonard Busher nothing is known except that he was a member of the Spitalfields Church. He was sufficiently educated to read his Greek New Testament. In 1614 he addressed to James and the High Court of Parliament then sitting, a Treatise *Religious Peace : A Plea for Liberty of Conscience.*

" But your Majesty and parliament may please to understand, that the Scriptures do teach, that the one true religion is gotten by a new birth, even by the Word and Spirit of God and therewith also it is maintained and defended . . . and no king nor bishop, can or is able to command faith . . . you may force men to church against their consciences but they will believe as they did afore when they come there . . . I read that Jews, Christians and Turks are tolerated in Constantinople . . . and how much more ought Christians to tolerate Christians . . . shall we be less merciful than the Turks . . . the bishops betray great ignorance when they persuade the king and parliament to force prince and people to church by persecution . . . the bishops should understand, that it is preaching and not persecuting, that getteth people to the church of Christ . . . therefore persecution for difference in religion is a monstrous and cruel beast and hindreth the gospel of Christ . . . be not your bishops' executioners in burning, banishing, hanging and imprisoning of harmless and peaceable Christians ; but let them enjoy freedom of the gospel and liberty of conscience ". " From a dingy meeting-house ", says Masson in his *Life of John Milton,* " somewhere in Old London, there flashed out first in England the absolute doctrine of Religious Liberty . . . not to the Church of England . . . nor to Scottish Presbyterianism, nor to English Puritanism does the honour of the first perception of the full principle of liberty of conscience, and its first assertion in English speech, belong. That honour has to be assigned, I believe, to the Independents generally, and to the Baptists in particular ".

Any account of the return of the exiles from Holland must include the name of Jacob. As a Puritan he had signed the petition to James in 1603 on his journey from Scotland. In 1604 he was in the Clink for his views. He had contended with Francis Johnson but became a convinced Congregationalist and a member of the Church in Leyden. Like Helwys, he thought the exiles should return to their native land, and with John Robinson's blessing Jacob arrived in London in 1616 with certain members of the Leyden fellowship. After a day of fasting and prayer, each one made open confession of his faith and joined hands and covenanted to walk together in all God's ways and ordinances, according as He had revealed them or should further make them known. This was the "Pilgrim Church" founded in New Kent Road, of which Jacob was pastor—the third Congregational Church to be founded on English soil.[1]

[1] Powicke, p. 383 ; Dale, p. 213 f.

CHAPTER V

OPPRESSIONS IN RELIGION

THE Nonconformist conscience had uttered its voice and the principle of the Free Church had been proclaimed. To win religious freedom, however, was to involve a long and unrelenting struggle. The alliance of Church and State, of Charles I and Laud, was like a formidable mountain across the road to religious and political freedom. The Presbyterian Puritans were strong, but the Nonconformists were still few in number. The absolutists in Church and State had been unifying and consolidating the forces against them and fortunately a new and powerful ally now came to the aid of the reformers—the House of Commons accepted the challenge of battle for the rights of the English people.

I

The chronic constitutional conflicts during the Stuart period were due to religious as well as political tension. Throughout the strife between king and Parliament the religious question was mainly dictating events. The Stuarts were obsessed by the divine right of their kingship, and they assumed the Church existed to sustain such rights ; they felt more securely seated on the throne when the Church exalted kingship as a divine institution, and obedience as a sacred duty. Likewise, the Church believed its privileges could only be maintained when the authority of ruler was firmly established. Thus absolutism in Church and State buttressed each other. Laud magnified the supremacy of the king over the church because he knew the king would protect the church for the sake of the State. It was against this ecclesiastical and political absolutism that Parliament during the reigns of James I and Charles I fought for its own existence ; and included in the Parliamentary ranks were orthodox churchmen as well as Puritans. But when Parliament was contending for the rights and liberties of the English people against the king, the bishops supported the king. Likewise, when Anglican Churchmen and Puritans were resisting the grievances and abuses of the Church, the Bishops could rely on the support of the Stuarts.

The storm centre of the Stuart period was that " Rex was Lex ." James boasted of " having broken the necks of three Parliaments one after another ". And he had done so by claiming that " he was above law and that it was treason to affirm that he was not ". When Coke, his Lord Chief Justice, accused him of interference in the administration of the Law, James retorted : " as for the absolute prerogative of the Crown, that is no subject for the tongue of a lawyer, nor is it lawful to be disputed. It is atheism and blasphemy to dispute what God can do . . . so it is presumptive and high contempt in a subject to dispute what a king can do, or to say what a king cannot do." To this absurd demand for supremacy in Church and State, the Parliament, Puritans and People of England were expected to submit. And when this supreme ruler in the church issued his Book of Sports and permitted glaring immoralities at his Court, Puritans and Nonconformists who protested, were " harried out of the land ".

" There are three things I will not part with," said Charles I, "the Church, my crown and my friends ". In the end, he lost the three things, but not until he and friends had provoked two civil wars. His Royal Supremacy included the right to rule the Church and the Episcopate, and he pursued his tortuous diplomacy to this end. Whatever was expedient was manipulated to give Charles the control of the bishops and the clergy. It never occurred to Charles that deceit and double-dealing might be inconsistent with his ideas of divine right : " He appears to have acted on the belief that, as the divinely appointed king, he need have no moral scruples in dealing with those who tried to thwart his will ".[1] Petitions poured into Parliament against the tyrannies of his reign. Repeated appeals were addressed to him to acknowledge the rights of Parliament in the English Constitution, but Charles feared and hated the Puritans in and out of Parliament. " Predestination was the root of all Puritanism",

[1] *John Pym,* by S. R. Brett, p. 69.

he said, "and Puritanism was the root of all rebellion". For the " rabble " of the Nonconformists his contempt was brutal. He could trust Laud to take care of them. Thus Charles ruled England ; he was evasive, slippery, playing off his opponents against each other by intrigue and delaying devices, while his scornful attitude to Parliament is measured by the eleven years when he governed the country without it.

II

In the service of such arbitrary government, Laud was the friend of Charles. As for the king he was not without a sense of humour : but Laud's nature was sour and malicious. His conception of his duty was to establish and expand the divine right of Episcopacy at whatever cost to his victims. Could any policy have been more stupid, and more certain to provoke revolution, than the determination of Laud and Charles to thrust Prelacy on Scotland ? But they persisted from 1633, when Charles was crowned King of Scotland in Edinburgh, until what Episcopacy there was in Scotland had been abolished. Such an imperious attitude against a nation cradled in Presbyterian principles kindled revolt throughout the land. Without consulting the Scots, Charles issued a royal warrant that all Presbyterian ministers should wear episcopal robes when conducting worship : then followed a Book of Canons and a Book of Common Prayer to be used in all the churches. No Presbyterian minister was to be permitted to preach until he had subscribed to the Canons. When the Presbyterian leaders objected, Charles commanded them " not to dispute, but vote " ; he added " I mean to be obeyed ". The scene in St. Giles, Edinburgh when the Anglican service was introduced on 23rd July, 1637, was a tumult in which stools and Bibles and other things were hurled at the head of the Dean of Edinburgh. And when the Scots demanded the withdrawal of the Prayer Book and the Canons, Charles answered : " I will rather die than yield to these impertinent and damnable demands ". When the Scots began to arm and told Charles there would be bloody war, he affirmed his divine supremacy, " Our right is from God ". But Charles and Laud had over-reached themselves. The Scots did arm and

Leslie was soon ready to march into the North of England with 30,000 men "to defend their religion and their liberties". Charles only escaped from the trap into which he and Laud had blundered by signing the Treaty of Berwick on 18th June, 1639. A few months afterwards he decided to summon Parliament.

Meanwhile, Laud had pursued his episcopal policy in England. He became Archbishop of Canterbury in 1633 and Chancellor of the Exchequer in 1635. Armed with such ecclesiastical and civil authority, he soon had his finger in every political pie. He used his power ruthlessly to destroy his opponents: " It is, " said Laud, " for the king and episcopate to judge in questions of religion ". Thus he attempted to enforce episcopal authority and forms of worship on Puritans and Nonconformists. His methods of extirpating the views of his enemies were equally " thorough "; he set up a rigid censorship of the Press, he made it seditious to preach, he used the Star Chamber and Court of High Commission as engines of his despotism. We give a few examples of his methods of repressing his victims.

Alexander Leighton, father of a future Archbishop of Glasgow, a graduate, a physician and a preacher, wrote a pamphlet, *Sion's Plea Against the Prelacy,* in which he sought to prove to the English people that Episcopacy was anti-Christian " and cannot consist in a nation with soundness of doctrine and sincerity of worship ". He called upon Parliament to smite the " infernal hierarchy ". Coming from a Scot, Laud resented this advice to England and ordered Leighton's ears to be cut off, his nose to be slit, in addition to a fine of £10,000.

Prynne was a prolific pamphleteer. In his *Histriomastic or Scourge of Players* he identified Charles I with Nero and the Queen with Herodias. For which Pyrnne lost his ears and was fined £5,000.

Henry Burton, a Yorkshireman, who was at Cambridge in 1595, was a far more serious writer. For two sermons in 1636 he was accused by Laud of sedition. Before the Star Chamber, Burton pleaded the right of conscience to preach the Word of God. Between his summons and his appearance before the Star Chamber, Burton describes how Laud's agents pestered him at home: " those barking beadles ceased not night nor day to watch and rap and ring at my doors . . . nor yet to search and hunt all the printing houses about London ". For such preaching Burton was fined £5,000 ; he was put in the pillory and had both ears cut off. Prynne, Burton, and Bastwick, who had similar treatment and fines, were imprisoned for life as a warning to others. Their foreheads or cheeks were branded. Laud's ferocity towards the Nonconformists was implacable. As Burton left London for lifelong imprisonment a hundred thousand people gathered to say farewell and express their resentment against his persecutors. Four days after the Long Parliament met in November, 1640, Prynne, Burton and Bastwick were freed and commanded to appear at the bar of the House of Commons to certify that they had been mutilated and branded. Let Clarendon tell of their triumphant reception : " When they came near London multitudes of people of several conditions, some on horseback, other on foot, met them some miles from the town ; many having been a day's journey ; and so they were brought, about two of the clock in the afternoon, in at Charing Cross, and carried into the city by above 10,000 persons, with boughs and flowers in their hands ; the common people strewing flowers and herbs in the ways as they passed, making great noise and expressions of joy for their deliverance and return : and in those acclamations mingling loud and virulent exclamations against the bishops who had so cruelly persecuted such godly men ".[1]

The result of these oppressions of Laud was twofold. His victims became popular in the country and prepared the ground for the growth of Protestant and Nonconformist principles. Every prosecution won public sympathy with his victims and rebounded with curses on Laud's own head. The second result was to drive thousands of Englishmen into exile to seek refuge in New England, where they founded a colony without a king and a church without bishops.[2]

Nortwithstanding the policy to silence his opponents in the pulpit and the Press, Laud was beaten in the battle of the pamphlets. When the Long Parliament met in November, 1640, Thomason, a bookseller, began to collect controversial tracts, and he had soon accumulated over a thousand. Laud had for-

[1] Clarendon, *History*, I, p. 283 f.
[2] cf. G. M. Trevelyan, *History of England*, p. 393 f. ; H. A. L. Fisber, *History of Europe*, II, p. 650 f.

bidden his own followers to defend him in the Press; but at last he commissioned Bishop Hall of Norwich to write on *Episcopacy by Divine Right Asserted*. It was quickly answered by five Puritan preachers and writers known under the name of Smectymnus. But at this stage Milton, the greatest literary genius of the Commonwealth period, was drawn into the controversy. Milton had gone to Cambridge in 1625 intending to enter the Anglican Ministry; but the methods of study, the curricula, the books which reeked " of monkish cells ", the futility of disputations, ever debating and " never able to come to the knowledge of the truth "—the result being " to make you a more finished fool and cleverer contriver of conceits and to endow you with a more expert ignorance "—led him to abandon the idea of entering the Church. " Truth ", said Milton, " had fled back to heaven and left error supreme in the schools ". No longer was Cambridge the nursery of great Puritan preachers and scholars as in the reign of Elizabeth.

Milton left Cambridge in 1632, and in 1638, when he wrote Lycidas, we can read his contempt for Laudian churchmanship and its deplorable results :

> How well could I have spared for thee, young swain,
> Enow of such as for their bellies sake
> Creep, and intrude, and climb into the fold ?
> Of other care they little reckoning make
> Than how to scramble at the shearer's feast,
> And shove away the worthy bidden guest ;
> Blind mouths ! that scarce themselves know how to hold
> A sheep-hook, or have learn'd aught else the least
> That to the faithful herdman's art belongs !
>
> The hungry sheep look up, and are not fed,
> But swollen with wind, and the rank mist they draw,
> Rot inwardly, and foul contagion spread.

Milton answered Hall in 1641 and 1642, and his remedy for the spiritual diseases of the Church was that Presbyterianism should displace Episcopacy. Let Presbyterianism be established. and it would be Utopia indeed ! But this was in 1641.

Pym was mistaken in the House of Commons when he

attributed Romanist intentions to Laud, who could not, dare not, admit the supremacy of the Pope over the Church, and declare the supremacy of Charles at the same time. But Laud was the founder of the Anglo-Catholic tradition in the Anglican Church : he believed in the right of Prelacy to persecute and torture, and he encouraged the ritualistic excesses which have brought one section of the Church of England to the verge of Romish doctrine and worship. Laud did Rome's work so well that a secret offer of a Cardinal's Hat was made to him—a gesture which revealed the expectations of the Vatican.

Yet books are written to exalt Laud as a martyr. Bishops openly announce that they are in the Laudian High Church Tradition : he is said to have been " a typical Englishman with his distrust of fanaticism " and one " who resisted spiritual dictatorship—a model example of all present-day lovers of the Church of England ". Does such eulogy mean that while Anglo-Catholics are more kindly, they are as exclusive as ever— never reading a book which tells of the travail of good men who were imprisoned, exiled, and in an earlier period burnt at the stake rather than submit to men of the Laudian type ? " A man superstitious, and of limited intelligence, he neither perceived the effects of his own acts nor understood the temper of the people he was called upon to rule ".[1] A hard ecclesiastic who defended and upheld the divine right of King Charles— to do wrong.

III

These oppressions in religion and the Scots' army in the north had created such reactions to the rule of Charles and Laud, that the King summoned Parliament in April, 1640 ; but when Parliament insisted on its rights before voting money for Charles, he dismissed it after three weeks. The condition of the country, however, was becoming so desperate that another Parliament was summoned for 3rd November, 1640 : when the Long Parliament, as it came to be called, met, it proceeded at once to secure guarantees of its own rights and privileges. The

[1] *Cambridge Modern History,* IV, p. 277.

Triennial Act was passed limiting the duration of future Parliaments to three years ; also that no interval between two Parliaments should exceed three years. The next step was to prevent the dissolution of Parliament without its own consent. The Star Chamber and Court of High Commission were then abolished—Acts which fundamentally changed the Tudor Constitution.

Eight days after Parliament met John Pym struck hard and swiftly at Charles's political friends. Having moved that the door of the House of Commons be locked, he impeached Strafford, and the Lords sent him to the Tower. On 18th December Pym impeached Laud of high treason, and he also was committed to the Tower. A week previously, 11th December, a monster petition, signed, it was said, by 15,000 Londoners, had been presented to the Commons demanding the abolition of Episcopacy : " That whereas the Government of Archbishops and Lord Bishops, Deans and ArchDeacons, etc., with their Courts and Ministrations in them, have proved prejudicial and very dangerous both to the Church and Commonwealth. . . . We therefore most humbly pray and beseech this Honourable Assembly, the premises considered, that the said Government with all its Dependencies, Roots and Branches, may be abolished, and Laws in their behalf made void, and the Government according to God's Word may be rightly placed amongst us ".[1] Pym was an orthodox Anglican, one for whom Presbyterianism had no attraction, not had he any use for " Nonconformist Anarchists ". It is sufficient to point out that Pym represented the attitude of many orthodox members of the Church of England towards the policy of Laud and Charles.

When, by the above measures, the House of Commons had won the battle for its own existence, it proceeded to deal with Laud's " oppressions in religion ". The person and pocket of the individual had been protected against an arbitrary monarch : what could now be done to protect the conscience of the individual from religious tyranny ? If Parliament could establish final authority over the King, what was to hinder the abolition of the royal supremacy over the Church ? It was at this point that reformers in Parliament revealed their differences. The

[1] Pym, ibid., p. 162.

House of Commons had been agreed on measures to safeguard its freedom and existence. On the issue of ecclesiastical reform the House was divided. When the Root and Branch groups moved to abolish episcopacy the conservative church party rallied to the King.

It was admitted that the condition of the Church was deplorable. Laud had supplied Charles with a list of the clergy marked " O " for Orthodox and " P " for Puritan : and Charles had promoted the former class and penalised the latter class. By this method of appointment, scandalous, illiterate and incompetent men were placed in the churches—Laud's hirelings, who were insulted in the streets. Still, at this stage, Pym and others were not in favour of abolishing episcopacy, but of reforming it. Lord Digby agreed with Pym's attitude. At the same time he desired " to clip the wings of the Prelates whereby they have mounted to such insolence." Lord Falkland agreed : " under the pretence of Uniformity the bishops had brought in superstition and defiled the Church . . . allowing the Romanists to celebrate their Mass in security, but making it a crime for Puritans to attend a Conventicle ". Such orthodox Anglicans preferred to reform episcopacy rather than abolish it and accept the Presbyterian polity. The Puritans, however, had suffered so long and so severely they could no longer trust the bishops. And at last the stubbornness of the bishops drove Pym and others to vote for the abolition of episcopacy.

" It would therefore seem that Pym took the view that if a soundly Protestant Church was unattainable with bishops, it must be attained without bishops. Faced with a choice of evils, he chose the less : that is, he sacrificed what after all was a matter of ecclesiastical administration in order to secure fulfilment of fundamental religious principles. It was the decision of a statesman shaping means to ends, and conceding—however reluctantly—a practical point in order to realise a principle to which all his life he had inflexibly adhered ".[1] The Bishops' Exclusion Bill became law 13th February, 1642 : and twelve Bishops who had supported Laud's " oppressions " were impeached and imprisoned.

The Long Parliament had achieved two victories : the first was political and broke the divine right of the king : the second

[1] Pym, ibid., p. 182.

victory was religious and broke the royal supremacy over the Church, and the divine right of Episcopacy. Parliament was now the supreme authority in the Church. How the House of Commons approached a new religious settlement will reveal the tension of the religious and political ideas of the laymen of the seventeenth century.

CHAPTER VI

PARLIAMENT ESTABLISHES PRESBYTERIANISM

THE civil war began on the 22nd August, 1642. The supremacy over the Church which had been exercised by the Tudors and Stuarts now passed to Parliament. Charles had repeatedly refused his royal assent to any reform of the Church : a prerogative he himself would never surrender, nor would he recognise its exercise by others. Parliament, however, was determined to settle the religious question on its own authority. On the 1st September, 1642, the House of Commons resolved : " That the government of the Church of England by Archbishops, Bishops, the Chancellors and Commissaries, Deans, Deans and Chapters, Archdeacons, and other ecclesiastical officers hath been found, by long experience, to be a great impediment to the perfect reformation and growth of religion, and very prejudicial to the state and government of this Kingdom : and this House doth resolve that the same shall be done away ". As Parliament was unable to conceive any substitute for episcopacy other than a national Church, what was the next step ? It proceeded to endorse its own recommendations which had been embodied in the Grand Remonstrance of 22nd November, 1641 : namely, that any substitute for episcopacy must commend conformity throughout the whole realm : " And we do here declare that it is far from our purpose or desire to let loose the golden reins of discipline and government in the Church, to leave private persons or particular congregations to take up what form of divine service they please, for we hold it requisite that there should be throughout the whole realm a conformity to that order which the laws enjoin according to the Word of God. And we desire to unburden the consciences of men of needless and superstitious ceremonies, suppress innovations, and take away the monuments of idolatry ".[1]

Hence, on 9th May, 1642, a Bill was passed in the House of

[1] Gee and Hardy, *Documents Illustrative of English Church History*, p. 561.

Commons " for calling an Assembly of godly and learned Divines, to be consulted with by the Parliament, for the settling of the Government and Liturgy of the Church, and for the vindicating and clearing of the doctrine of the Church of England from false aspersions and interpretations ". On three occasions this Bill was passed, and when Charles still refused his assent, Parliament called the Assembly on its own authority. The Assembly was constituted of several bishops, but their attendance was infrequent, about a hundred Presbyterians and five Congregationalists. There was no Baptist representative. The terms of reference were to " confer and treat among themselves of such matters and things touching and concerning the Liturgy and discipline and Government of the Church of England, or the vindicating and clearing of the doctrine of the same from all false aspersions and misconstructions as shall be proposed to them by both or either of the said Houses of Parliament, and no other ; and to deliver their opinions or advices of, or touching, the matters aforesaid, as shall be most agreeable to the Word of God, to both or either of the said Houses from time to time, in such manner and sort as by either or both of the said Houses of Parliament shall be required ". All members were pledged to secrecy of the proceedings : and these godly and learned divines were exhorted to remember that their functions were to do no more than advise Parliament. The Assembly met at Westminster on 1st July, 1643 : its last session was on 22nd February, 1649 : it sat on 1,165 occasions.

The Solemn League and Covenant had been drawn up by the Scottish Assembly to resist the attempt of Charles and Laud to force Episcopacy on Scotland : this covenant the Assembly revised and on 5th February, 1644, it became the law for all Englishmen over eighteen years : it included a vow " to extirpate prelacy, superstition, heresy, schism, profaneness and whatever shall be found contrary to sound doctrine and the power of godliness . . . to preserve and defend the true liberties of the Kingdom, to reform doctrine, worship, discipline and government according to the Word of God ". The Covenant was taken by members of Parliament, by Sunday congregations in London, and commanded by Parliament to be taken throughout the land by all over eighteen years. It was the test of loyalty to the authority of Parliament.

The Assembly began its work by revising the Thirty Nine Articles. The Presbyterian majority controlled its decisions, though the five Congregationalist members made a gallant witness to their own principles. When vital theological differences emerged there were stormy scenes. The Scots were watching proceedings and were eagerly interested : " it was my advice ", says Baillie, " to eschew a public rupture with the Independents till we were more able for them. As yet a Presbyterie to this people is conceived to be a strange monster . . . with Independencie we propose not to meddle in haste till it please God to advance our armies, which we expect will much advance our arguments ".[1]

The clash of principles came as the Assembly began to discuss the nature of the Church and the Ministry. Many " scandalous clergy " had been ejected from their livings and controversy arose over the ordination of ministers to fill their places. The Presbyterian principle was that ministers should be examined, approved and ordained by Presbytery. It was the Congregational principle that representatives of the whole Church should test and approve, and that ordination should follow the call of the local Church to the minister. What constituted Church membership proved equally divisive. Following Calvin, the Presbyterians welcomed to the Lord's Table any except " known evil livers ". The Congregationalists welcomed all who confessed Jesus Christ as their Lord and Saviour.

The truth was, the Presbyterians were afraid of the " Sects " —a horrible word—and used by them in derision, a term which Troeltsch has unfortunately used to distinguish the Free Churches from Churches using the name Catholic. The Presbyterian majority had derived from Calvin their ideals of a national Church with a definite order of worship and government : and it appeared to them that " Brownists and Baptists " were individualists and anarchists. They consented that the five Congregationalists of the Assembly were to be trusted to behave themselves : but they feared the individualism of the rebellious " Sects ".

When it became clear to the five Congregationalists that further controversy was useless, they decided to make a direct appeal to Parliament, which they did in a noble pamphlet.

[1] Mackinnon, *History of Modern Liberty*, III, p. 463 f.

They recorded their sufferings for their faith, the sorrows of exile, the desire to be loyal in faith and worship to their convictions of New Testament principles : under episcopal rule they had been imprisoned and exiled ; what was to hinder them from being imprisoned and exiled again if Presbyterianism became the established religion ? Nye's closing speech in the Assembly was a masterly defence of Congregational principles, but to no avail. Advice was given by the Assembly to Parliament to establish Presbyterianism in England. Parliament accepted this recommendation and on 28th January, 1645, Presbyterianism became the National Church. The Prayer Book had already been abolished and the Presbyterian Confession of Faith and Directory of Worship were substituted. Tolerance, however, was extended to Congregationalists.

CHAPTER VII

THE ARMY ESTABLISHES RELIGION

THE religious settlement by the House of Commons was far from acceptable. The Presbyterians had used their majority in Parliament as they had used it in the Westminster Assembly : but the Nonconformists far outnumbered them in the Army. Further, the Presbyterians resented the intention of Parliament to retain its own supremacy over the Church. To make matters worse, quarrels and jealousies began to embitter the relations between the Scots and Nonconformists : they had fought together for victory at Marston Moor, but the Scots Army accused the Parliamentary leaders of treachery and intrigue with Charles. The fact was, that since the Westminster Assembly had met in 1642 the whole political scene had changed. Cromwell and the New Model Army had been winning battles : the Nonconformists were now masters of the military and political situation. For the New Model was mainly composed of Congregationalists and Baptists : " such men as had the fear of God before them and make some conscience of what they did . . . the plain russet-coated captain that knows what he fights for and loves what he knows ". And these men had fought for religious freedom.

Again, relations between the Army and the Presbyterian majority in Parliament had become severely strained. The Army had never accepted the decision of Parliament to establish Presbyterianism in England. And when Parliament attempted to disband the Army it met with a flat refusal and a sharp demand for arrears of payment. Both before and after the second Civil War the Army had repeatedly insisted on religious freedom. To this end the New Model had overthrown its enemies. To trace the attempts of the Army to reach " a religious settlement " will again reveal the difference between the lay and ecclesiastical mind. The Army was primarily interested in religious experience which had its sources in personal relationship with God in Christ. But the Army had not yet outgrown the conception of a State Church. How to legislate for religious freedom and define the scope of religious toleration in relation to an endowed and national Church became a controversial issue which ended in a compromise unacceptable to the Levellers.

First: In "The Heads of Proposals" in 1647 the Army leaders demanded the abolition "of all coercive power, authority and jurisdiction of bishops and all other ecclesiastical officers whatsoever, extending to any civil penalties upon any : and also the repeal of all acts . . . enforcing the use of the Book of Common Prayer, or attendance at Church, or prohibiting meetings for worship apart from the regular Church . . . but stood out in any case and all cases, for Liberty and Religious Dissent ".[1]

The Army group, known as the Levellers, presented their document, "The Agreement of the People". "The Levellers' Case", says John Buchan, " had a terrible cogency. Oliver and Ireton, they said, had striven to reach an agreement with the King and Parliament and had notably failed. As practical men, therefore, they must look elsewhere and appeal to the People ".[2] Cromwell did his utmost to control these agitators, but nine regiments of cavalry and five of infantry urged " The Agreement " on the Army Council demanding an unchangeable law which would secure religious freedom. At this stage, however, the Levellers had not conceived a Church free from State control and said Parliament could establish and endow any form of religion except Popery or Prelacy. " The Agreement " was categorical that the national Church should be Protestant; that any who dissented from such a State Church should have freedom to worship according to his own conscience.

Second: In 1651 leading Congregationalist ministers sent a Petition to Parliament concerning the " Propagation of the Gospel " and made fifteen proposals. They still requested a law requiring all people to attend worship on Sunday " except such as have scruple of conscience ". Even so, such dissenters must notify a magistrate of the place where they worship. After prolonged discussion of the Petition, Parliament resolved " that

[1] cf. Articles XI–XIII.
[2] *Cromwell*, p. 253.

the magistrates hath power in matters of religion for the Propagation of the Gospel ".

Third : In 1653, during a discussion on a new Franchise and Distribution Bill, the Army leaders became so angry over the proposals that Cromwell walked into the House, spoke with great passion and said : " You are no Parliament : I say you are no Parliament ; I will put an end to your sitting " : whereupon the musketeers walked in and cleared the House.

Cromwell now summoned a new House of Commons on his own authority, " men fearing God and of approved fidelity and honesty." Its first meeting was 4th July, 1653, and it only survived for five weeks. It was known as Barebone's Parliament after a leather merchant named Barebone, a Baptist. Included in its membership were a number of able men, but the attempt at the religious settlement wrecked it. Its main significance was that by slight majorities it voted to abolish patronage and tithes, and by fifty-six to fifty-four votes rejected the principle of any established and endowed Church in England. For the first time an English Parliament had voted against a State Church. Such a vote, however, was so unsatisfactory that the majority handed Cromwell their resignation.

Fourth : The Parliamentary impasse led the Council of Officers to invest the supreme executive power of the State in a " single person " and Cromwell was sworn in as Lord Protector of England, Scotland and Ireland on 16th December, 1653. Fifteen other persons were also appointed to work with Cromwell. Upon this Council now rested the responsibility of the " religious settlement " : it decided to establish and endow the Christian Religion as contained in the Scriptures. This curious attempt to eliminate the term " Church " and substitute the " Christian Religion " can only be explained as a revolt against the entangling ecclesiastical controversies of the past : it was the layman's preference for religious experience rather than endless theological debate ; that ethics is more practicable than dogma. No particular Church was to be national : all who professed themselves Christians according to the Scriptures were free to preach and worship as far as they kept the peace and " did not promote Popery or Prelacy ".

Fifth : In the Humble Petition and Advice to the Protector (1657) Article XI defines the Christian Religion as " the true

Protestant Christian Religion as it is contained in the Holy Scriptures of the Old and New Testaments, and no other, be held forth and asserted for the public profession of these nations ". A Confession of Faith was drawn up on the above basis and no persons were to be allowed " maliciously or contemptuously to revile or reproach " it. Ministers and Preachers who agreed with the Confession, " although in their judgment and practice they differ in matters of worship and discipline ", could hold any living, and could receive tithes and other endowments which constituted " the public maintenance appointed for the Ministry ". The Confession demanded faith in the Trinity, in the Deity of Christ and the Scriptures as the revealed will and Word of God.

In March, 1654, a Commission of forty-three members—thirty-three ministers of religion and ten laymen—was appointed to examine and approve all ministers for service in the Church. Congregationalists were in the majority, the rest were Presbyterians and Baptists. The Commissioners were known as Cromwell's Triers. They found it necessary to eject " scandalous ministers " and there is no valid argument why they should not have been ejected. The evidence of the work of the Triers is all on the side of justice, even generosity when circumstances deserved it. Baxter was not likely to flatter the Triers, but he testifies that the clergy were treated fairly, that good and acceptable men, orthodox episcopalians, were allowed to remain in their livings. Severe criticism has been directed against the Triers and there is wide divergence regarding the numbers who were ejected from their livings. Walker, who grievously exaggerates, says the number was about 10,000 ; Stoughton says 2,000 to 2,500 ; Neal is nearer the truth after carefully checking the figures which he estimates at 1,200 to 1,400.

From other critics objection has been raised to the continuance of Tithes for the maintenance of the ministry. But on this matter Cromwell was extremely sensitive that poor and godly ministers should be worthily sustained. Until some other sure source of income was available to maintain the ministry, he insisted on retaining Tithes.

The Articles of the Petition and Advice set a limit to toleration which appears somewhat inconsistent with Cromwell's own

spirit : his " settlement " by no means satisfied many who had
looked to him to release religion from every vestige of State
control or endowment : it has also prompted many later critics
to cast cynical aspersions on Cromwell's motives. It does not
occur to these critics that Cromwell was risking the resistance
of the radicals of the Army. No one knew better than Oliver
that the country had to be governed—a task which he faced
without calculating fear or favour. Cromwell knew the way
he took. He had the Englishman's respect for Law and knew
the peril of furiously driving the nation. In his spirit there was
a magnanimity which embraced the poor and all victims of
injustice and tyranny : " I have plucked many out of the raging
fire of persecution which did tyrannise over their consciences
and encroach by arbitrariness of power over their estates ."[1]
The paradox of Cromwell perplexed his own contemporaries
and continues to perplex men still : " Some see in him the
apostle of liberty, the patron of all free communions, forgetting
his attempt to found an established church and his staunch
belief in a national discipline " :[2] even so, Buchan rightly says :
" this religious settlement was the most tolerant yet seen in
England, the most tolerant to be seen for many a day. Beyond
doubt it was far in advance of public opinion, since it offended
alike the rigid voluntaries and the rigid Presbyterians. It could
not endure, for its exclusion of episcopacy limited the State
Church to a section of the nation, but it was an honourable
effort to raise the spiritual life of the nation ".[1] And he adds :
" We shall not understand Oliver unless we realise that he was
in essence a mystic, and that the core of his religion was a mystical
experience continually renewed ".[3]

" If ' the liberty of the Spirit ' involves tolerance, the ' government of the spirit ' involves toleration". This Cromwell realised
from the first, and the attainment of toleration, in a measure then
without parallel, he counted his chief claim to reputation. As
early as 1644 he said : ' To seek to maintain our opinions in
religion by force . . . we detest and abhor '. In the following
year he proclaimed it to be fundamental that ' for brethren, in
things of the mind we look for no compulsion, but that of light

[1] Buchan, *Cromwell*, p. 443.
[2] ibid., p. 20.
[3] ibid., p. 67.

and reason '.   In his speech opening the Nominated Parliament he said : ' If the poorest Christian, the most mistaken Christian, shall desire to live peaceably and quietly under you—I say, if any shall desire but to lead a life of godliness and honesty, let him be protected '."[1]

[1] Nuttall, *The Holy Spirit in Puritan Faith and Experience*, p. 126 f.

CHAPTER VIII

THE LEVELLERS

" When the Court New Book told the world of the swarms of Anabaptists (Baptists) in our armies ", wrote Baxter, one of Cromwell's chaplains, " we thought it had been a mere lie . . . but when I came to the Army, among Cromwell's soldiers, I found a new face of things which I never dreamt of. I heard the plotting heads very hot upon that which intimated their intention to subvert both Church and State. Independents and Anabaptistry were most prevalent—I found that they took the king for a tyrant and an enemy and really intended to master him or ruin him—but their most frequent and vehement disputes were for liberty of conscience, as they called it ; that is, that the civil magistrate had nothing to do to determine of anything in matters of religion by constraint or restraint, but that every man might not only hold, but preach, and do, in matters of religion what he pleased ".[1]

These radical reformers in the Army were known as the Levellers.[2] The name itself, as the name Anabaptist in the sixteenth century, has prompted all manner of ill-informed judgments. John Lilburne, the arch-agitator of the New Model, has been represented as the re-incarnation of John of Leyden, " as if he had been spit out of his mouth." The exact relations of the Levellers to the Congregationalists and Baptists are not easily ascertainable. There can be no doubt, however, that the political philosophy of the Levellers was a development of the implications of the Nonconformist principle of religious freedom. John Lilburne was a Nonconformist : as a victim of Laud, he

---

[1] Woodhouse, *Puritans and Liberty*, p. 387 f.

[2] The English Levellers of the seventeenth century were the successors of the spiritual, political and social reformers of the sixteenth century. For the Anabaptist and Peasant background of the Levellers cf. p. 255.

had been imprisoned in the Fleet by order of the Star Chamber. Writing from prison in 1638, he says he was " acquainted with very few of them that publicly confess the same truth for which I suffer . . . being never yet in any of their congregations in England ". (He had been an exile in Holland.) He also writes of the contemptible ones of the world in whose society his soul had found delight, and the friends who had given him spiritual eyes and understanding. Among these friends was Edmund Rozer, a Baptist preacher : " My pastor, or teacher to the congregation when I was a member ". Another friend especially in his younger days was William Kiffin, who later became pastor of the Baptist Church now at Devonshire Square, London. In 1649, however, Rozer, Kiffin and other Baptists publicly repudiated all connection with Lilburne and the Levellers. And Baptist historians have been too readily inclined to accept the contemporary estimate of the Levellers, as they have been to accept contemporary views on the Anabaptists. But historical research by non-Baptists has considerably vindicated both the Levellers and the Anabaptists as radical reformers far ahead of their own contemporaries.

John Lilburne was a skilful and furious pamphleteer. Oft in prisons, he used his pen to inform and inflame public opinion against Laud's censorship of preaching and the Press ; and he was able to get his pamphlets printed and circulated. After the ejection of the Bishops from Parliament, Lilburne wrote with passion against the idea of monarchy and demanded the abolition of the House of Lords. His central theme was the " Sovereignty of the People " : and this in an age when the common man had neither part nor lot in the Government which ruled him. When, in 1647, Parliament proposed to disband the Army which had rid the people of Stuart persecution and tyranny, Lilburne seized his opportunity : he believed God had delivered such enemies as the Peers and the Monarchy into the power of the People—and the instrument of the People was the Army. On four occasions in 1647 a Petition " The Case of the Army truly stated ", drawn up mainly by Lilburne, was presented to Parliament. On the third occasion Parliament showed its contempt by a vote of ninety-four to eighty-six and burnt it. When it was submitted a fourth time Parliament took fright at the rising anger of the Army leaders : it was a revolutionary document requesting the dissolution of Parliament and the recognition that all power resided in the People.

Then followed, on 28th October, 1647, the first document, " The Agreement of the People ", and the famous debates in Putney Church between the Army leaders and elected representatives of regiments. The proposals were :

1. No further discussion with Charles.
2. The Supremacy of the People.
3. England to be divided into electoral areas.
4. The present Parliament to be dissolved on 1st September, 1648.
5. Biennial Parliaments in the future.
6. Religious and political freedom.
7. Abolition of conscription.
8. Indemnity for all who had suffered in person, or loss of goods, under the tyranny of Laud and Charles.
9. Equality before the Law for all people.
10. Manhood Suffrage.

These revolutionary proposals provoked vehement discussions in Putney Church between the Council of Officers and the representatives of the Army. Ireton asked the meaning of the words, " The People of England ". Did they mean that every Englishman was equal in the sense that he was entitled to vote at Parliamentary elections ? He was told the words meant " Manhood Suffrage ". Rainsborough argued that every man who is governed by others should have an opportunity of electing the Government : the poorest man in England was under no obligation to any Government unless he had put himself under it willingly. Ireton replied that no person had any right to vote unless he had a permanent fixed interest in the Kingdom— property was the qualification of the Franchise. " I do not find ", retorted Rainsborough, " anything in the law of God that a lord shall choose twenty burgesses, and a gentleman but two, or a poor man shall choose none . . . but I do find that all Englishmen must be subject to English laws . . . and the foundation of all laws lies in the people ".[1] Sexby argued

[1] Mackinnon, *History of Modern Liberty*, IV, p. 35 f.

against Ireton on the grounds of the sacrifices of the Army and its service to the nation : " We have engaged in (behalf of) this kingdom and ventured our lives and it was all for this— to recover our birthrights and privileges as Englishmen . . . it seems now, except a man hath a fixed estate in this kingdom, he hath no right in this kingdom. . . . I am resolved to give my birthright to none . . . the poor and mean in this kingdom have been the means of the preservation of this kingdom ". For sake of peace, honesty and quietness, Ireton was ready to part with a good deal of his birthright : " Eventually Cromwell was ready to widen the existing franchise to include copyholders by inheritance and Ireton agreed to a more equitable distribution of seats ".[1] The Council of Officers met the Levellers by extending the Franchise to all home-born Englishmen except servants and beggars. Cromwell was far from convinced that these proposals of the Levellers were practicable. And it was the realisation in government of these theories which explained his attitude. Why pass legislation which was likely to be unworkable ? He did consent that no further approaches should be made to Charles.

After the execution of the king on 30th January, 1649, it seemed to the Army that the way was now open to effect drastic changes in the Constitution. A revised programme of " The Agreement of the People " was submitted ; its aim being to give the nation fuller representation in Parliament as far as political circumstances permitted. The proposals were :

1. The present Parliament must dissolve within three months.
2. Biennial Parliaments and redistribution of seats.
3. Extension of Franchise to all ratepayers and householders. and those over twenty-one years of age, servants and paupers to be excluded.
4. No servant of the State in receipt of public money should be eligible for Parliament.
5. Parliament might establish a National Church excluding popery and prelacy : with full religious freedom for dissenters.

[1] ibid., p. 37.

This revised " Agreement " was the work of Ireton : but it did not satisfy Lilburne and the Levellers. Lilburne therefore drew up his own Programme. It included additional demands, not stated earlier :

1. Universal Franchise for all over twenty-one years.
2. Annual Parliaments.
3. No coercion whatever in religious belief and worship.
4. Freedom of Trade ; no tax on Food ; no imprisonment for debt.
5. No Tithes : Universal Education ; Provision for old age.
6. No Death penalty except for murder and treason.
7. Religious belief to be no disqualification for civil service.

Whatever judgment was passed on the Levellers by their own contemporaries we cannot deny that they were resolved to fight for full freedom of conscience. They were prophets of the political democracy and the social justice which are now the basis of the civilisation of the West. Apart from Annual or Biennial Parliaments the above proposals are now the rights in Law of the common man. But these demands in the seventeenth century worried Cromwell ; he dreaded lest the Sovereignty of the People might mean anarchy. One of Oliver's early speeches in Parliament was a plea for Lilburne's release from prison, and in those days he had patiently smiled on the agitator. Now Cromwell was in power he thought the plans of the rebels were utterly impracticable ; he visualised these theorists rocking the State to confusion until no Government on earth could control it. Against the Levellers in the Putney debates, Cromwell had used two arguments : first, it was impossible to make a Constitution " *de novo* ", to ignore many of the ancient customs and traditions of England ; second, the Levellers should ask whether their proposals were practicable. And when unrest in the Army continued and the ringleaders were getting beyond control, Cromwell consented to the order of the Council of State to arrest Lilburne and other revolutionaries : " You have no other way to deal with these men but to break them or they will break you ". At last, to check the spread of mutiny and restore discipline in the Army, Cromwell shot three of the Levellers.

The Levellers were far advanced politically beyond their contemporaries ; they were exponents of full religious and political toleration ; they stood for constitutional democracy. They were not anarchists. They had suffered and were determined to end the rule of tyrants. They stood on the rock of the liberty of conscience and saw that religious freedom was the inspiration and dynamic of all other freedoms. Such principles were the application to political structures of the New Testament value of the individual and the doctrine of the Priesthood of all believers.

After the Westminster Assembly in 1643, Milton changed his views on the Presbyterianism of the seventeenth century as a substitute for Episcopacy. The Assembly angered him by its attitude to his arguments concerning divorce : he met its recommendation for the strict licensing of the Press with scathing denunciation. His judgments on the Assembly and the Presbyterian majority in the Long Parliament were not published until after his death. " By 1649 he had come to believe that the great opportunity of reforming England and its religion had been missed and had led to a ' ridiculous frustration '. Liberty had been put ' like a bridle into the hands ' of Parliament and the Assembly, but they had failed to use it ".[1] Dr. Hutchinson says Milton expressed the " English mind in his life-long advocacy of freedom. It is for freedom—civil, political, religious—that the English people have made their most determined struggles. Milton is also very English in the importance which he always attached to moral issues ".[2] He undoubtedly expressed the English Free Church mind. His methods were far removed from those of Lilburne : but he came to hold and to advocate the ideas and principles of Free Church order and worship according to the Congregationalist polity. (I cannot refer here to his theological views). He stood for the complete self-government of the Church ; while loyal to Cromwell he was also critical, he disapproved of tithes, endowments and patronage. No minister of the Church should hold a civil office. It

[1] Hutchinson, *Milton and the English Mind*, p. 100.
[2] p. 1.

was the inward calling of God that made a minister. The people should be free to choose their own ministers and such choice is the only basis for ordination. Any minister so chosen and so ordained has " authority to ordain other ministers and deacons ".

Note : Miss Gibb's book, *John Lilburne,* was published too late for reference in this brief chapter.

CHAPTER IX

"RUPTURES OF THE COMMONWEALTH"
Milton

CROMWELL died on 3rd September, 1658, and the rifts in the Commonwealth Constitution soon became serious. By patience with irritable friends, by magnanimity towards White-locke, Ludlow, Vane, and men who were hostile and ambitious, the Protector had striven to broaden the basis of his government. " What can you desire more than you have ", he asked Ludlow ? " That which we fought for, that the nation might be governed by its own consent ", was the reply. " I am as much ", said Oliver, " for a government by consent as any man but where shall we find that consent " ? For nearly ten years Cromwell was attempting the political structure by which the nation would be governed by its own consent. Absolutist theories in Church and State were utterly alien to his nature. He believed in the rights of a representative Parliament and only dismissed the " Rump " because it had long ceased to represent the nation : " unlike others who have founded Republics he began and he ended his career as a believer in the uses of constitutional king-ship ".[1] This judgment is confirmed by Oliver's attitude in the Putney debates, in his defence of the " Heads of Proposals " and by his personal refusal of kingship when it was offered to him. But ten years are as a tale that is quickly told when it comes to changing ancient customs and a system of government. We have seen that Cromwell would stand no rebellion from the Army. Yet, if he had lived another ten years, the conditions were so unsettled, he could not have ruled without the Army. Has any ruler, considering the period and the clash of parties, used the weapon of Force more humanely ? He " obtained in the field of religion a reconciliation of all the various Puritan

---

[1] G. M. Trevelyan, *History of England*, p. 429.

forces which he had signally failed to obtain in politics ", but he had sought to obtain it. " The Roman Catholics were less molested under the Protectorate than under Presbyterian or Anglican Parliaments and though the Mass was not legally tolerated the Recusancy laws were repealed ".[1]

To attempt any explanation of the fall of the Commonwealth is an absorbing theme. But the question arises : why were Nonconformist principles of religious and political freedom so soon rejected ? The achievements of toleration had been progressive, why were the gains so quickly lost ? One explanation is that the Idea of Freedom had not yet become embodied in Institutions capable of conserving it. The Nonconformists had won battles on the field, but as churches they were still comparatively few in number. Prior to 1660, Jordan has counted 297 Baptist Churches in England and Wales. The Congregational Assembly of Elders and Messengers which met at the Savoy in 1658 represented 120 Churches : and it is computed that nearly 400 Congregationalist ministers were ejected from their livings in 1662. Against these progressive forces we must set the strength of the Anglican tradition, the royalist landowners, and the innate conservatism of the masses of the people who rarely know history, and do not know that the price of their freedom and security is eternal vigilance. The conservation of the best spiritual and political results would have been possible if Presbyterians, Congregationalists and Baptists had been reconciled to each other. But radical Nonconformists had been unable to convince the Presbyterians of the stability of their motives ; on the other hand, the Presbyterians, with their high doctrine of Law and Order, never forgot that the New Model Army had broken their ascendancy : nor did they recover from the shock of the execution of the king ; to the end, with all the evidence of Stuart duplicity and cunning, they stood for the divine right of the office and hereditary principle of kingship. Hence, the Puritan forces were too divided to consolidate the gains which had been won during the Commonwealth period.

" I like not the democratic forms," said Baxter : and the Presbyterians shared his view. In his *Holy Commonwealth*, Baxter has a disappointing estimate of the intelligence and political capacities of The People. He thinks "democratic government is the worst

[1] Trevelyan, *History of England*, p. 431.

of all forms ", and the sovereign is above all the positive laws of the Commonwealth. The anger and sorrow of Milton over the return of the Stuarts remind us of the Hebrews who had been delivered from Egypt, and but for the leadership of Moses would have returned to the bondage of Egyptian flesh-pots. "That a nation should be so valorous and courageous to win their liberty in the field, and when they have won it should not know how to use it or value it, but basely and besottedly to run their necks again into the yoke which they have broken, and prostrate all the fruits of their victory at the feet of the vanquished, will be such an example as kings and tyrants never yet had the like to boast of ".[1]

II

On 25th April, 1660, General Monk's Parliament met with the intention of recalling Charles II from Breda. The Presbyterians and the Anglicans were mainly responsible for the negotiations conducted through Monk. Before and after Cromwell's death, Monk had taken an oath to resist the return of the Stuarts ; but his correspondence with Charles reveals conclusive treachery : " I hope the king will forgive what is past both in my words and actions . . . for my heart was ever faithful to him, but I was never in a position to do him service till this present ". A deputation of Presbyterian ministers waited on Charles at Breda ; on 25th May he arrived at Dover and on 28th entered London. A tumultuous welcome greeted him. Twelve Presbyterian ministers were in the procession and when Charles was presented with a Bible he said it would be the rule of his life. The Roman Catholics assured him of their loyalty, the Congregationalists and Baptists " generally " accepted the Restoration of the monarchy. A London resident who was present when Charles entered the city wrote to his friend in Paris : " were you here, you would say, Good God, do the same people inhabit England that were in it ten or twenty years ago ! Believe me, I know not whether I am in England or no, or whether I dream ".[2]

[1] *Prose Works*, II, pp. 102–6.
[2] Gooch and Laski, *English Democratic Ideas in the Seventeenth Century*, p. 271.

The Declaration at Breda appealed to the imagination of Britain. It seem to herald the dawn of a new age, as though Charles II had learned all the lessons to be drawn from his father's political follies and slippery tricks. Recalling the religious quarrels of the past and the divided condition of the nation, he declared, " a liberty to tender consciences ; and that no man shall be disquieted or called in question, for differences of opinion in matters of religion which do not disturb the peace of the kingdom." If every party interpreted these words in relation to its own tender conscience the welcome to London is easily understood. But the old tensions remained, nor had the main parties shifted their ground. The Presbyterians and the Bishops did not trust one another and still regarded the Nonconformists as individualists, rebels and regicides. True, Charles qualified his promise by the statement that no one must " disturb the peace of the kingdom ". How, then, did he begin to extend " liberty to tender consciences " ?

He began by appeasing the Presbyterians for they had recalled him and they were the strongest party in Parliament. His first decision was to appoint a number of their ministers as royal chaplains—whom he invited shortly afterwards to prepare a document stating the grounds on which Presbyterians and Anglicans could unite in a National Church. The document was mainly similar to the Admonitions drawn up by Cartwright and submitted to Parliament in the reign of Elizabeth, and the Book of Discipline associated with the name of Walter Travers. The Bishops, however, refused to meet the Presbyterians and would only consent to three of their suggestions. The King then announced that he intended to make a Declaration of Indulgence and a draft of the same was seen and revised by Baxter and his friends. Further, on 22nd October, 1660, the King presided over a meeting of twenty-two representatives at Worcester House—six Bishops, seven Presbyterians and several Statesmen. When Clarendon had read the Declaration each party was requested to make any objections to it. But before any decision was taken, Baxter says Clarendon introduced a Petition to the King from the Independents and Baptists, which Clarendon said he did not " very well like ". He read his suggested reply to the Petition which was : " That others also (meaning Roman Catholics) be permitted to meet for Religious Worship, so be it, they do it, not to the disturbance of the Peace : and that no Justice of the Peace or Officer disturb them ". On this reply to the Congregationalists and Baptists, Clarendon sought their advice. But neither Bishops nor Presbyterians would speak. If they agreed to Clarendon's reply tolerating Congregationalists and Baptists how could they refuse similar toleration to Romanists ? If the Presbyterians refused to agree, it meant, " that all sects and parties would be against us ". The Presbyterians were in a dilemma : even their silence would implicate them with Anglicans and the Nonconformists. Baxter at length broke the silence, and referred to the Papists and Socinians as " intolerable parties " : to which His Majesty replied, " there were Laws enough against the Papists ". And the conference ended.

Two Presbyterians and two Anglicans were then invited to revise the document read by Clarendon, and on 25th October the Declaration was published. To the amazement of the Presbyterians most of their proposals were accepted, and the union of Presbyterians and Anglicans in the National Church seemed near achievement : so near, Charles appointed Reynolds, a Presbyterian, to the see of Norwich : Baxter refused the Bishopric of Hereford until the Declaration had been ratified by Parliament. When the Bill was introduced into the House of Commons to give legal authority to the Indulgence there was criticism—it would offend the Roman Catholics. When the statement was added that it was contrary to the King's own wishes that the Bill should become Law, it was lost by 183 votes to 157. Charles had raised and dashed the hopes of the Presbyterians and Nonconformists. Why ? The answer is that he was desirous of obtaining toleration for Roman Catholics and discovered that neither Anglicans, nor Presbyterians, nor Nonconformists would consent. Presbyterians and Nonconformists chose to suffer indignities, imprisonment and loss of goods, rather than agree to legal protection for Romanists. Charles was not yet a Roman Catholic himself, but his mother and his wife were : and the bribes which he had accepted from the French King were powerful incentives to subtlety and treachery in his dealings with Parliament and the nation.

III

After failure to authorise the Declaration of Indulgence a new Parliament met in May, 1661, packed by Clarendon with supporters of the Church and the King. It entered at once on a period of vindictive legislation which aimed at nothing less than the destruction of Nonconformity. After a brief interval, cruel persecution was initiated which continued till 1688.

The Corporation Act became Law in 1661. Its intention was to buttress the Church of England by excluding all men from civil, military and municipal offices unless " within a year before appointment they should have received the Lord's Supper according to the ritual of the Church of England ". Likewise such men must take the oath of supremacy and the oath " that it is not lawful, under any pretence, to take arms against the King ". The Quakers who, on principle, refused to take any oath, were fined, brutally treated in prison, and transported.

The Bill for the " Uniformity of Public Prayers and Administration of the Sacraments " was introduced to the House of Commons on 29th June, 1661. The House was in haste to pass it and restore all the ancient privileges of the Anglican Church. Delay, however, was necessary, because, in his Declaration, Charles had promised a revision of the Prayer Book. And in order " to review the Book of Common Prayer and to prepare such Alterations and Additions as they thought fit ", a Commission of twelve Bishops, twelve Presbyterians and nine others met at the Savoy in April, 1661. It was soon obvious that the Bishops were in no mood for revision of the Prayer Book and the Commission dissolved. Charles next requested Convocation to undertake the task of revision. A number of unimportant changes were made, but no vital concession was offered to the Presbyterians. Baxter said the work of Convocation made the Book worse. The House of Commons accepted the amendments of Convocation and the Uniformity Bill became Law and received the royal assent on 19th May, 1662. The Act came into operation on 24th August, 1662—a day of cruel affliction throughout the land—and as annual tithes were due to be paid at the end of September, 1,800 to 2,000 ministers who refused to conform lost a year's income.

" An Act for the Uniformity of Public Prayers, and Administration of Sacraments, and other Rites and Ceremonies ; and for establishing the Form of Making, Ordaining and Consecrating Bishops, Priests, and Deacons, in the Church of England ". All the coercive instruments at the disposal of Church and State were again to be used to compel Englishmen to worship God according to the Prayer Book. The Introduction to the Act was malicious in its oblique references to Nonconformists, showing how formal and traditional divine worship was to its authors : " A great number of people in divers parts of this Realm, following their own Sensuality, and living without knowledge and due Fear of God, do wilfully and schismatically abstain and refuse to come to their Parish Churches and other public places where Common Prayer, Administration of the Sacraments and Preaching of the Word of God is used . . . ." Dale says " this remarkable description of Nonconformists remains unchanged in the Statute Book ". The House of Commons said the Act was passed " to the intent that every person in this realm may certainly know the rule to which he is to conform in public worship ".

Every Parson, Vicar, or other minister whatever, on, or before 24th August, 1662, must vow before his congregation : " I do hereby declare my unfeigned assent and consent to all and everything contained in and prescribed in and by the book entitled The Book of Common Prayer. . . ." Every one holding an ecclesiastical office must take the oath, every curate, college chaplain, university fellow, professor, tutor, schoolmaster : " I will conform to the Liturgy of the Church of England as it is now by Law established ".

Under the supervision of Cromwell's Triers, the Presbyterians, Congregationalists and Baptists had been appointed to livings, but they had not been episcopally ordained. On 24th August they were ejected. The exact figures are difficult to ascertain but between 1,800 and 2,000 ministers were driven from their churches. These were " godly ministers ", preachers of the Word, men who loved their congregations and were loved by them in return. As we have stated, Cromwell's Triers ejected " scandalous ministers " but those ejected in 1662 were men of God. In their decision on 24th August we see the character and majesty of the Nonconformist conscience. There was no lie in their soul. They knew their vocation and their New

Testament and no worldly gain could seduce them. " We cannot so lie ; no, not to save the homes of our wives and children ; not to save ourselves from beggary ; not to win deaneries and bishoprics ; no, nor even that we may still be able to bind up broken hearts, to sustain good men in righteousness, to rescue wicked men from sin and eternal death. First of all we must be honest men. God help us for the rest ".

Such brave men were reduced to the verge of starvation. " Hundreds of able ministers ", wrote Baxter, " with their wives and children had neither house nor bread, for their former maintenance served them but for the time, and few of them had laid up anything for the future . . . the people's poverty was so great that they were not able much to relieve their ministers. The jealousy of the State and the malice of their enemies were so great that the people that were willing durst not be known to give to their ejected pastors, lest it should be said that they maintained schism or were making collections for some plot or insurrection ".[1]

The Act of Uniformity was re-enforced by the First Conventicle Act of 1664, making illegal any meeting of more than five persons in addition to the family in the house. The penalty for the first offence was five pounds or three months in prison : ten pounds or six months in prison for the second offence : one hundred pounds for the third offence or transportation to a foreign plantation for seven years.

The Five Mile Act was the next penal legislation against Nonconformists. Unless ejected ministers were willing to take the oath that they would not take up arms against the King or " endeavour any alterations of Government in Church and the State ", it was illegal for them, except on a journey, to come within five miles of any place where they had exercised their ministry. The fine for the offence was forty pounds. Nor could such ministers open a school or act as tutors to the members of any family to whom they had formerly ministered.

The Second Conventicle Act was passed in 1670. The penalties were not so heavy as under the former Act except they could now be levied on the goods and chattels of the convicted person. If the offender was too poor to pay, the fine was transferred to some wealthier member of the congregation.

[1] *Reliquiæ Baxterianæ*, Part II, p. 385.

The fact that a third of the fine was paid to any informer led to incredible and disgusting scenes. " Informers were everywhere at work, and having crept into religious assemblies in disguise, levied great sums of money on ministers and people. Soldiers broke into the houses of honest farmers, under pretence of searching for conventicles, and where ready money was wanting they plundered their goods, drove away their cattle and sold them for half-price. Many were plundered of their household furniture ; the sick had their beds taken from under them and themselves laid on the floor. These vile creatures were not only encouraged, but pushed on vehemently by their spiritual guides ".[1]

These penal laws, however, did not prevent Nonconformists from preaching and the people from worshipping. Large congregations gathered in towns and cities and smaller numbers gathered in lonely places. As the brutality of the German armies during the World War drove loyalists into underground activities on the Continent, so the Conventicle Acts helped to sustain a fighting and a conquering faith in the ranks of the Nonconformists of the seventeenth century. During the Plague in 1665 and the Great Fire of London in 1666, when many clergy deserted their posts and Parliament moved to Oxford, Nonconformist ministers rendered needy service to the sick and destitute : they preached to large congregations in the churches, deserted by the clergy. But the Penal Acts were not in the least relaxed against them.

IV

The Church had used Parliament as its legal instrument to break the Nonconformists ; but political forces elsewhere were shaping the strategy of the King, and it was now time for him to act. He had early commenced his intrigue with Louis XIV of France. In 1670 he entered into a secret alliance with Louis against Holland, a Protestant State : by this Treaty Charles agreed to accept £200,000 a year as the price of betraying Protestantism in England and declaring himself a Roman Catholic " as soon as circumstances permitted ". He misused money, voted by Parliament for the Dutch War, to maintain his licentious

[1] cf. Mackinnon, *History of Modern Liberty*, IV, p. 189.

court. When the Dutch defeated the English, Charles must at all costs divert the anger of the nation from himself. Hence, his Second Declaration of Indulgence, affirming that the coercion of Nonconformists had failed, and that over twelve years the persecutions had yielded " very little fruit ". In March, 1672, it was, therefore, Charles' pleasure that penal laws against Nonconformists be immediately suspended ; also " that a sufficient number of places, as shall be desired ", shall be available for them " to meet and assemble in order to their public worship and devotion ". Nonconformist teachers and places of worship were to be licensed, but Romanists must meet " in their private houses only ". In ten months 3,500 licenses were issued for Nonconformist places of worship—figures which alarmed the Anglicans. A long conflict, however, now began over the Indulgence, which was never intended for the sake of the Nonconformists, but to further his Catholic schemes with Louis. When the House of Commons resolved that " Penal Statutes in matters ecclesiastical cannot be suspended but by Act of Parliament ", it was upholding the authority of Parliament against the prerogative claimed by the King : and though Charles pressed his ecclesiastical prerogative Parliament refused to acknowledge it or surrender its own rights. Whereupon the licenses issued for Nonconformists places of worship were cancelled. The House of Commons was inclined to relax the penal laws and a Bill was introduced to exempt Nonconformists from penalties if they would subscribe the doctrinal articles of the Anglican Church : then they could meet for worship, and ministers who took the oaths of allegiance and supremacy could obtain a license to preach. The Bill passed the Commons, but before it had received the consent of the Lords, Parliament was adjourned and later prorogued by Charles ; and the Bill was lost.

Now began the conflict between the House of Commons and the King and his Romanist intentions. Parliament passed the Test Act, 1673, which made it impossible for Roman Catholics to hold any civil, municipal, or military office. Every holder of such offices must receive the Lord's Supper according to the usage of the Church of England and declare on oath " that there is no transubstantiation in the Sacrament of the Lord's Supper or in the elements of the bread and wine, at or after " the priestly prayer of consecration. With such opposition from Parliament the King withdrew his Indulgence.

In the Parliament of 13th April, 1675, Charles had promised : " I will leave nothing undone that may show to the world my zeal for the Protestant religion as it is established in the Church of England, from which I will never depart ". This statement must be judged by the revelation in the House of Commons in 1678 during a debate between Danby and Montague, ex-ambassador to the French Court. Charles went to the House and said he had caused the papers of Montague to be seized. Whereupon Montague produced a letter signed by Danby at the command of Charles, requesting from Louis a subsidy of 6,000,000 livres to make himself independent of Parliament in order to pursue his Romanist aims.

Parliament carried defiance a stage further by attacking the Duke of York's marriage with Princess Modena, a Roman Catholic. The Duke was heir to the Throne and a Romanist, and it was resolved in the Commons to bring in a Bill to exclude him from the succession : " If we do not something relating to the succession ", said Lord Russell, " we must resolve when we have a prince of the popish religion to be papists or burn " : " As long as the Duke is heir to the crown, the kingdom is unsafe ", said Hungerford : " For us to go about to tie a popish successor with laws for the preservation of the Protestant religion ", said Hampden, " is binding Samson with withes. He will break them when he is awake ".[1] Charles prevented the Bill from being introduced by proroguing Parliament.

During the later years of Charles II the Whig and Tory parties emerged, the Whigs inclining to toleration to the Nonconformists, the Tories becoming the bulwark of the Church and the monarchy. The Whigs holding " the damnable doctrine " that Sovereignty is derived from the people : the Tories, with the Church and the Universities answering that the King held his crown " by a fundamental hereditary right of succession which no religion, no law, no fault can alter or diminish ".[2]

The character of Charles II raises serious ethical questions regarding his Supremacy in the Anglican Church. What was it in Anglican theory and practice which led the Church to

[1] Mackinnon, IV, p. 217.
[2] ibid., IV, p. 227.

tolerate such glaring wickedness in a King who was destitute
of any religious principle, and who flouted all the ethical standards
which the Church of God surely exists to maintain ?   This ethical
test in relation to the Church was decisive for Nonconformists.

Trevelyan says Charles was an " expert hedonist ".   But he
was a cynic as well as an epicurean.   In 1669, at St. James's
Palace, Charles confided to the Duke of York, Clifford, Arlington
and Arundel, " that he desired to reconcile himself to the Catholic
faith and to turn England Catholic with him " : he assured the
French Ambassador a few months later that he intended " to go
over ".   " For only under a Catholic Constitution might a King
of England hope to be absolute ".   Further, Charles' immoral
Court was a byword to his generation.   While Nonconformists
were being persecuted under the penal laws, Charles was amusing
" himself with two new mistresses, the two most famous of the
thirteen mistresses whose names have been preserved.   Nell
Gwynn did not cost the nation above £4,000 a year in revenues ;
the other, a young Breton lady, who had come to England with
Henrietta of Orleans, soon became Duchess of Portsmouth and
drew an income of £40,000 a year beside gifts amounting to
many times that sum ".[1]   Were the Presbyterians, Congregationalists and Baptists right in standing for a purer church,
ministry, and ethic ?   On one side we find treachery, perjury,
bribery, kings and prelates entangled in the wretched business
of persecution and immoral indulgence ; on the other side we
see men contending and suffering for a High Churchmanship
and ethic according to the measure of the New Testament.

V

James II was a Roman Catholic when he succeeded to the
throne.   In the Stuart tradition he began his reign by promising
to maintain government in Church and State as by Law established.   He would " maintain the Church which he knew to be
loyal, and laws which made him as great a king as he wished
to be ".   His secret motive was far otherwise than his promises.
He became king on 6th February, 1685, but on 26th March,
Barillon, the French Ambassador, wrote to Louis XIV : " I have

---

[1] *Cambridge Modern History,* V, p. 205.

had a long conference with the King of England in which he explained to me to the bottom his plans and the state of his affairs. He told me that he knew the aversion that the people of England had for the Catholic religion, but that with the aid of Your Majesty he hoped to surmount this obstacle ; that his only aim was to work for this end ; that he knew well enough that he would never be entirely safe till the Catholic religion was established in England so firmly as never to be destroyed ; that this required time and great precautions for the future . . . that the re-establishment of the Catholic religion in England can only succeed under the protection and by the assistance of Your Majesty ".[1] On 29th October, 1685, Barillon reported to Louis a further conversation with James : " he added that his design was to obtain from the Parliament the revocation of the Test Act and the Habeas Corpus Act, the first of which destroys the Catholic religion, the other the royal authority ".[2] On 6th July, 1686, James was flattering himself on the success of his preparations and Barillon wrote to Louis : " The King openly testifies his joy at finding himself in a position to strike bold and authoritative strokes. He receives with pleasure the compliments which people make him on this score. He has spoken much to me of it and has given me to understand that he will never relax ".[3] Mackinnon has examined and verified the Barillon correspondence in the archives of the French Foreign Office. Could any evidence be more conclusive of the deliberate intention of James ; first, to seize arbitrary power ; second, to use such power to establish Roman Catholicism in England ?

His methods of reaching his goal were as degrading as his treachery to the Laws and Constitution of the realm. As James said, the legal obstacle in his path was the Test Act, which excluded Roman Catholics from municipal, civil, military or any other paid office in the State—the Act which demanded an oath denying Transubstantiation. The King must, therefore, get rid of the Test Act or its penal clauses. Parliament was as hostile to James on this issue as it had been to Charles II, whereupon James claimed the supremacy of his ecclesiastical

[1] Mackinnon, *History of Modern Liberty*, IV, p. 335 f.
[2] ibid., IV, p. 348.
[3] ibid., p. 361.

prerogative over the authority of Parliament. To support his claim he stooped to bribery and intimidation : as he himself had received the bribes of Louis, he was sure the votes and intrigues of members of the House of Commons could also be bought : he intimidated the Bench. In June, 1686, in the case of Sir Edward Hales, Chief Justice Herbert delivered judgment : " The laws of England are the King's laws. Therefore it is their inseparable prerogative to dispense with penal laws in particular cases and upon particular necessary reasons. Of these necessities and these reasons the King himself is the sole judge. This is not a trust invested in or granted to the King by the people, but the ancient remains of the sovereign power and prerogative of the kings of England, which never yet was taken from them nor can be ".[1] With this judgment ten Justices agreed, only one dissenting. Confirmed thus, James proceeded to defy Parliament and cancel the penal clauses of the Test Act. Roman Catholics were appointed to church livings, to University Presidencies, chairs and other offices. " In 1685 ", says Trevelyan, " the Privy Council, the rural and municipal magistrates, the Lords Lieutenant and the Sheriffs were almost without exception Tories and High Churchmen. Three years later, on the eve of the Revolution, Tories and High Churchmen had been excluded from positions of central and local authority as thoroughly as if Oliver himself had been at work. James attempted to replace them by Roman Catholics, all laws to the contrary notwithstanding ".[2]

Towards his objective James now made a bid for the support of the Nonconformists who were still victimised under the penal laws of Charles II : in doing so it is certain that the King was influenced by Penn's writings. But whereas Penn was a Quaker who had suffered twenty years for his principles, and for which he had been expelled from Oxford University— tolerance advocated by the King's Indulgence was suspect. Penn has been misunderstood by reason of his acclamation of James and his Declaration of Indulgence—as though Penn was a man given to fawning and flattery. As it was, he had had unusual personal relations with James and had been a frequent visitor at the Palace when his father was an Admiral of the

[1] ibid., IV, p. 363.
[2] G. M. Trevelyan, *History of England*, p. 470.

Fleet. James had promised Penn's father to protect the young Quaker, as far as possible, in view of his religious convictions, which promise James scarcely fulfilled, seeing that Penn was in Newgate prison during the reign of Charles II : there he wrote in 1671 *The Great Case of Liberty of Conscience*, in which he reasoned that persecution was alien to the teaching of Christ, an invasion of the rights of human personality and that it undermined the stability of the State. Penn used his personal relations with James on behalf of religious freedom, sacrificing any advantage of his standing at Court, " choosing rather to suffer affliction with the people of God ". His noble spirit is revealed, as founder of the Commonwealth of Pennsylvania, in the opening sentences of its Constitution : " In reverence to God, the Father of light and Spirits, the Author as well as the object of all divine knowledge, faith, and worship, I do, for me and mine, declare and establish, for the first fundamental of the government of this country, that every person that doth or shall reside therein shall have and enjoy the free profession of his or her faith and exercise of worship towards God in such a way and manner as every such person shall in conscience believe is most acceptable to God ". The man who could so plan a Constitution was not likely to fawn and flatter the Stuarts.

Penn had no sympathy with Romanists, but he would give them liberty to worship. In 1686 he addressed to James " A Persuasive to Moderation " and pleaded that toleration could be granted to Romanists without peril to the State, but that it should be granted by Act of Parliament. Hence, on April 4th, 1687, James published a Declaration of Indulgence, and could not but heartily wish that all his people were members of the Catholic Church : " it hath of long time been our constant sense and opinion that conscience ought not to be constrained, nor people forced in matters of mere religion. It has ever been directly contrary to our inclination . . . and finally that it never obtained the end for which it was employed ". All this is excellent argument, just as it was, on the lips of Charles II, also plausible expediency. Penn, the Quakers, Presbyterians and Nonconformists were grateful for any suspension of the penal laws—they offered their thanks to the King. How could they do otherwise than rejoice though they had been disillusioned so frequently by the Stuarts ? At the same time they knew that it was wiser to wait and rely on an Act of Parliament than fall into the hands of James II.

The next step led to crisis. On 20th May, 1688, James commanded the Bishops and clergy to read a Second Declaration of Indulgence in all London churches, also in provincial churches on 3rd and 10th June. But by this time the Catholic appointments in Church, State and the Universities had alarmed the Bishops as it had previously alarmed Parliament. The Bishops refused to read what they called a Declaration of Indulgence to Catholics. In relation to the Catholic propaganda of James this refusal of the Bishops is easily understood : but it was also consistent with long standing hatred towards the Nonconformists whom the church had persecuted without mercy. Unfortunately, the Bishops had not distinguished until now between the demands of the Nonconformists for religious freedom and the subversive intentions of the Jesuit advisers at James' Court. " They preached prerogative and the sovereign power to the highest pitch, while it was favourable to them, but when they apprehended the least danger from it, they cried out as soon as the shoe pinched, though it was of their own putting on ". Now the attitude of the Bishops underwent a change : they began to appreciate the steady moral and intellectual qualities, and suffering patriotism of the Nonconformists whose support they sought. In their refusal to read the Declaration, James had clearly overrated the loyalty of the Bishops. But worse was to follow. After anxious debate the Bishops decided to petition the King—an unlawful step to take. When the Bishop of St. Asaph handed to him the document, stating the grounds of their attitude to his Indulgence, James was furious and accused them of rebellion : " God has given me the dispensing power and I will use it ".

The result of this interview was a summons to the Bishops to appear before the Privy Council when they were told they would be charged before the Court of the King's Bench : as they refused to find bail for their appearance they were sent to the Tower. A week later they were tried for publishing " a false, malicious and seditious libel under the form of a petition ". They were found " not guilty ". The excitement of the London crowds can be measured by the fact that for two nights and a day they rang their bells and lit their bonfires.

After this aquittal, Sancroft, Archbishop of Canterbury, publicly advised the bishops and clergy to show " tender regard to their brethren, the Protestant Dissenters : to visit them, to persuade them, if it was possible, to join the Church ".   The Bishops made it known that they were going to adopt a new policy towards Dissenters : " I am certain that the Bishops will never stir from their petition ; but that they will, whenever that happy opportunity shall offer itself, let the Protestant Dissenters find that they will be better than their word ".[1]   This change of attitude was welcome.   Would that it had continued !

The Church and the Tory party, who had been ardent supporters of the throne, were now fully persuaded that James would not hesitate at using any means to subvert Protestantism. James had driven Tories, Whigs, Bishops and Nonconformists to the conviction that they must close their ranks if Protestantism was to survive.   The religious issue was now more clearly defined than at any previous period in English history : it was Protestantism and the rights of Parliament against Romanism and an outmoded and arbitrary conception of kingship.   If Protestantism was to survive the Stuarts must go.

A remarkable change had taken place in the religious situation. The policy of penal legislation had defeated itself ; persecution as a weapon against conscience had been discredited ; it had been a long and tortuous road and now it seemed that Nonconformists had entered their Land of Promise—which was religious toleration.   For religious toleration had now become a national and a political necessity : it had also become an economic necessity if England was to develop industrial and commercial leadership. It is interesting to learn the concern of the Church and the Tories regarding the attitude of the Nonconformists.   What response would they make to the Declarations of James ?   There was Lord Halifax's *Letter to a Dissenter* : " You act very unskilfully against your visible interest if you throw away the advantages of which you can hardly fail in the next probable revolution. Things tend naturally to what you would have . . . the Church of England, convinced of its error in being severe to you ; the Parliament whenever it meeteth sure to be gentle to you . . . so that in truth all things seem to conspire to give you ease and satisfaction, if, by too much haste to anticipate your good fortune,

[1] cf Skeats and Miall, *History of the Free Churches of England*, 1688–1891, p. 72 f.

you do not destroy it ".[1] Thus Halifax pleaded with Nonconformists to refuse a present consolation from James lest they
lose the future blessings which the Church and Parliament would
bestow. And it is proof of the sound spiritual and political
judgment of the Nonconformists that they stood with the
Bishops against the King. A minority of Nonconformists
snatched at James's offer to suspend the Test Act : but if some
of them doubted the promises of their persecutors regarding the
future, Protestantism counted no stalwarts more loyal than the
Nonconformists.

So James went. The Tories and most of the Bishops would
have preferred a Regency in James's name, but they finally
agreed to the change of succession in favour of William and
Mary, the power being vested in William. On 5th November,
1688, William sailed into Torbay carrying at his masthead the
English flag, inscribed with the words : " The Protestant
Religion and the Liberties of England ".

[1] Mackinnon, IV, p. 377.

CHAPTER X

ARRESTED REFORM

IN view of the promises and good wishes of the Church and Tory parties during the crisis under James II, how did the Nonconformists fare ? " The Tory forces in Church and State ", says Trevelyan, " lost little by the Revolution, except the power of persecuting their rivals ". The various parties reverted to many of their former differences as soon as it came to the settlement with William of Orange. The two Archbishops and five bishops who met with the Peers on 11th December, 1688, declared they would work with William " for the protection of the Church and due liberty of conscience to Dissenters ". Sancroft, Archbishop of Canterbury, when reminded of his pledge to secure relief for Nonconformists from the penal laws of Charles II, said the Bishops would keep their promises but such a matter must be settled by Convocation. There is no doubt of the good faith of Sancroft and other bishops. But the religious controversy, as usual, became entangled with other issues on which old party differences revived. When both Houses of Parliament met and the vote was taken whether William and Mary should be King and Queen, twelve Bishops out of fourteen voted against it. Later, Sancroft and several Bishops and four hundred clergy refused to take the Oath of Allegiance to William as King of England : they desired him to be no more than Regent, to mediate between themselves and James II, and having settled the Church of England question against Romanism, they wished to recall James and see William depart for Holland. They claimed their oath to James was inviolable. William was magnanimous towards these Non-Jurors, as they were called, but Parliament was firm : it was resolved that unless the Non-Jurors took the Oath of Allegiance to William before or on 1st August, 1689, they should be dispossessed of their livings, and failing to take the oath, Sancroft and five Bishops and many clergy were deprived of their benefices. " I think," said Maynard in the House of Commons, " that the clergy are out of their wits, and I believe if the clergy should have their wills, none of us would be here again ".

The attitude of the Nonconformists was far otherwise. Upwards of a hundred ministers were introduced to William and pledged their loyalty : they would continue to pray for " the success of his future endeavours for the defence and propagation of the Protestant interest throughout the world ". William was a staunch Protestant but he lacked the pleasing manners of the courtier : he was stern and unemotional in his relations with his advisers and his subjects. In Holland he was known as a Presbyterian ; although as King he attended the Church of England and received communion. His aim to secure full religious freedom for Nonconformists may have estranged him from the Church and Tory party ; it is curious, however, that after years of lying, treachery and dissolute living at the courts of the Stuarts, so many Anglo-Catholics should have worked for the return of James, rather than give their loyalty to William, whose principles had won him the unique position of the leading Protestant Statesman of Europe.

On 16th March, 1689, William addressed Parliament and urged the repeal of the Test and Corporation Acts : but Parliament refused to repeal any of the penal Acts of Charles II against the Nonconformists ; the sacramental test was throughout the debates the stumbling-block—a test which had deprived the country of the service of many capable men, had encouraged insincerity, and made a profanation of the sacrament itself.

A Toleration Bill, however, was introduced in the House of Lords in February, 1689, and passed without opposition. The Commons had its own Bill, " An Act for Liberty and Indulgence to Protestant Dissenters ", which passed its second reading. Then the Commons accepted and passed the Bill from the Lords. It was a mean Act, extending nothing more than the bare minimum of toleration ; as though Nonconformists must ever be under the supervision of Bishops and magistrates, and as though every Nonconformist place of worship must be licensed by the aforementioned representatives of Church and State. Nor must the doors of Nonconformist chapels be locked, bolted or barred during worship. The Act demanded that all English people should go to worship on the Lord's Day. Nonconformist ministers escaped the penalties of the Five Mile Act if they took the Oaths of Allegiance and Submission to William and subscribed to the Thirty-Nine Articles, with the exception of thirty-four, thirty-five, thirty-six and a clause of the twentieth. Baptists were exempt from subscribing to the Article on Infant Baptism. Quakers could make an affirmation in place of the oath, and when there was controversy and reluctance to grant this relief to the Quakers, Parliament was reminded of their sufferings, that " they have been in the shambles these twenty years ". Unitarians and Romanists were excluded from the benefits of the Act.

A Comprehension Bill was introduced into the House of Lords on 11th March, 1689: " An Act for uniting their Majesties' Protestant Subjects ". There was considerable discussion on matters of doctrine, worship and church government, for men desiring to minister in the United Church ; it was finally agreed that men seeking ordination must declare that they " submit " to the constitution of the Church, rather than declare " approval " of doctrine, worship and form of government. An ordained Presbyterian minister was not required to be re-ordained. Other Nonconformist Ministers must be re-ordained. This attempt to achieve a united Church makes the declaration interesting to present-day Free Church ministers : " I . . . do submit to the present Constitution of the Church of England. I acknowledge that the Doctrine of it contains all things necessary to Salvation, and I will conform myself to the worship and the government thereof as established by Law, and I solemnly promise in the exercise of my Ministry to preach and to practise thereto ". Concessions were made to well-known Presbyterian objections of the past. The surplice need not be worn except in Royal chapels, Cathedrals and College Churches : the sign of the cross was not necessary in baptism, and kneeling at the communion was optional.

Considering the disputed questions and changes involved by the Comprehension Bill, the Lords petitioned their Majesties to appoint a Royal Commission of Bishops and Clergy to suggest changes in liturgy, canons, ecclesiastical courts, and to present their recommendations to Convocation. The Commission met on eighteen occasions and Archbishop Tillotson drew up concessions to Nonconformists which he was prepared to defend.

When the Bill reached the House of Commons it was agreed that it should lie on the Table; rather than discuss it the Commons requested the King to summon a meeting of Convocation. It was hoped that Tillotson, who was most liberal in his views towards the Nonconformists, would preside at the Convocation, but the Anglo-Catholics and Jacobites had canvassed so well that Tillotson was not elected. The Lower House of Convocation was in no conciliatory mood to receive Tillotson's suggested concessions to Nonconformists: rather it was antagonistic to any attempt at Comprehension. Hence convocation was prorogued, Parliament was dissolved, the Bill was lost and never revived.

" The Glorious Revolution " had delivered England from the Stuarts, but it had brought the Nonconformists small gains. The Church and Tory parties had grown hostile to William and also arrested the progress of religious toleration. For more than a hundred and fifty years Nonconformists were still to suffer ecclesiastical and political injustices. The failure of reform was mainly due to the reactionary clergy. South, the Prebendary of Westminster, who hated Dissenters and taunted them as schismatics, " said what five-sixths of the clergy felt ". Sancroft, Tillotson and Burnet were anxious to remove all penal laws and give Nonconformists a wider freedom. But the Whigs and the Presbyterians were far too indifferent both within and without Parliament. Nonconformists were depressed by years of persecution and by reason of hopes deferred: they had no political unity, nor organisation whereby to attack the State where it was most vulnerable, namely in Parliament. It appeared that the forces most potentially progressive at the close of William's reign were already showing signs of the apathy which afflicted the eighteenth century.

CHAPTER XI

THE EIGHTEENTH CENTURY
ABUSES: REVIVAL: REPEAL

Dᵁᴿᴵɴɢ the early years of the eighteenth century Non-conformity suffered from the general " leave things as they are " attitude, widespread in all sections of the community. Queen Anne was rude to the deputies who presented their Address on her accession to the throne. Before her death, two Bills had been passed which foreboded more suffering for Non-conformists. Burnet, one of the kindliest Bishops, always considerate toward contemporary Nonconformists, intimated to Calamy that good men were of the opinion that Dissent would die out with the generation then existing. The Presbyterians were losing ground and Congregationalists and Baptists were barely maintaining it. A strange lethargy was slowly disintegrating theological conviction and ethical standards. It was an age of Reason, yet neither Theology nor Philosophy registered any startling triumphs. The influence of Philosophy tended to disturb the certainties of Christian belief. According to the Deists, Philosophy released Christianity from the encumbrance of Miracle and Mystery. Bishop Butler answered them in his *Analogy*, but his Probabilism never warmed the heart of anybody ; his attitude to vital religion can be estimated by his remark to George Whitefield whose evangelism was pure flame : " pretending to be inspired by the Holy Ghost was a horrid thing, a very horrid thing ". The Cambridge Platonists sought to introduce sweet reasonableness into religious controversy ; they were known as the Latitude Men, whose aim was to divert eighteenth-century thought from superstition on the one hand and enthusiasm on the other. They stood for moderation ; equally disliking political Puritanism and Tory High Churchism. They were thinkers whose piety belonged more to the cloistered life than to the tumultuous arena of world affairs.

It was in such an atmosphere, that in 1730, an anonymous pamphlet appeared : *An Enquiry into the Causes of the Decay of the Dissenting Interests in a letter to a Dissenting Minister*. The writer stated two main causes of the decay of Dissent. First : the ignorance among Nonconformists of their own principles. Second : Nonconformists did not attend well to their own interests : they were ceasing to defend their Churches and to fight for their rights. He did not think the Puritan spirit of liberty had been lost, but ministers should be allowed more liberty in their preaching. The pamphlet was relevant enough to draw replies from Doddridge, who knew of flourishing congregations in the Midlands ; also from Isaac Watts, who said the decay of vital religion was not confined to Nonconformists ; he agreed that there had been little success of late in the conversion of sinners. He was concerned at the tendency towards public-drinking, amusements and profane comedies. Watts urged his contemporaries to recover the habits of worshipping twice on the Lord's Day, also strict commercial integrity—both noble Puritan virtues.

I. WESLEY AND THE NONCONFORMISTS

The Evangelical Revival was the outstanding religious event of the century. George Whitefield had been a beer cellarman in Bristol but became " a poor scholar " at Oxford ; there he joined the Holy Club and met the Wesleys. It was Whitefield, at twenty-three, who began to preach in the fields : " finding that the pulpits are denied me and the poor colliers are ready to perish for lack of knowledge, I went to them and preached on a mount to upwards of two hundred ". His fame spread till enormous crowds of twenty and forty thousand gathered to hear him preach. Whitefield was a devout member and an ordained clergyman of the Anglican Church, but his preaching was banned and hindered. The Chancellor of Bristol diocese reminded him that it was illegal to preach without a bishop's license as Whitefield was doing in the city ; his answer was " there is a canon which forbids all clergymen to visit taverns and play cards : why is not that put into execution " ? The Vice-Chancellor of Oxford University threatened to lay him by the heels for preaching in other men's parishes. A favourite device was to ring the Church bells to drown his voice. Whitefield was a Calvinist and therefore accepted the doctrine that Christ died only for those elected to salvation ; but such a limited or " particular " view of the Atonement never affected the evangelical appeal of White-field any more than it did the appeal of Spurgeon in the nineteenth century. Whitefield's converts became the Calvinistic Methodists of Wales, and were also constituted into the Countess of Hunting-don's connexion in England. But many of the Churches founded by Whitefield, says Dale, " gradually adopted the Congrega-tional polity, so gradually it would be difficult to know when the change took place ".

John Wesley was a High Churchman and ever loyal to the Church of England. His home and schooling, his classical training at Oxford, his Fellowship at Lincoln College, his share in the Holy Club, are all so different from Whitefield's hard school of experience. His conversion at Aldersgate Street on 24th May, 1738, about a quarter before nine, when his heart was strangely warmed, and he testified there what he now first felt—all this passed into the history of the eighteenth century. For fifty-two years, Wesley was preaching what he had felt that night. His amazing physical endurance, his journeys, his fear-lessness and confidence, his converts, his societies and lay preachers, seeking first to rescue the perishing, the great world-wide Methodist Church—the imagination cannot measure the wonders of God's Grace in and through John Wesley.

I cannot pause longer over this mighty event which redeemed the eighteenth century from much that was sordid and " safe " in ecclesiasticism. But the Church of England was hostile to Wesley and his work. Bishop Butler tried to prevent him from preaching at Bristol : he was refused the Sacrament at Epworth where he was born ; the incumbent at Wednesbury stirred up the people to riot against him. On the other hand, the evan-gelicals in the Anglican Church were greatly blessed through his work.

Wesley was an Arminian and believed that Christ died for all men. On this matter Whitefield joined issue with him, and their arguments covered the well-worn themes of the Calvinist-Arminian debate. Happily, more happily than some of their followers, they remained to the end the firmest of friends.

I

How did the Evangelical Revival affect the Nonconformist Churches? During the latter half of the century the older churches experienced a remarkable growth in membership. On 27th February, 1810, Viscount Sidmouth referred in the House of Lords to the alarming increase of Nonconformist preachers and places of worship and called for official returns. These were made from licenses issued by the Bishops, though a number of small places of worship may have been omitted; but in towns with more than a thousand people the Nonconformist places of worship outnumbered Anglican Churches by 3,457 to 2,655. This convincing progress was due to the quickening spiritual forces of the Revival. So alarmed were the High Church Tories that they persuaded the Government to vote £100,000 for the building of Anglican Churches; and such grants were renewed until over a £1,000,000 of public money was spent in erecting Churches "against the growth of Dissent". The Revival affected both the theology and the preaching of Congregationalists and Baptists. There was no little controversy between them and the Methodist societies; believers' baptism or infant baptism was a lively issue and strong language was used. The lay preachers of Methodism stimulated lay work in the older churches. Dale points out how Congregationalists and Baptists had been disciplined in the methods of increasing Church Membership: " they did not deny the possibility of sudden conversion but they were unfamiliar with it. They found it hard to believe that a man might go into a Methodist meeting, a swearer and a drunkard, and be ' born again ', and ' find peace ' and rejoice in ' full assurance ' of his salvation, before the meeting broke up ".[1] Again, there is no doubt that the Revival stimulated the Older Churches to a wider and more glorious vision of service for Christ. I can but mention here, and draw out its significance later; The Baptist Missionary Society was founded in 1792; the London Missionary Society in 1795; the Church Missionary Society in 1799; the British and Foreign Bible Society in 1804; the Wesleyan Missionary Society in 1813.

[1] *History of English Congregationalism*, p. 584.

II. "AN ACCUMULATION OF SOCIAL EVILS"

"The religious and social condition of the masses under the two Georges is the severest condemnation of the religious life of the period. The masses were ignorant and brutalised, and their numbers and demoralisation rapidly increased".[1] Every writer on the eighteenth century agrees concerning the distressing social and moral standards of the nation. We have pointed out the decay of Dissent : in the next section evidence of the deplorable state of the Bishops' Bench and clergy will be produced. But it is desirable, however briefly, to indicate the ignorance, poverty and wretchedness of the greater part of the population throughout the century.

Hannah More's revelation of conditions in the West of England is typical. She records haunting scenes in Cheddar and district : within fifteen miles of her home, thirteen parishes were without any resident clergyman. When she gathered children, to teach them during the days of the week, she was opposed by farmers who were " as ignorant as the beasts that perish, intoxicated every day before dinner, and plunged in such vices as made me think London a virtuous place ". She visited every home in Cheddar and found each a place of " the greatest ignorance and vice. There was but one Bible in all the parish. No clergyman had resided in it for forty years. Children were buried without any funeral service and out of a population of two thousand, eight persons at the morning service and twenty in the afternoon, was considered a good congregation ". The living was in the gift of the Dean of Wells ; but the incumbent lived as far away as Oxford, and his curate lived at Wells, twelve miles distant. " At Wiveliscombe the incumbent was intoxicated about six times a week and was very frequently prevented from preaching by two black eyes honestly earned in fighting ". When Hannah More gathered poor children to school at Wedmore she was finally prosecuted in the Ecclesiastical Court. But her reforming and educational devotion achieved remarkable results. Upwards of seventeen hundred children were reclaimed by her labours : " so that in the parish of Blagdon, at two assizes, there was no prosecutor nor law-breaker ". But worldly clergymen were

[1] *Cambridge Modern History*, VI, p. 80.

hostile " if she had attempted in their parishes what we do in some others ".

In this period John Howard was visiting dens of iniquity and gaols, and startling sensitive souls by his revelations : his facts shocked his generation. He was a Congregationalist who often worshipped, when in London, at the Baptist Church in Little Wild Street. As a Nonconformist he was under the ban of the penal laws of Charles II. In 1787, when an attempt was made to repeal the Corporation and Test Acts, Beaufoy quoted in the House of Commons Burke's eloquent tribute to John Howard : " He has visited all Europe not to survey the sumptuousness of palaces, or the stateliness of temples, not to make accurate measurements of the remains of ancient grandeur, nor to form a scale of the curiosity of modern art ; not to collect medals nor to collate manuscripts ; but to dive into the depths of dungeons, to plunge into the infection of hospitals, to survey the mansions of sorrow and pain ; to take the gauge and dimensions of misery, depression and contempt ; to re-member the forgotten, to visit the forsaken ; and to compare and collate the distresses of all men in all countries ". And Beaufoy proceeded to say that John Howard as a Nonconformist was denied the common rights of an Englishman in his own country.

The eighteenth century " was a brutal age, an age of the press gang, of the whipping post, of gaol fever, and all the horrors of the criminal code ; an ignorant age, when the popula-tion, lords and louts alike, drank with great freedom and reckoned cock-fighting, among the more innocent joys of life ; when education . . . was hardly thought of ; a corrupt age, when offices and votes were bought and sold, and bishops owed their sees to the king's women ".[1]

III. PLURALISM AND ABSENTEEISM

We expect the ministry of the Church, directly and indirectly, to promote good government, and to do so by insisting on a high standard of political morality. The Tudors and the Stuarts had rewarded episcopal service with the wealth of the Church

[1] Augustine Birrell, *Essay on John Wesley*.

and State. How did the Episcopate re-act to the political pressure of rulers in the eighteenth century? After the religious upheavals of the civil war and the opportunity of the Revolution, did the Church put her house in order? William III was not deeply interested in ecclesiastical appointments, but Queen Anne never paused to conceal her prejudice. During her reign, whether Whigs or Tories were in power, the Bishops' bench in the House of Lords was a political party machine. The Queen admitted that she appointed her favourite bishops to dish the Whigs: " I know the principles of the Church of England and I know those of the Whigs, and it is that, and no other reason, which makes me think as I do of the last ". Without consulting her ministers she appointed Bishops to Exeter and Chester in 1707. When the Whigs protested at her unconstitutional action she defended herself vigorously: " All the clamour which is raised against them (the two Bishops) proceeds only from the malice of the Whigs. . . . I do assure you these men were my own choice ". Confiding her ideas of William III to the Duchess of Marlborough, the Queen declared that no one would divert her from the political policy of ecclesiastical appointments: " As to my saying the Church was in danger during the last reign, I cannot alter my opinion. For though there was no violent thing done, everybody that will speak impartially must own that everything was tending toward the Whigs. And whenever that is, I shall think the Church beginning to be in danger ". Anne informed Archbishop Sharp in 1705 " that she would always desire that the bishops she put in should vote on the side that they who call themselves the church party, do vote on ". One of the most notorious examples of such political support was when Walpole's government was threatened with defeat over the " malodorous question of the South Sea Company ", and was saved by the " steadiness of the Bishop's bench ". Out of twenty-six bishops the votes of twenty-four were " for the Court ".

The Pluralism of the bishops and clergy during the century was an open scandal—when one person holds a number of livings, drawing the incomes and paying a miserable stipend to a curate who does the work, or drawing large sums for several offices which demand only occasional service, or receiving incomes from livings which he never visits, absenteeism well rewarded—discreditable to the Church and the State. The abuses of medieval pluralism and clerical corruption continued under the Hanovers and their Ministers.

For example, Lord Barrington had several brothers who had already been well rewarded by the State, but he was anxious for the welfare of Shute, who had been but two years in the priestly office : and to the Duke of Newcastle, Prime Minister under George II, he wrote thus : " I have but one anxiety in this world, my youngest brother remains still without any provision, which is the more distressful to me because every other brother I have is most happily provided for . . . he has been two years in priest's orders and will be one of the first King's chaplains that are made. Anything in the Church not under £300 would make both him and me completely happy. As we belong to Berkshire, a stall at Windsor would be peculiarly acceptable ". The advance of Shute Barrington was astounding. He duly became a chaplain to George III, which office was regarded as a sure stepping-stone to a bishopric. In 1760 Lord Barrington pressed his claims on the Duke and suggested Shute for the Deanery of Bristol : an appeal which failed. But in 1761, seeing Shute was now twenty-seven, he was nominated to the fifth stall of Christ Church, Oxford, which added £400 a year to his income; in 1761-2 he was presented with two stalls at Hereford Cathedral ; in 1768 another stall was given him at St. Paul's ; in 1769 he became Bishop of Llandaff, in 1782 of Sarum, and in 1791 he was made Bishop of Durham with an annual income, on three years' average, of nearly £22,000. The cumulative sums of such pluralism were enormous. How could this mingling of political patronage and ecclesiastical obsequiousness do other than demoralise the Church and the Ministry ? The example just related is only one of others from Professor Norman Sykes' chapter, " The Ladder of Preferment" in his book, *Church and State in England in the Eighteenth Century*.[1]

It is not surprisng that these evils led to vigorous denunciation and demands for the reform of the Church. And when the House of Commons was reformed in 1832 the nation began to press for other reforms. The Church was regarded as no less

[1] cf. p. 158ff. J. K. B. Masterman admits in his small volume, *The Church of England*, that a third ot the clergy were pluralists, p. 25.

corrupt than Parliament. The active hostility of the episcopate to the Reform Bill had roused the anger of the people. The bishops were accused " of being interested partisans, and of having entered into an alliance with the opponents of political reform, in the hope of warding off an attack upon their own privileged position. The Reformers complained of the condition of the Church of England, and a demand was made for a searching inquiry and prompt removal of alleged abuses ".

These abuses were set forth in the *Black Book*, first issued in 1820 and re-published in 1831 :

" It is unseemly, we think, and inconsistent with the very principles and purposes of Christianity, to contemplate lofty prelates with £20,000 or £40,000 a year, elevated on thrones, living sumptuously in splendid palaces, attended by swarms of menials, gorgeously attired, and of priests to wait upon their persons, emulating the proudest nobles, and even taking precedence of them in all the follies of heraldry. Beneath them are crowds of sinecure dignitaries and incumbents, richly endowed with worldly goods, the wealthiest not even obliged to reside among their flocks ; and those who reside not compelled to do one act of duty beyond providing and paying a miserable deputy just enough to keep him from starving. Contrasted with the preceding is a vast body of poor, laborious ministers, doing all the work, and receiving less than the pay of a common brick-layer or Irish hodman ; but the whole assemblage, both rich and poor, paid so as to be a perpetual burden upon the people, and to wage, of necessity, a ceaseless strife with those whom they ought to comfort, cherish and instruct ".

Examples are given of the extent to which particular families were enriched by favouritism. Bishop Sparke, of Ely, is said to have " owed his promotion to the circumstance of having been tutor to the Duke of Rutland " ; and the provision secured for himself, his sons, and his son-in-law, is thus set forth :

The Bishop's See of Ely and Dependencies[1] - - - £27,742
The Rev. J. H. Sparke, the Bishop's eldest son, holds the living of Leverington, the sinecure rectory of Littlebury.

[1] Extraordinary Black Book, p. 25.

the living of Bexwell, a prebendal stall in Ely Cathedral, is steward of all his father's manorial courts, and chancellor of the diocese. The estimated value of the whole -   -   £4,500

The Rev. E. Sparke, the Bishop's youngest son, holds the consolidated living of St. Mary and St. Nicholas, Feltwell, the vicarage of Littleport, a prebendal stall in Ely, is Registrar of the diocese, and examining chaplain to his father, the estimated annual value of his appointments not less than -   £4,000

The Rev. H. Fardell, the Bishop's son-in-law, holds the living of Waterbeach, the vicarage of Wisbech, and a prebendal stall in Ely Cathedral. The estimated annual value of his preferments - - - - - - £3,700

Total income of the Sparke family -   - - £39,942

The unscrupulous nepotism of Archbishop Sutton is similarly set forth.[1] Among seven of his family were " shared sixteen rectories, vicarages and chapelries, besides preacherships and dignities in cathedrals ". One son-in-law is said to have received, " in about as many years, eight different preferments, estimated to be worth £10,000 per annum ". Statements like these could not fail to influence the public mind, and to call forth a demand for the reform of Church abuses.

It is not surprising, therefore, that the reformed Parliament speedily resolved to ascertain the facts. After much discussion a Royal Commission was appointed to inquire into the state of the Established Church. The Reports of this Commission were duly presented to Parliament. In the first of them, made in 1835, the Commissioners give the annual income, on a three-years' average, of the Episcopal Sees ; from which it appeared that, while some of the bishops were in the receipt of enormous incomes, others received only comparatively small amounts. The following figures sufficiently indicate the inequality which was shown to exist :

DIOCESE.		INCOME.	DIOCESE.			INCOME.
Canterbury	-	£22,216	Oxford	-	-	£3,106
York	-	£13,798	Rochester	-	-	£1,523
London	-	£15,133	St. David's	-	-	£2,490
Durham	-	£21,991	Llandaff	-	-	£1,008
Ely	-	£12,627				

[1] ibid., p. 26.

The gross income of all the bishops was found to amount to £181,631 per annum, giving an average income to each bishop of £6,727. The disproportion between the incomes of the parochial clergy was no less striking. It was found that upwards of 150 beneficed clergymen were in the receipt of the following incomes :

NUMBER OF CLERGYMEN.		INCOMES.			
134	above	£1,000	and	under	£1,500
2	,,	£1,500	,,	,,	£2,000
9	,,	£2,000	,,	,,	£2,500
4	,,	£2,500	,,	,,	£3,000
2	,,	£3,500	,,	,,	£4,000
1	,,	£4,843	,,	,,	
1	,,	£7,306			

In addition to this it was reported that there were seventy sinecure rectories with no duties whatever attached to them, yielding a gross revenue of £18,622 per annum. On the other hand, it was shown that there were nearly 5,000 beneficed clergymen who were in receipt of less than £200 per annum. Thus of the incomes of the clergy :

297	were under	£50	per annum.	
1,629	,,	,,	£100	,, ,,
1,602	,,	,,	£150	,, ,,
1,354	,,	,,	£200	,, ,,

It was further reported that there were 5,230 curates, with an average stipend of £81 per annum ; 4,224 of whom were employed by non-resident incumbents, who gave an average salary of £79 per annum.

Cathedral Revenues

The revenues of the Cathedral bodies were shown to be equally in need of reform. The report gives the gross annual income of these bodies as £284,241 ; the net income divisible amongst the deans and chapters at £208,289 ; and the gross annual separate incomes of the dignitaries and other clerical members of the cathedral at £75,854. The report further showed that these cathedral dignitaries were required to keep only a brief residence, and that their sole duties consisted in preaching once or twice yearly in the cathedrals ; and that besides the incomes which they derived from the capitular estates the deans and canons commonly held livings of great value, and in many instances were possessed of other offices.

Creation of Permanent Commission

In 1836 the Government of Lord Melbourne brought in a Bill to constitute the Ecclesiastical Commissioners a permanent Corporation, and to carry out the recommendations of the Committee of Inquiry. Lord John Russell justified the proposal by urging the necessity for making provision for the spiritual destitution of populous districts. The Government Bill passed, and the title of this Act is suggestive :

> " An Act for carrying into effect the Reports of the Commissioners appointed to consider the State of the Established Church in England and Wales, with reference to Ecclesiastical Duties and Revenues, so far as they relate to Episcopal Dioceses, Revenues, and Patronage ".

This important Act is commonly known as the " Bishops' Act ", for beside constituting the Ecclesiastical Commission a permanent corporation, in 1836 it fixed the future salaries of the bishops as follows :

Abp. of Canterbury	- £15,000	Bp. of Ely - - £5,500
,, ,, York	- £10,000	,, ,, St. Asaph
Bp of London	- £10,000	and Bangor £5,200
,, ,, Durham	- £8,000	,, ,, Worcester - £5,000
,, ,, Winchester	- £7,000	,, ,, Bath and
		Wells - £5,000

Out of the funds accruing from the excess of income from the property attached to these Sees over the stipends thus fixed, the Commissioners were instructed to make the " average annual incomes of the other bishops respectively not less than four thousand pounds, nor more than five thousand pounds ". The

Act also directs : " That a copy of every order of His Majesty in council made under this Act shall be laid before the House of Parliament in the month of January in every year ".

Other legislation on the same lines followed. In 1840 " the Cathedral Act " gave legal effect to the recommendations of the Commission concerning deans and chapters. In 1856 the powers of the Church Building Commissioners were transferred to the Ecclesiastical Commission. Four years afterwards the Legislature vested episcopal estates in the Commission and provided that the income from property attached to the episcopal sees should be carried to, and form part of, the Common Fund, and be applicable to the purposes of that fund.

The Bishop of Durham in his recent book, *The Anglican Tradition in the Life of England*, says the *Black Book* of 1820 and the *Extraordinary Black Book* of 1831 were beyond measure abusive and inaccurate. The Bishop admits " indefensible ecclesiastical abuses ",[1] but he adduces no details of their nature. I have quoted the stark facts of Pluralism, and the figures are those of a Royal Commission presented to Parliament. I do not understand how these facts and figures, submitted to and by a Royal Commission, are inaccurate or abusive. The Bishop of Durham agrees that " the majority of Churchmen, whatever their virtues, seemed to be more concerned to resist change than to put their house in order ". Exactly ! It was the immoral ramp of Pluralism, and a system of patronage by rulers and statesmen, who bought the votes of Bishops in the House of Lords, which enraged the nation. No one can defend such shameful and corrupt practice in the Church of God. While it worked, statesmen and Bishops united to resist reform in Church and State. How justifiable was Dr. Johnson's criticism ! " No man can now be made a bishop for his learning and piety, his only chance for promotion is his being connected with somebody who has parliamentary interest ".

To these Pluralists and Absenteeists the spiritual needs of the masses meant nothing ; they drew their revenues and neglected the spiritual work for which they were paid. A further result of the system was the impoverishment of the clergy who did the work for which Pluralists drew the incomes. Bishop

---

[1] p. 82. J. H. B. Masterman : *The Church of England*, p. 25, says the *Black Book* was hostile but well informed.

Horsley found in his diocese " many curacies of the value of £10 a year, for the improvement of which he laboured ".[1]   In an ordination sermon Paley commended poverty to the curate since it placed him, " upon a level with the greatest part of your parishioners, you gain access to their conversation and confidence, which is rarely granted to the superior clergy. . . . I put you in mind of this advantage because the right use of it constitutes one of the most respectable employments not only of our own order, but of human nature ; and leaves you, believe me, little to envy in the condition of your superiors, or to regret in your own ".[2]

This section is painful reading ; but it is a statement of abuses which called for abolition : I must do justice to Nonconformists who suffered under these religious and political injustices during the eighteenth century : moreover, these facts are essential to any understanding of the national urge towards the Great Reform Bill of 1832.

IV. THE PLAN TO DESTROY NONCONFORMITY

After the death of Queen Anne in 1714 the Protestant succession was by no means secure.   Anne had not discouraged the Jacobites who detested the prospect of a German Lutheran prince on the throne, as bitterly as they had hated William III and all his ways and works.   The High Church Tory Party had plotted with the Pretender : even Walpole had corresponded " safely " with him.   But Nonconformists had resolved never to have another Stuart to reign over them : they knew that nothing less than massacre would be their lot under such a restoration.   In 1715 the Pretender was proclaimed as King James III, and it appeared to many that George I was sitting on a rocking-chair rather than on the throne.   His coronation was the occasion for the clergy and Tory die-hards to stir up riots against Nonconformists, their homes and places of worship. At Oxford, Birmingham, Newcastle-on-Tyne, Wrexham, and in Lancashire, Presbyterian, Congregational and Baptist churches were burnt and wrecked.   It was this outbreak of violence

[1] Sykes, p. 207.
[2] ibid., p. 230.

which led Parliament to pass the Riot Act in 1715. The Non-conformists began to arm, determined to fight for the Protestant succession. At Newcastle-on-Tyne seven hundred men, mainly Nonconformists, were prepared for action. In Lancashire a minister named Wood equipped and armed four hundred men and held them in readiness for action at Preston. " The body of James II lay in State in the church of Faubourg St. Jacques, unburied and surrounded by flaming tapers, awaiting the day when the Jacobites could lay it to rest in English earth ".[1] Even Susanna, John Wesley's mother, was a Jacobite : when Samuel, her husband, learned that she had never said " Amen " to his public supplications for William III there was a domestic scene : and when Mrs. Wesley refused to transfer her loyalty to William III, husband and wife separated for a year, until William died.

Another venture was made in 1745 to re-establish Stuart rule in England. The young Pretender landed in Scotland and five thousand Highlanders rallied to his standard : they crossed the Border and reached as far south as Derby when the officers refused to march further. They knew that English forces were being drawn from the Continent and the retreat to Scotland began. Near Culloden a British force under Cumberland defeated and scattered the Scots. This 1745 rebellion was the end of Stuart intrigues in British politics : but the Government was so alarmed that eighty plotters were executed and three hundred and fifty rebels were transported. Again, the High Church Tory Party made no secret of sympathy with the Pretender : but the Nonconformists were firm in their support of George II. The Committee of Dissenting Deputies called upon Nonconformists in all parts of the country to carry arms. Ministers became recruiting officers. Doddridge of Northampton, gentlest of men, urged the members of his church to enlist for the King. In Parliament, forty-five years later, Charles James Fox, speaking in support of the repeal of the penal legislation against the Nonconformists, said that " a candid examination of the history of Great Britain would, in his opinion, be favourable to the Dissenters. In the rebellions of 1715 and 1745 this country was extremely indebted to their exertions. At both these periods they stood forward as the champions of British

[1] *Cambridge Modern History*, VI, p. 43.

liberty . . . their exertions then were so magnanimous that he had no scruple to assert that to their endeavours we owed the preservation of Church and State. . . . Gentlemen should remember that, at the times alluded to, the High Churchmen did not display such gallantry, for many appeared perplexed and pusillanimous ". On another occasion, in Parliament, it was stated that " two hundred thousand Nonconformists had volunteered for the defence of the Kingdom when an invasion seemed imminent ".

In 1660, Charles II had promised liberty to tender consciences. Then came the Corporation Act in 1661 and the Test Act in 1673. The former Act made it possible for borough-mongers to pack Parliament. The Duke of Newcastle could reckon the votes of nearly fifty members through his control of municipalities—men who had taken the sacrament and could be trusted to vote for their master. Both the Corporation and Test Acts treated Nonconformists as less than Englishmen. On the other hand scandalous and depraved characters would take the sacrament to secure salaried positions in the State. " I was early with the Secretary Bolingbroke ", writes Swift, " but he was gone to his devotions . . . to receive the sacrament. Several rakes did the same. It was not for piety but employment, according to Act of Parliament ".[1] But as long as they were only " rakes " and not Dissenters, Swift's party saw no profanation. A few Nonconformists succumbed to the temptation. Sir Humphrey Edwin was elected Lord Mayor of London in 1697 and attended Pinners' Hall, used as a Congregational Church, in all his regalia. Sir Thomas Abney, became Lord Mayor in 1701 and qualified for the office by receiving the sacrament in the Church of England, afterwards worshipping at the Presbyterian Church. There was an angry outcry by the Anglicans against such occasional conformity for offices in civil life. Daniel Defoe, a Nonconformist who often used his weapon of satire to the annoyance of his friends as well as his enemies, protested vehemently that these occasional acts of conformity were inconsistent with the Nonconformist conscience and a reproach to the Christian religion : " how can you take it as a civil act in one place, and a religious act in another ; is not this playing ' bo-peep with God Almighty ' " ? Baskerville, a Baptist, had been elected to the

[1] G. M. Trevelyan, *History of England*, p. 501.

common council of the City of London and qualified by receiving the sacrament. When he was rebuked for his violation of principle and defended himself, the Church in Unicorn Yard took counsel with the Baptist Board, and it was resolved that Baskerville ought not to be allowed to remain a member of the Church. There was an occasional protest against the Test Act from the Anglican side : " to make the celebration of this institution," said Bishop Hoadly, " which was ordained and confined by our Lord Himself to the serious remembrance of His death in the assemblies of churches of Christians, to be the instrument of some particular sort of Christians (as well as of infidels and atheists) getting into civil offices, and to be the bar against other sorts of Christians, is debasing the most sacred thing in the world into a political tool and engine of State ". Yet, Lord North as late as 1787 defended the Corporation and Test Acts " as the great bulwark of the Constitution, and to which they owed those inestimable blessings of freedom they now happily enjoyed ".

But there was more penal legislation in the reign of Anne to buttress the Church. In 1711, by a sordid bargain between the Whigs and Tories, the Occasional Conformity Bill was passed : that all mayors, aldermen, councillors, and persons in the service of the State, who should attend Divine worship in a Nonconformist Church, or any meeting at which more than ten persons were present, should on conviction forfeit his office and pay a fine of £40 to the informer. But worse legislation was to follow. In 1714 the Schism Bill was passed " to prevent the growth of Schism and for the further security of the Church of England as by law established ", forbidding any person to teach or keep a public or private school, until he declared that he would conform to the liturgy of the Church of England and submit to the sacramental test. This Bill was a cruel and malicious blow at the Dissenting Academies, which, under many difficulties, had achieved excellent educational results. It was intended to destroy all possibility of Nonconformist children receiving an education anywhere but in a Church of England school, where they would be taught the catechism of the Prayer Book. " The Tories believed that if they could destroy the Dissenting Academies they would put an end to Dissent ; the Dissenting congregations of the next generation would have no educated ministers . . . only the poor and ignorant would continue to attend the conventicles ; and Nonconformists would become too weak and too contemptible to trouble the Church any longer ".[1] I shall refer to the place and work of the Academies in the chapter on Education. Notwithstanding petitions and protests the Bill passed and was due to come into force on 1st August, 1714 ; the day when Bradbury, Congregationalist minister at Fetter Lane, met Bishop Burnet, who asked why he looked so sorrowful : referring to the Schism Act he replied, " I am thinking whether I shall have the constancy and resolution of that noble company of martyrs whose ashes are deposited in this place ; for I most assuredly expect to see similar times of violence and persecution, and that I shall be called to suffer in a like cause ". That morning, Queen Anne died, and the Schism Bill died with her.

V. REPEAL ! REPEAL !

Throughout the eighteenth century, Nonconformists were subject to the penal legislation of the Corporation and Test Acts. True, the Toleration Act of 1689 had made concessions but their places of worship must still be licensed by a Bishop or magistrate ; their ministers must still subscribe, with certain exceptions, to the Thirty-Nine Articles. The sacramental test had closed the door to all national and municipal service on the part of Englishmen who were Nonconformists, including the Unitarians. The whole penal legislation was the work of men who were determined to maintain their wealth, privilege and power, and to do so by using the Church and State to disfranchise and crush the " inferior population ". But Nonconformists had proved themselves loyal Englishmen : they had suffered for their country, their homes and their principles. The Quakers especially had been victimised. By 1736, 1,180 Quakers had been prosecuted, 300 had been imprisoned and some had died in prison, under the penal Acts. Yet, the Corporation, Test, Conventicle, Five-Mile and Occasional Conformity Acts were still unrepealed. The Nonconformists who were now growing conscious of their political power, were determined to wipe these Acts off the Statute Book.

[1] Dale, *History of Congregationalism*, p. 503.

In 1736 a Bill was introduced into the House of Commons to repeal the Corporation and Test Acts: it was defeated. In 1739 another Bill was introduced and defeated. In 1772 a Bill was introduced to release Nonconformist ministers from subscribing to any of the Thirty-Nine Articles ;[1] it was proposed that they should be permitted to declare their belief in the Holy Scriptures as containing the revelation of the mind and the will of God ; and to affirm the Scriptures as the rule of their faith and practice. High Churchmen were shocked that the Scriptures should be substituted for the Articles. The Archbishop of York and five Bishops voted against the Bill and it was defeated. The Archbishop accused Dissenting ministers as men prompted by " a close ambition ", a remark which drew a caustic rebuke from the Earl of Chatham : " this is judging uncharitably ; and whoever brings such a charge without evidence, defames. The Dissenting ministers are represented as men of ' close ambition ' : they are so, my lords ; and their ambition is to keep close to the college of fishermen, not of cardinals ; and to the doctrines of inspired apostles, not to decrees of interested and aspiring bishops. They contend for a scriptural and spiritual worship ; we, (Anglicans) have a Calvinistic creed, a Popish liturgy, and an Arminian clergy. The Reformation had laid open the Scriptures to all ; let not the Bishops shut them again. Laws in support of ecclesiastical power are pleaded, which it would shock humanity to execute. It is said religious sects have done great mischief when they were not kept under restraints ; but history affords no proof that sects have ever been mischievous when they were not oppressed and persecuted by the ruling Church ". Despite such a rebuke the Tories and the episcopate killed the Bill. In 1773 a similar Bill was introduced into Parliament and defeated. In 1779 the Bill, slightly modified, was passed by both Houses of Parliament. It was the first concession for ninety years towards toleration for Nonconformists.

But the Corporation and Test Acts still remained. In 1787 another Bill to repeal the Acts was brought into Parliament. The Committee of Dissenting Deputies was now organising the repeal campaign. Pitt was alarmed : " The Church and the State are united upon the principles of expediency, and it

[1] cf. p. 125.

K

concerns those to whom the well-being of the State is entrusted to take care that the Church be not rashly abolished ". Fox retorted that the sentiments of the Bishops and the clergy should not set the standard of the political action of the House of Commons. The Bill was defeated. In 1789 another attempt at repeal was made. When the Nonconformists were accused of disloyalty to the State, Fox defended their religious teaching as promoting civil liberty and said that no government had the right to inquire into private opinions : " the comparative moderation of sentiment in the Church itself was owing to the Dissenters, who had compelled the members of the Establishment to oppose argument, instead of force, to argument ". The Bill was defeated by twenty votes. In 1790 another Bill for repeal was brought into the House of Commons. Fox made a powerful plea, also warning the House that the demand for reform would not cease with the repeal of the penal Acts : " the cause of the Dissenters was one with the universal rights of mankind ". The Bill was rejected ; one important factor contributing to the defeat of the Bill on this occasion was the sympathy of many Nonconformists with the French Revolution.

Not until 1827 did the Nonconformists organise their resources for another attempt to repeal the obnoxious penal Acts. The Committee of Dissenting Deputies, the Board of Congregational Ministers, the British and Foreign Unitarian Association, the Baptists uniting through the Protestant Society, prepared the final attack. The Methodists now came to the help of the Nonconformists. Meetings were held throughout the country. Liberal members of Parliament were interviewed and canvassed. And on 26th February, 1828, Lord John Russell introduced the Repeal Bill. He appealed to the House of Commons " to render this act of justice to three millions of their fellow subjects ". Representing Tories and High Churchmen, Peel opposed the measure : he afterwards agreed to vote for it if a declaration was made by all who should occupy municipal offices that they would refrain from doing anything to subvert the Church of England. The Bill passed and received the Royal Assent on 9th May, 1828. For a hundred and fifty years the penal Acts had remained on the Statute Books and during this long period, Nonconformists had been excluded from all employment, civil, naval, or military, under the Government. For the first time in English history,

Nonconformist ministers and places of worship were free from interference or control by the Anglican Church or the State. From now onwards they are not known as Dissenters or Nonconformists. They are Free Churchmen. The repeal of these Acts marked the rising political power of the Free Churches in the State, a guarantee of further victories over remaining religious and political injustices.

CHAPTER XII

FREE CHURCHMEN: THE AMERICAN WAR:
THE FRENCH REVOLUTION

THE repeal of the penal laws was long delayed, and the demand for reform was stolidly resisted, by reason of the attitude of Nonconformists towards the American War in 1774 and the French Revolution in 1789. From 1774 to 1832 Nonconformists were changing the thought and character of the English people; and the evidence that they did so, is the slow disintegration of Tory High Church rule until the Reform Bill of 1832 was placed on the Statute Book. I am not dismissing lightly, and will try to do justice to other agitations for reform, but the religious tensions of the period account for the contrast between the French and English revolutions—the difference between intellectual and social anarchy in France and revolution by slow Parliamentary procedure in England.

The first hindrance to reform was the American War. In 1774, George III and his Cabinet resolved to tax the American colonists before obtaining their consent. As many of the colonists were descendants of the Puritans who had fled from the tyranny and arbitrary taxation of the Stuarts, they were in no mood to submit to the English Parliament and events drifted on to civil war. On one side was the unbending stubbornness of George III; on the other side was the uncompromising attitude of the American radicals led by Adams, to whom separation from England gradually appeared desirable and essential. But we are concerned with the division of religious opinion in England. Porteus, a court preacher, delivered a sermon before the King and defended the policy of taxation without consent, for which he was soon afterwards rewarded with a bishopric. Speaking in the House of Lords, the Duke of Grafton found it necessary to chastise the " despotic " zeal of the clergy, and, in particular, that of Archbishop Markham. " Twenty-four Bishops ", wrote

Benjamin Franklin, " with all the lords in possession or expectation of places, make a dead majority (in the Lords) that renders all debating ridiculous ".

Nonconformist opposition to the King, the government and the Church was led by Dr. Joseph Priestley, a Unitarian-Presbyterian minister, a brilliant philosopher and scientist, whose studies had gained him the Fellowship of the Royal Society ; he was a man of lovable disposition, simplicity of character and purity of life, who kept controversy at its highest ethical levels. He had been one of the earliest Nonconformists to declare that religious equality demanded the disestablishment of the Anglican Church. In 1774 he published an *Address to Protestant Dissenters of all Denominations with regard to the State of Public Liberty in General and of American Affairs in Particular*, appealing to Nonconformists to remember that religious liberty could never be maintained except on the basis of civil liberty ; he declared that George III and his ministers were taxing the colonists because they were Dissenters and Whigs. Priestley prophesied that the Americans would teach mankind a lesson similar to that which Cromwell's Ironsides had taught their own generation. Dr. Richard Price, a Unitarian-Presbyterian, relates the situation : " From one end of North America to the other they are fasting and praying. But what are we doing ? We are ridiculing them as fanatics and scoffing at religion. We are running wild after pleasure and forgetting everything decent at masquerades. We are gambling in gaming-houses, trafficking for boroughs, perjuring ourselves at elections, and selling ourselves for places ". Before the civil war began, Benjamin Franklin wrote from London to the colonists, " the Dissenters are all with us ".

But a greater obstacle to reform was the French Revolution of 1789. France was nearer England and the ruling classes were terrified lest the Revolution should spread across the Channel. Again, the religious forces in England were in conflict. The continuous advocacy of reform, says Professor Sykes, was finally extinguished by the outbreak of the French Revolution : " The unhappy generation from 1793 to 1826 contributed more than any of its predecessors to the ill-repute of the eighteenth century by its policy of repression and reaction, which, though resolute in opposing all who laid even the mildest hands upon the established order in Church and State, allowed the accumulation of anomalies and abuses in such magnitude as to provoke the radical reform epoch which succeeded. 'Since the miserable event of the French Revolution', observed Bishop Watson, 'it may be said to every man in England and Europe who attempts to reform abuses either in Church or State—*desine, jam conclamatum est*'".[1] Political differences in England were acute, but the fury and malice of religious strife led to serious consequences. The Revolution had disestablished the Roman Catholic Church in France, and it is not surprising that the "Church in danger cry" was heard again in England. Burke's *Reflections on the French Revolution* had attempted in glittering rhetoric, to excite the envy of the French and the pride of the English over the condition of the Anglican Church : "they can see, without pain or grudging, an Archbishop precede a Duke. They can see a Bishop of Durham, or a Bishop of Winchester, in possession of ten thousand pounds a year, and cannot conceive why it is in worse hands than estates to the like amount in the hands of this Earl or that Squire ". In reply to Burke's statement, Professor Sykes quotes many of the financial details recorded in the preceding chapter ; "to the imaginative mind of Burke such things, far from being an occasion of shame or apology, constitute a title to praise and congratulation ".[2]

The *Reflections* prompted Price and Priestley to defend the rights of the people against such despotic governments and churches as those of France. On the other hand, Priestley regarded the events in America and France as signs of a new era of liberty for the peoples of the world. Price published a sermon on the three national blessings of intelligence, virtue and liberty, warning all governments to read the signs of the times. In the House of Lords, Bishop Horsley went so far as to denounce Nonconformist conventicles and Sunday Schools as places of sedition and atheism—an accusation which drew the fire of Robert Hall (1764–1831) "the greatest preacher in the Free Churches and the leading Baptist of his time "[3] who had referred to the French Revolution as the most splendid event in history. Hall began his ministry at Broadmead Chapel, Bristol, and was already famous as a thinker and orator of the first rank ; he

[1] *Church and State in England in the Eighteenth Century,* p. 407.
[2] ibid., p. 408 f.
[3] *Cambridge Modern History,* VIII. p. 764.

answered Horsley that while the Free Churches were centres of Biblical instruction they also stood for religious equality and reform. Horsley had proclaimed to the nation the duty of passive obedience to rulers, and argued that to deny the divine right of the King was the highest of all treasons. As the chief protagonist of the Bishop, it will be well to quote Robert Hall's reply : " it is not a little extraordinary, that Bishop Horsley, the apologist of tyranny, the patron of passive obedience, should affect to admire the British Constitution, whose freedom was attained by a palpable violation of the principles for which he contends. He will not say that the Barons at Runnymede acted on his maxims, in extorting the Magna Charta from King John, or in demanding its confirmation from Henry III. If he approves of their conduct he gives up his cause . . . We owe him an acknowledgment for the frankness with which he avows his decided preference of the clergy of France to dissenters in England—a sentiment we have often suspected, but have seldom had the satisfaction of seeing openly professed before . . . the extreme tenderness he professes for the fallen Church of France is well contrasted by his malignity towards dissenters. Admirable consistency in a Protestant Bishop, to lament over the fall of that anti-Christ whose overthrow is represented by unerring inspiration, as an event most splendid and happy ! It is a shrewd presumption against the utility of religious establishments, that they too often become seats of intolerance, instigators to persecution, nurseries of Bonners and Horsleys ".[1] When the Bishop described dissenters as miserable men, in the gall of bitterness and in the bond of iniquity ; Hall says it is time to turn from this disgusting picture and priestly insolence and deal with Horsley's attitude to the Press : " The political sentiments of Dr. Horsley are in truth of too little consequence in themselves to engage a moment's curiosity, and deserve attention only as they indicate the spirit of the times. The freedom with which I have pointed out the abuses of government, will be little relished by the pusillanimous and interested. In the present crisis of things, the danger to liberty is extreme, and it is necessary to address a warning voice to the nation, that may disturb its slumbers, if it cannot heal its lethargy. When we look at the distraction and misery of a neighbouring country we behold a

[1] Halls' *Works*, IV, p. 55 f.

scene that is enough to make the most hardy republican tremble at the idea of a revolution.   Nothing but an obstinate adherence to abuses can ever push the people of England to that fatal extremity.   But if the state of things continues to grow worse and worse, if the friends of reform—the true friends of their country, continued to be overwhelmed by calumny and persecution, the confusion will probably be dreadful, the misery extreme, and the calamities that await us too great for human calculation. . . . In the field of government, as in that of the world, the tares of despotism were sown while men slept.   The misfortune on these occasions is that the people, for want of understanding the principles of liberty, seldom reach the true source of their misery ; but, after committing a thousand barbarities, only change their masters, when they should change their systems ".[1]   When Hall was accused of being a radical reformer, a revolutionist and a republican, he vigorously denied the two latter charges ". " But a radical reformer ", he said, " is one that goes to the root of the evil, that proposes not merely to palliate, but to extirpate it.   And what is that reform worth that proposes less.   He who labours under an inveterate malady wishes for a radical cure . . . if, by styling me a radical reformer, he intends to impute revolutionary views, I say it is a calumny and a falsehood ; and I challenge him to produce a single sentence from my publications which sustains such a charge or which convicts me of hostility to the existing order of things, as consisting of King, Lords and Commons ".[2]

The controversy issued in violence.   " Down with the abettors of the French Revolution ", and " Down with the Dissenters ", cried the clergy as the mob in Birmingham fired Priestley's house and library and destroyed his scientific apparatus.   In many other places Nonconformists had their homes wrecked and burnt ; they began to arm themselves in defence of their homes. The chief instigator of the Birmingham riots was Madan, rector of St. Philips.   George III expressed his pleasure when he heard of the attack on Priestley and he made Madan a bishop.   But from Derby, Bath, Bristol, Exeter, Essex and other centres resolutions of sympathy were forwarded to Priestley.   Three years later, owing to threats, he sought a home in America where he received honourable hospitality.

[1] ibid., pp. 57, 99.   [2] ibid., p. 138.

I. "I KNOW THE DISSENTERS : THEY CARRIED THE REFORM BILL"

After the close of the French War at Waterloo in 1815 there was widespread misery and disillusionment. A huge national debt, soaring prices and masses of unemployed gave renewed impetus to the demand for reform. But the policy of the Government was to resist every attempt at improvements and change. In the past, history had known military, political and religious revolutions which had shaken society to its foundations ; but the Industrial Revolution which had been changing the face of the Northern and Midland counties of England was a portent which the Government did not understand—it was the beginning of the machine age and the clash of human values, the end of which still baffles us. The mushroom growth of the northern towns is evidence of the swiftly-changing English scene. About 1770 Bradford was a small place with grass growing in the streets, but in 1837, when Queen Victoria came to the throne, it had a population of 50,000 : during the following seventy years the population grew to 150,000 : the numbers employed in the cotton mills in and around Manchester rose from 40,000 to nearly a million in the same period. The mills were running in bitter rivalry with each other. When there was no foreign competition the manufacturers competed with each other and drove wages down to a starvation level. Men were dismissed and children trained for their jobs. Robert Hall told of thousands of smallholders and farmers distrained for rent, dragging their furniture on wagons and carts as they moved from one place to another seeking employment.

The defeat of Napoleon was thus followed by indescribable wretchedness. The extreme wealth of the few was in marked contrast with the extreme poverty of the workers. Bread riots broke out and mill machinery was smashed. When the starving workmen began to form clubs and societies to defend their rights to live and work, or when they held meetings to demand reform, the Government passed the Combination Acts, suspended Habeas Corpus, and the Seditious Meetings Bill made it illegal to hold meetings or arrange lectures without a magistrate's license. The freedom of the Press was attacked.

Repression, not reform, was the attitude of the Government. Unemployment and hunger led the workers in the cotton towns to organise a meeting on 16th August, 1819, in St. Peter's Fields, near Manchester, the site on which the Free Trade Hall was afterwards built. It was estimated that upwards of 60,000 workers marched in orderly ranks, carrying banners, demanding " Repeal of the Corn Laws ", " Universal suffrage ", " Votes by ballot " ; for Manchester was then the most populous town in England except London, but had no representative in Parliament. The Government had not forbidden the procession, nor was any persuasive attempt made to disperse it. There was no suggestion nor intention of violence from the marchers. But as soon as Hunt began to speak the Yeomanry, with drawn swords, charged into the crowd. A frightful stampede prevailed, eleven were killed, four hundred were wounded, a hundred and thirteen being women. The organisers of the procession were arrested and convicted and Hunt was sent to gaol for two years and six months. The attitude of the Court and the Government is revealed in the Regent's " high approbation " of the " exemplary manner " in which the Yeomanry " assisted and supported the civil power with great satisfaction ". Such were the congratulations bestowed on armed forces against the unarmed workers at Peterloo. Tumults and agitation, however, continued till 1830, when the Court and Tory rulers cloud no longer resist the growing forces of reform. The Duke of Wellington, " as far as he was concerned, as long as he held any station in the Government of the country, he should always feel it his duty to resist such measures (of reform) when proposed by others ". A speech which marked the end of fifty years of Tory and High Church government in England. Archdeacon Paley saw no necessity for reform : " We have a House of Commons composed of 558 members in which number are found the most considerable landowners and merchants of the kingdom ; the heads of the army, the navy and the law ; the occupiers of the great offices in the State ; together with many private individuals eminent by their knowledge, eloquence and activity. If the country be not safe in such hands, in whom may it confide its interests ? . . . Does any new scheme of representation promise to collect together more wisdom or to produce firmer integrity " ?

In November, 1830, the Tory Government resigned and a Whig Ministry succeeded it. On 1st March, 1831, Lord John Russell introduced his Reform Bill in the House of Commons : he thrilled and startled the House as he expounded the scope of reforms the Government meant to undertake. Macaulay's vivid description of the scenes in Parliament is famous. But the defenders of the rotten boroughs defeated the Bill in committee, and after considerable arguments with William IV Parliament was dissolved. In the new House of Commons Russell brought forward a second Reform Bill. On this occasion he warned the Tories against the penalties of destroying it, or assuming that a faction could prevail against the voice of a nation. The Bill passed the Commons by large majorities, but the House of Lords threw it out by a majority of forty-one votes, twenty-one bishops voting against the Bill. This action of the Bishops inflamed the reformers. The rebuke of *The Times* deserves mention : " Will no question occur to the people of England touching my lords, the bishops ? Will nobody ask, what business have they in Parliament at all ? What right have these Tories ex-officio to make or mar laws for the people of England ? Let them confine themselves to superintending the souls of the faithful, and let them begin with their own ". Meetings in the country demanded their exclusion from the House of Lords : " They were hooted wherever they went and burnt in effigy by the mob ". Rioting broke out in the country. Nottingham Castle was burnt down : the Mansion House was fired. Clubs and societies multiplied to agitate for reform. In December, 1831, the Third Reform Bill was introduced in the House of Commons and passed ; but the second reading in the Lords only received the majority of nine votes, and on 8th May, 1832, the Lords again rejected the Bill. Thereupon the Government resigned and the Duke of Wellington tried to form a Ministry but failed. The Whig Government returned, and for the fourth time the Reform Bill was introduced : it passed both Houses of Parliament and received the royal assent on 7th June, 1832. Throughout the country rang the exulting cry, " The Reform Bill has passed ". Later in life Lord John Russell paid his tribute : " I know the Dissenters. They carried the Reform Bill ".

II. CHARTISTS AND ROBERT HALL

I have indicated the conditions of the Industrial Revolution and the battle for the Reform Bill that I might relate the contribution of the Free Churches to the spiritual and political progress of the period. The nature and scope of their constructive work during these tragic years are mostly overlooked. While they were patiently seeking religious equality they were teaching the nation the true principles of political progress : their consistency of worship and activity proceeded without noise or advertisement, but they were leavening the social life of England and creating a new type of citizenship.

Other groups were, of course, working for reform, and I gladly, but briefly, refer to them. Mention must be made of Robert Owen (1771–1858) to whom industrial democracy was far more important than political democracy : whose theories of co-operative labour, aided by science and machines aimed at finally abolishing private property. Radicals like Cobbett and Hunt hated every form of injustice and profoundly influenced the masses who were suffering under industrial depression. " Orator " Hunt, as he was known, was the speaker at Peterloo. Cobbett was a restless and prolific journalist : his popularity with the workers was such that the mill hands in Lancashire would turn out of the mills to buy his " Political Register " : he was often inconsistent and his economic theories were often crude. There was no lack of pamphleteers to stimulate the reform programme among the workers. Most important of all was the Chartist Movement with its direct aim of Parliamentary reform. The National Charter was drafted by Richard Place and had six objectives ; adult male suffrage, votes by ballot, annual parliaments, abolition of the property qualification for members of the House of Commons, payment of members, equal electoral districts. Among Chartist leaders were atheists and agnostics and Nonconformists, men like Thomas Cooper, whose memorial church in Lincoln still stands. My own great-grandfather, a Baptist, a hand-framework knitter in Nottinghamshire, was a Chartist. The anti-religious tone of some Chartists led the Wesleyan preachers in Bath in 1839 to exclude from their fellowship any Methodist who joined himself to the Chartists.

The Congregationalist minister at Horton Lane, Bradford, denounced Chartists who were "infidels and blasphemers of our religion". But there were noble men among them. The weakness and failure of Chartism came through the quarrels of the leaders and the attitude towards the Corn Laws; they stood aloof from the Anti-Corn Law League, nor had Chartism any leaders comparable to Cobden and Bright.

Robert Hall was a devoted friend of the Hand-Framework Knitters. Stockingers, they were called, the Midland framework knitter in the house, corresponding to the hand-loom weavers in the north. His memorable debate with Cobbett over the Framework Knitters' Union indicates the different attitude to reform during the period. Cobbett tried to persuade the Leicestershire operatives to boycott the Union: he alleged that the distress of the workers was due to the accumulation of taxes "which from beginning to end is his darling theme", said Hall. The first aim of the workers should be, according to Cobbett, to attack "the herd of sinecureists and pensioners, the eaters of taxes . . . he seems to think that if the working classes can get beer and bacon they should rest satisfied, no matter how abject their state of drudgery and subjection to their fellow men ".[1] The Knitters' Union was a means of self-defence: by the exercise of foresight and self-denial a fund was established as the most efficient expedient to aid the unemployed and to maintain an adequate rate of wages: "The skill and labour of the poor man constitute his whole possession and he has a right to place it to the best advantage . . . and a right to set aside a portion of his earnings towards securing the means of a just and natural remuneration of his industry ". "Cobbett was ", said Hall, " a popular disclaimer, not a philosopher; a firebrand, not a luminary. He emits fire and smoke in abundance, like a volcano, but the whole effect is to desolate, not to enlighten . . . whatever the inhabitants of this country may think of the Framework Knitters' Union, he plainly sees in the consequences of its failure the materials of ferocious delight; he sees without the aid of inspiration an inundation of miseries to follow, paupers crowding by thousands to the doors of overseers, parishes dismayed and perplexed, the poor clamouring for bread which cannot be given them, and rushing upon the point of the bayonet to avoid a

[1] Hall, *Works* IV, p. 187 ff.

more cruel and lingering death, the commencement of that tempest . . . to shake all that is stable, to prostrate all that is great, and to accumulate a pile for the elevation of future demagogues ". Cobbett wanted the revolution which was destructive, but which would inevitably submerge the workers in its wreckage : Robert Hall stood for reform which was creative of permanent well-being for the workers.

We pay tribute to the men who agitated for political and economic revolution, but whose objective was neither prompted nor inspired by the religious motive. These men made a great impact on their age. It was a period of fierce controversies, and no one disputes that these men were contending for the rights of the poor and for better social conditions. They were desperate men : and it was a miracle how the country escaped civil war. The Reform Bill had not enfranchised the lower working classes. The Bill adjusted the relations between the landlord class and the manufacturers : but when the shouting of the masses over the passing of the Reform Bill ceased, the working classes found they were left without a vote. Instead, however, of smashing their own means of livelihood and plunging the nation into civil war, they revealed the discipline which has often saved and distinguished the British people in times of crisis. And the subtle revolution in the ideas of the workers went on.

III. A SIGNIFICANT CENSUS

Anglican historians who write on their Church during these years admit its low spiritual levels, its corruption, its self-seeking and unpopularity. On the other hand, the Free Churches were growing numerically and they stood for human and creative moral values. In 1851 the Government census returns were : Church of England buildings, 14,077 ; all other denominational buildings were 20,399.

Attendance at Public Worship

	Morning	Afternoon	Evening
Anglican - - - - -	2,541,244	1,890,764	860,543
Other Denominations - -	2,106,238	1,293,371	2,203,906

Between 1801 and 1831 Nonconformist Church sittings increased by nearly two millions ; and between 1831 and 1851 by just short of another two millions. In the manufacturing districts the Nonconformists were everywhere in the majority. These Government figures in 1851 caused a sensation, and Wilberforce, Bishop of Oxford, was most offensive in his attack on the Free Churches : it was painfully incredible to him that they should have grown so rapidly while the National Church was well-nigh static.

Further evidence of the numbers of Sunday school scholars under Free Church influence is furnished in the Report of the Manchester Statistical Society in 1834.

	Man-chester	Salford	Liver-pool	Birming-ham	Bristol
Free Church - -	19,032	6,250	8,350	11,830	8,477
Church of England -	10,284	2,741	6,318	4,500	2,631
Roman Catholic -	3,812	613	700	—	—

In Free Church Sunday schools young people were instructed in the Scriptures, which was a most valuable training in character building. The only education many children received in these days was from Sunday school teachers. I take a typical illustration of Free Church vitality from the Baptist Sunday school at Baxtergate Church, Loughborough. There were eight hundred scholars and about seventy teachers. The British and Foreign Bible Society was not yet able to distribute cheap editions of the Scriptures. By no means was every scholar provided with a copy of the New Testament. Yet Biblical teaching was thorough: the Christian virtues of speaking the truth and abhoring a lie ; of honesty and the sin of stealing ; of kindness and the avoidance of cruelty ; of honouring parents and the shame of disgracing those who loved them—such was the teaching which urged children and adolescents to build their character and their friendships on the truth as it is taught in the Bible. Further, the moral example of the minister and teachers embodied such verbal instruction. It was in such schools, under the influence of good men and women, that young people found the centre of the only social life they knew. Loughborough was a town with a population probably not exceeding 12,000, but there were few houses into which children did not carry the influence of Sunday school teaching. And what was happening in a town like Loughborough was happening over most of the country. The Free Churches and Sunday schools were leavening the family and social life of the working classes. Parents who never attended divine worship insisted on their children attending Sunday school. And when every protest has been heard against such Victorian parental control, the cumulative effect of this quality of worship, work and influence, led on to the golden age of Nonconformity in the latter half of the nineteenth century.

CHAPTER XIII

RELIGIOUS EQUALITY AND A FAMOUS LAW SUIT

AFTER the passing of the Reform Bill of 1832 the long struggle began for religious equality. A church which perpetrates any form of injustice, to any section of the community, is misrepresenting the nature and ethic of the Gospel. Conservatism, political and ecclesiastical, in possession of privilege and revenues, has always known how to fight to the last ditch for what it possesses. Ancient institutions, when attacked, know all the weapons of defence; they are masters of rearguard strategy and delayed action; of dividing or tripping the opposing army; of enlisting every auxiliary force to fight their battles. If they can sit on the fence, or do anything to preserve their interests, there is always the possibility of reformers weakening or quarrelling or dying off. When surrender involves the loss of income which others are compelled unjustly to provide, ancient customs and institutions are like ancient fortresses before the invention of artillery—they can stand a long siege.

After 1832 the demands for religious equality began to disturb the life of the nation and they have not yet been finally conceded. In 1930 the Archbishops appointed a " Commission on the relations between Church and State ", and the Report was presented in 1935. This Report will receive attention later: but to indicate the long drawn-out conflict against injustice I quote from the evidence of Bernard Lord Manning, Fellow of Jesus College, Cambridge, a distinguished Free Churchman: he had been stating the responsibility of the Established Church for political and ecclesiastical injustice; how it had led to " a store of ill-will and the desire for revenge. . . . The interests of religion and the visible Church in a country like ours, where in the long run public opinion rules, are best served (we think) if the whole Church can say, as the Free Churches can say, to the anti-clericals and non-Christians : ' Thank you for nothing ;

we don't owe you a penny; and you owe the Church everything'. Incidentally, Free Churchmen consider that if feeling is less bitter in England against the Establishment than it has been in certain countries, and if the Established Church is therefore likely to escape the worst effects of such a sense of injustice, as there is here, no small service has been rendered to the Established Church by the Free Churches in working for a gradual diminution of the political and educational and social privileges of the Establishment ". Manning then proceeded to point out that the Established Church, as a fact of history, had caused political and ecclesiastical injustice to Churches not established : " the political injustices are mostly remedied, though unhappily not by generous gesture on the part of the stronger and established section of the Church, but by a bitter hand-to-hand conflict not yet completely ended. The ecclesiastical injustices for the most part remain. As far as we can judge, they are likely to remain, because no redress seems likely to come from the Anglican side ; and although we were willing, and sometimes glad, to fight injustice in the political arena, we are increasingly unwilling to fight for ecclesiastical rights to the scandal of the unbeliever ". Bernard Lord Manning had in mind the tragic conflicts during the nineteenth century which I must discuss in all fairness to the claims of the Free Churches on the nation.

The revolt against Church Rates began in 1834 and led to incalculable bitterness until 1868. In 1827 the amount accruing to the Church of England from the rate was £519,000 ; all ratepayers were compelled to find the sum demanded or suffer distraint of goods and sometimes imprisonment. The money raised was towards the repair and maintenance of church buildings. As Free Churchmen bore the cost of erecting and maintaining their own places of worship they resented paying compulsory rates towards the repairs of Church of England property. The Anglicans resorted to the curious argument that the buildings used by the National Church were the property of the nation and as members of the nation, Free Churchmen should pay the rate. This admission that Anglican buildings were the property of the nation was well known to Free Churchmen, but they replied that people who used the property should maintain it. When such cities as Manchester, Birmingham and Leeds refused to levy the rate the larger towns began to do likewise, and the income from the rates fell in 1859 to £261,000.

The parish vestry meetings, which parishioners were entitled to attend, became occasions when political and religious feeling divided the local population. Throughout the land there were scenes of intense excitement. When the majority of the parishioners at the Braintree Vestry meeting in 1837 refused to authorise the rate, the churchwardens attempted to overrule the vestry meeting and levy the rate; and a famous lawsuit followed. Mr. Samuel Courtauld was Chairman of the Anti-Rate Committee of Braintree and initiated legal proceedings against the Churchwardens. The Case went from one Court to another. The Bishop's Court decided that the levy of the Churchwardens was legal; the Court of the Queen's Bench ruled the levy was illegal. For sixteen years the dispute was fought out in the Courts. Finally, in 1853, the House of Lords pronounced the levy of the Churchwardens illegal and invalid—on the ground that the majority of parishioners had refused to authorise it. For his services to the cause of religious equality Mr. Courtauld was presented at a public dinner in Braintree with a silver testimonial valued at seven hundred guineas. The spirit in which he had fought the case was manifest, when the parish church at Braintree, which had fallen into decay, was restored at a cost of £4,000, all raised by voluntary gifts.

The controversies in Parliament can be imagined when between 1834 and 1868 something like sixteen Bills were introduced for the Abolition of Church Rates. John Bright, Edward Miall, and other Free Churchmen led the movement in the House of Commons; the Whigs who were elected by Free Church votes were often unwilling to support the cause of abolition. If a Bill arrived at the House of Lords it was thrown out. Even Disraeli, who had known how to raise the cry of " the Church in danger " rebuked the Archbishop of Canterbury : " the church rate question was a matter to be settled by statesmen and not by Archbishops ". Anti-church rate committees, as at Braintree, were formed throughout the country and were the means of educating the nation in matters of religious and political equality. In 1864, at an Exeter bye-election, when the Liberal Candidate refused to support Abolition, he was defeated through the abstentions of Free Church voters; a sensation which awakened the Liberals to the strength of the Free Church vote. In 1865, after the defeat of the Bill, *The Times* told the militant Bishops and clergy : " the Church Rate is gone and nothing can save it. Let people subscribe for the parish church as they do for many thousand district churches and chapels, and the parish church will be all the better for the alteration ".[1] The end came through Gladstone, who had recently joined the Liberal Party ; he introduced the Abolition Bill in the House of Commons in 1868 and it received the royal assent.

Gladstone had not always supported the Abolition Bills. When he did so, his son Herbert wrote to say that he thought his father should defend all the privileges and possessions of the Church ; that one concession to the Free Churches would lead to others until the end would be the destruction of the Church. If Gladstone's reply had been the policy of the Church of England, the nineteenth century would have been spared many religious quarrels : " in the first place it is sometimes necessary in politics to make surrenders of what, if not surrendered, will be wrested from us. And it is very wise when a necessity of this kind is approaching, to anticipate it while it is yet a good way off; for then concession gets gratitude and often brings a return. The kind of concession which is really mischievous is just that which is made under terror and extreme pressure ; and unhappily this has been the kind of concession which for more than two hundred years, it has been the fashion of men to make who call themselves the ' friends of the Church '. I believe it would be a wise concession, upon grounds merely political, for the Church of England to have the law of the church rate abolished in all cases where it places her in fretting conflicts with the dissenting bodies . . . as to disruption . . . the Church of England is much more likely of the two, to part with her faith than with her funds. It is the old question : which is the greater, the gold or the altar that sanctifies the gold. Had the question been more boldly asked and more truly answered in other times, we should not have been where we are now. And by continually looking to the gold and not the altar, the dangers of the future will not be diminished but increased ".[2]

[1] Skeats and Miall, p. 594.
[2] Morley, *Life of Gladstone*, II, p. 159.

CHAPTER XIV

THE FREE CHURCHES AND EDUCATION

I. THE DISSENTING ACADEMIES

THE history of the attitude of the Church of God to Education is still waiting to be written. How have the National Churches of Christendom used, or misused, their opportunity to educate the nations? The Christian religion can never be divorced from education without serious injury to the Church on the one hand and the peoples on the other. In the motive of God the church was intended to be the teacher, as well as the preacher, of the Gospel: " Go ye, therefore, and make disciples of all nations, baptizing them into the name of the Father, the Son and the Holy Ghost : *teaching* them to observe all things whatsoever I commanded you ". After baptism, whether of infants or believers, the church has often neglected the function of teaching. Further, the question arises, what kind of teaching ? The Church is the custodian of truth as it is revealed in Scripture ; and truth is not something upon which children and adolescents and adults stumble ; they need to learn the truth by hearing the Word of God and by the ethical example of the Church and its members. Such teaching and learning penetrate to the secrets of personality : the thought, emotion and volition of the learner responding to the truth embodied in the personality of the teacher.

It is tragic that the relation of the Church to education in Britain has been nothing less than one of fierce conflict. For over two hundred and fifty years, the nation, and especially the children, have been the victims of this strife. Nor can anyone compute the losses to the Church or the impediments to the spread of Christianity in the land. In justice to the Free Churches I must relate the facts, for they establish one of the strongest claims of the Free Churches upon the gratitude of the British nation. It will set the conflicts over elementary education in the nineteenth and twentieth centuries in a truer perspective if I begin with the heroic struggle of the Dissenting Academies. The Uniformity Act of 1662 drove nearly two thousand ministers from their livings in the Church of England, but it also closed the universities to all Nonconformists. Moreover, such men were not only forbidden to preach; they were forbidden to teach; every curate, incumbent, master, tutor, professor or reader in the universities, every schoolmaster, every person instructing or teaching any youth in any house or private family, must take the oath to conform to the liturgy of the Church as by law established. Further, the Five-Mile Act of 1665 was passed, not only to prevent ejected ministers from living within five miles of the place where they had ministered; it was intended to make it impossible for such men to earn their living by teaching, or by acting as tutor, in the families of their former congregations. Numbers of ejected ministers had opened schools as their only means of livelihood, but the Act forbade them to teach anywhere under a penalty of £40. Yet, in spite of these penal laws, Nonconformist ministers founded Academies where youths were able to receive education for the professions, or a theological training for the Christian ministry.

In his book, *English Education under the Test Acts*,[1] Dr. H. McLachlan has made a most valuable contribution to our knowledge of these Dissenting Academies, the tutors and their qualifications, the students, the curricula, the methods of training in class and by seminar discussions. McLachlan names seventy-two of these Academies in various parts of the country; of a large number he gives illuminating historical details. They were often compelled to move from place to place under the stress of persecution, but they kept high educational ideals before the people. Richard Frankland (1630–1698) was appointed a tutor in Durham University by Cromwell. When he was ejected from his living he returned to his home at Rathmell, near Settle, in Yorkshire. There he founded in 1669 one of the earliest and largest Academies. Six times he was compelled to move the school, to Natland, Kirby Malham, Crosthwaite, near to Cartmel, Attercliffe and back to Rathmell. His reputation as

[1] I am indebted to Dr. Mclachlan for the details of the Academies.

a scholar, and that of his tutors, attracted students from afar. Twenty entered during the first year at Attercliffe. Eighty students were in attendance in 1695 at Rathmell. The course was five years. In one session six students proceeded to Edinburgh to take degrees. At his death, Frankland had educated more than three hundred students, the majority entering the ministry.

Carmarthen Academy, still a College, traces its origin in 1668 to the first Welsh Nonconformist Seminary founded at Bridgend by Samuel Jones, M.A., who had been educated at Oxford. He was an ejected minister : " a great philosopher " says Calamy, " a considerable master of the Latin and Greek tongues and a pretty good Orientalist ". This Academy was supported later by the Congregationalist Fund. " Among the most eminent Congregational scholars who founded Academies ",[1] says Dale, " was Charles Morton, a Fellow of Wadham College, Oxford ". Soon after his ejection he founded the Academy at Newington Green, London ; but he was persecuted so continuously that he went to New England in 1685 and became Vice-President of Harvard. Samuel, father of John Wesley, was a pupil at Newington Green : " It was the most considerable of any in England ", says Wesley ; it had about fifty students when he attended classes. Other Congregationalist scholars were Theophilus Gale, Thomas Rowe, Isaac Chauncey, son of Charles Chauncey who was driven from England by Archbishop Laud and became President of Harvard. After 1662, Isaac Chauncey became pastor of a Congregational Church at Andover, and later at Mark Lane, where Isaac Watts was one of his successors in 1701. Chauncey was tutor of the Academy founded by the Congregational Board at Moorfields, London. This Academy became Homerton College, one of the three institutions invited to form New College, now at London. Bristol Baptist Academy was associated in its origins with the Broadmead Church and minister. As early as 1689 its tutor was W. Thomas, B.A., an Oxford man, ejected in 1662. This Academy, which Robert Hall attended at fourteen years of age, and many others who bear honoured names in Baptist history, is now Bristol Baptist College. Reference must be made to Warrington Academy, one of the most famous. Here Joseph Priestley, whose house was burnt down by the mob in Birmingham, was a tutor, lecturing on Science and

[1] *History of English Congregationalism,* p. 499 f.

conducting research. Edinburgh University (a Scottish University could grant degrees to Nonconformists) in 1764 conferred the LL.D. on Priestley; in 1766 he was created a Fellow of the Royal Society in recognition of his scientific contributions, for he had discovered oxygen and other gases. At Warrington he taught Latin, Greek, French, Italian, Philosophy and Theology : " while he advocates a different type of education specially fitted to the needs of each class in society, he believes that the pursuit of truth and practice of virtue must underlie all education. One can trace alike the Nonconformist divine and the man of science in his recommendations ".[1]

It is clear from this all too brief survey of the work of a few of the Dissenting Academies that excellent educational work was being done. But in the reign of Queen Anne, savage attacks were launched by Anglicans against these training centres. Prebendary South, in a sermon in 1685 besought his hearers : " employ the utmost of your power and interest both with the King and Parliament, to suppress, utterly to suppress and extinguish, those private, blind, conventicling schools or academies of grammar and philosophy, set up and taught secretly by fanatics, here and there all the kingdom over ".[2]

Such academies were denounced for perpetuating a race of mortal enemies both to Church and State ; they were guilty of schism and sedition. Samuel Wesley attacked the Academies although he had received his education at Newington Green ; he accused them of drawing men away from the Church and endangering the prosperity of the two universities : Dissenters were " villains " and " hypocrites " and " murderers " : he estimated that " some thousands " among the pupils, " sons of the nobility and gentry who, but for these sucking Academies would have gone to Oxford and Cambridge ".[3] The most ferocious denunciations came from Dr. Sacheverell, whom Bishop Burnet described as " a bold, insolent man, with a very small measure of religion . . . but he resolved to force himself into popularity and preferment by the most petulant railing at dissenters and low-churchmen ". Preaching before the Lord Mayor of London in 1709, Sacheverell declared the Academies to be

---

[1] Barnard, *Short History of English Education*, 1760–1944, p. 34.
[2] Quoted by Dale, p. 502 f.
[3] Quoted by Dale, p. 503.

hot-beds of " Atheism, Deism, Tritheism, Socinianism, with all the hellish principles of fanaticism, Regicide and Anarchy "[1] taught in them. They were " fountains of lewdness " and this in a sermon before the judges at Assize. These critics believed that if they could destroy the Academies they could destroy Nonconformity. To prevent any training of men for the Nonconformist ministry would lead to the disappearance of Dissent. To this end on the 12th May, 1714, the Schism Bill[2] was introduced into the House of Commons " to prevent the growth of Schism, and for the further security of the Church of England as by Law established ". The intention of Parliament was to close all public or private schools or seminaries unless the teacher conformed to the liturgy of the Church of England. No person could teach without a license from the Archbishop or Bishop : no license would be granted without a certificate that the applicant had received the sacrament, at some parish church, within the previous twelve months. The Bill also sought to make it impossible for Nonconformist children to be taught anywhere, by anyone, except an Anglican teacher. Petitions against the Bill poured into Parliament but it was passed and was to become law on August 1, 1714. Nonconformists throughout the country were sorely distressed, anticipating another period of persecution. But Queen Anne died on 1st August and the Bill never became law.

Life and educational standards in the ancient universities were at a low ebb during these attacks on the Academies. Knox, who was Headmaster of Tonbridge School, and had been a Fellow of St. John's, Oxford, wrote on the *Present State of the University of Oxford*: " these houses which the piety and charity of the founders consecrated to religion, virtue, learning, everything useful and lovely, are become the seats of ignorance, infidelity, corruption, debauchery, . . . with respect to the state of morals, I firmly believe that in no department a worse state exists ".[3] The tribute to the Academies by Barnard, Professor of Education in Reading University, in his recent volume, is therefore as deserving as it is welcome : " It is possible that the importance of the Nonconformist Academies in English education

[1] Dale, p. 503.
[2] cf. p. 143.
[3] Barnard, p. 29.

has not always been sufficiently recognised. They doubtless vary in size and efficiency, in the breadth of their curriculum and the ability of their teachers ; and the academy at Warrington, and Priestley the Scientist, may represent the high lights of the general movement. But there were other excellent academies and first-rate teachers in them, and they kept the torch of true education burning at a time when the two national universities were dormant. The Nonconformist academies employed rational teaching methods, they encouraged freedom of inquiry . . . they are, indeed, the forerunners of our modern universities which have grown up in commercial and industrial centres ".[1]

II. DOGMA: SCRIPTURE. THE NATION: THE CHURCHES: THE CHILD

Hatred against the Dissenting Academies culminated in the Schism Bill which was intended to stamp out Nonconformity. Fortunately, George I did not approach the situation as an Anglican in religion and a Tory in politics, but as a Lutheran and a Whig, who was resolved to maintain the Church as by law established and at the same time extend toleration to Nonconformists. The Church of England, however, continued to assume that guardianship over all education was her sole prerogative. Any introduction to the controversy over elementary education in the nineteenth century must take this exclusive claim into account. The control over all national education was regarded as the inherent right of the Church. If any religious education was to be given in State schools it must be given under the auspices of the State Church. Moreover, if the State built or helped to build Schools where children learned the three R's, such education must not be divorced from the dogma and liturgy of the Church. The duly ordained clergy were alone authorised to teach religion and superintend education. According to Lord Stanley, the spokesman of the Church in Parliament : " education was the peculiar province of the clergy and was a spiritual matter to be entrusted to their superintendence ".

[1] Barnard, p. 35 f.

This dispute over religious education in the schools which runs through the nineteenth and twentieth centuries was an extension of the conflict which had raged through the seventeenth and eighteenth centuries. From Marston Moor and Naseby, the battle ground had shifted to the schools of the nation. After the Reform Bill, Parliament could no longer ignore the evils of child labour in the mines and the mills of the North of England. The Church had done nothing to attack these economic and social injuries to childhood, but as soon as the Government gave a grant in 1833 towards the building of schools, the religious controversy began to blaze up again.

I must here explain the nature of the issue : it was dogma, liturgy and tradition over against the teaching of Scripture. The Church possessed all the advantages of privilege, wealth, and political weapons ; the Nonconformists were poorer, growing in numbers as we have pointed out, but far from being well organised. What is dogma ? Theologians agree that dogma is Christian doctrine embodied in a Creed, which has received ecclesiastical sanction, as by the Council of Nicæa in 325, or by the Council of Trent in 1545–1563. But Kant has written wise words on this matter. Dogma, he says, is an opinion, the basis of which has not been critically examined ; it is the part setting itself up as the whole ; it seizes on some single principle, does not examine it critically, but uses it to explain what will serve a purpose rather than serve the truth ; it may explain phenomena within a limited range, but beyond such a range it fails. In time, a one-sided dogma is met by another one-sided dogma, until whatever can be asserted can with equal reason be denied. In this way, dogma gives rise to scepticism. Kant includes theological as well as philosophical dogma in his indictment ; and who can deny that in the history of theology one dogma has not given rise to another, and proved divisive of Christian communities ? Modern educational ideals have no room for such dogmatic mental drill ; it is the medieval method of instruction ; it assumes that the mind of the child is passive, something on which an impression must be *stamped* ; or an empty receptacle into which creeds and catechism must be crammed. The child does not understand such dogma, often in the light of advancing knowledge and mature experience he finds that he must unlearn what was forced into his mind as a child. Yet, the cry for more instruction in dogma is sounded by living writers, including Miss Dorothy Sayers and Mr. T. S. Eliot. Further, the habit of repeating creed and catechism must be enforced by the habit of liturgical worship, habits which have often stunted the whole personality. And when such methods are used by the Church to inculcate docility to priestly authority, we can trace the tragic consequences in the atheism and Bolshevism of the Soviets, and in the illiteracy, superstition and political corruption of the Latin bloc of nations. The Orthodox Church of Russia had nearly a thousand years to evangelise and educate the people in the ethics of Jesus, but it crammed dogma down the throats of the children and taught submission to priestly masters and political despots. The Papacy had longer to evangelise and educate the nations of Europe, but it forged, and has used, its weapon of infallibility to keep the people docile to ecclesiastical and political bondage.

Against dogmatic instruction in the schools at the public cost, Free Churchmen have consistently stood for the teaching of the Scriptures : they know the problem of authority in relation to the Scriptures, but they believe that a wayfaring man though a fool, can read, without erring, therein ; and it is better for children to learn that God's nature is love, to understand the tenderness and teaching of Jesus and their duties towards each other, than to memorise dogma and live in fear of hell. There was no dogmatic instruction in the methods of Jesus ; creeds and catechisms were not his methods of teaching. And for the Church of God, Jesus is the supreme example of the Teacher.

How did these conflicting methods of dogmatic instruction and Biblical teaching affect elementary education in England ? In the debates on the Schism Bill in 1714 Lord Cowper referred to Nonconformist Charity Schools which were doing good work in many parts of the country. In 1698, Charity Schools were founded by the Society for the Propagation of Christian Knowledge. In these schools the clergy taught the catechism. The picture of these schools, given by Dickens in his Sketches of Boz, is well known. Isaac Watts, pleading for the support of Nonconformist Schools, says that some Dissenters had subscribed to Anglican schools, but discovered a systematic attempt to train the children in the principles of Jacobitism ; " that the children were brought up in too many of these schools in principles of disaffection to the present government, in bigoted zeal for the word Church . . . it was time then for Dissenters to withdraw that charity (of theirs) which was so much abused ".

A pamphlet written in 1833 by Dr. James Kay led to the founding of the Manchester Statistical Society by a group of distinguished social workers ; through the investigations of this Society we have valuable information of the types of schools existing at the time in Lancashire.

The first type was known as the Dame's School and there were two hundred and thirty such schools in Manchester. Boys were taught to read and girls to sew. Many of these schools were held in dirty and ill-ventilated single rooms. " If I can keep a bit of quietness ", said one Dame, " it is as much as I can do and as much as I am paid for". Books were as scarce as fresh air : it was not uncommon for children to sleep through the afternoon : " they are quieter when asleep ". The average income of these schools was six shillings and ten pence per week.

The next higher type was known as the " common day school ", kept by the teacher who lived on what he earned. His charge was sixpence to ninepence weekly according to the range of subjects : the teacher of average ability was able to earn sixteen to seventeen shillings weekly. Reading, writing and arithmetic were taught. A few adventurous teachers based their appeals on a wider syllabus. One Manchester Master advertised the scope of his subjects as including Hydrostatics, Hydraulics, Geology, and Entomology. Regarding his syllabus an interested parent remarked, " this is *multum in parvo* " ; " yes ", replied the schoolmaster, " I teach that, you may put that down too ". One of these common day schools in Liverpool measured ten feet by nine, in which one teacher, one cock, two hens, three black terriers, and forty children somehow found space to live and learn.

The next type of school was maintained by public subscription and there were soon two rival societies supporting these schools.

In 1796, Joseph Lancaster opened a school for poor children in his father's house in Southwark. His remarkable success can be estimated when it is stated that in two years the scholars increased to a thousand. His school in Manchester numbered a thousand scholars, closely packed in one long room, with two masters and one mistress in charge. He used the monitorial method, placing an elder boy in control of ten other boys, thus using the elder scholars to teach the younger. There was, and may be still, a dispute on the origin of this method. It was said that Lancaster borrowed it from Dr. Bell who had used monitors in the Military School at Madras. But there were differences between the methods of the two men; and the claim of the *Edinburgh Review* was: " There is no one who has ever denied that he (Lancaster) was the first who established in England a system of education whereby one master can teach a thousand or even a greater number of children ". An Anglican critic of Lancaster's methods reproached him with being an Anabaptist, who probably forsook his original faith to marry a pretty Quakeress. His Free Church convictions, however, explain the principles on which his schools were founded. The Church of England was accused of neglecting the poor: "that some leading persons in the hierarchy were adverse to education cannot be doubted ", says the *Edinburgh Review*, " but, upon the whole, there was rather a want of diligence than of good-will, until the great exertions of the Dissenters stirred up a corresponding spirit in the Church ". Lancaster cared for the education of the poor, but the schools he founded were unsectarian, the Bible being read and taught. The schools opened and closed with Bible readings on which lessons were based. Free Churchmen and Liberals rallied to the support of these schools. When, later, a Society was formed in 1808 to spread schools of the Lancaster model, it was named the " British and Foreign Schools Society ". Lancaster's rapid success soon encountered opposition: Anglicans accused him " of educating the whole body of the common people without any regard to the religion of the nation . . . were Mr. Lancaster's plans to be fully adopted, the common people would not know that there is such a thing as an Established Church in the Nation ". Lancaster was attacked as " the Goliath of schismatics ": " the good which he has done is very great but it is pretty much in the way that the devil has been the cause of redemption ".

The controversy issued in 1811 in the formation of " The

National Society for promoting the education of the Poor in the Principles of the Established Church ". The aim of this Society was defined clearly enough and henceforth the battle of education was to be waged between those who sought ecclesiastical ends and those who sought religious ends. The aim of the National Society was to advance State religion rather than State education. In the early years of the nineteenth century the masses of Free Churchmen were poor ; yet they made remarkable sacrifices to pay school fees and support the Lancastrian Society ; on the other hand the National Society received the support of the wealth of the Established Church. For twenty years the two societies continued to depend on voluntary contributions, until 1833, when the Government made to them a grant of £20,000.

As the National Society could draw on the richer resources of the Church, its schools soon began to outnumber those of the British Society. But educationists pointed out that Government subsidies to these two voluntary societies could never meet the demands of the country ; and J. A. Roebuck proposed in the House of Commons in 1839 that the time had arrived when the Government should assume responsibility " for the universal and national education of the people ". The Government was clearly of the same opinion but feared that such an innovation would be sure to raise a storm ; it was decided, however, to avoid a debate in Parliament by an Order in Council, and on 10th April, 1839, the Crown established a Committee of the Privy Council " to superintend the administration of any sums voted by Parliament for the purpose of promoting Public Education ". This was the first central authority appointed in England to deal with the problem of education. But when the Government asked the House of Commons to sanction a Grant of £30,000 to be administered by the new Committee of the Privy Council, fury was let loose. The National Society denounced State interference in education. Even when in receipt of public money as building grants, Archdeacon Denison, speaking for the Society, declared that religious education was intended to build up the Church and must, therefore, be in the hands of the clergy. Lord Stanley attacked the Committee set up by the Order in Council and moved that Her Majesty be petitioned to revoke the Order : " The Committee would be irresponsible and despotic ;

to take education out of the hands of the clergy and to transfer it to laymen would lead to scepticism and national infidelity ". Lord Mahon was sure that education out of the hands of the clergy was a direct cause of crime. When the Bill reached the House of Lords, the Archbishop of Canterbury proposed an Address to the Queen that no general education should be established in the country without consulting the Peers. With the support of fifteen Bishops the Lords agreed by a large majority to petition Her Majesty lest the State should spend money on schools which were not controlled by the clergy. " Impelled by this fear ", says Kay-Shuttleworth,[1] " the Church, in defence of her traditional privileges, assumed the responsibility of resisting, by the utmost exercise of her authority and influence in the country, in both Houses of Parliament, and at the foot of the Throne, the first great plan ever proposed, by any Government, for the education of the humblest classes in Great Britain ".

The most extreme claims are often made on behalf of the Church of England in regard to elementary education in this country. It is sometimes implied that no other efforts were made to educate the children, or that the Church bore the responsibility for elementary education until the State made it compulsory. The facts are far otherwise. " The Liberals and Nonconformists ", says Dr. Braley, Principal of the College of the Venerable Bede, Durham, in his book, *A Policy in Religious Education*, " were the first in the field ".[2] The point here is to note how the battle of the schools began. The Anglicans aimed at the education of the poor in the principles of the Established Church ; Free Churchmen aimed at a system of Biblical education excluding instruction in any distinctive denominational principles, claiming that such teaching was the responsibility of the Churches. It is imperative to keep these differences of view in mind, and if we do so, we shall not consent that the issue was always a miserable squabble. Anglican leaders believed they were contending for principles vital to the Church of England. On the other hand, men like Dale, John Clifford and Sylvester Horne did not stoop to squabble. There are Free Churchmen who have gone to

---

[1] *Public Education as Affected by the Minutes of Council*, p. 3 f. Kay-Shuttleworth was the first Secretary of the Committee of the Privy Council.
[2] p. 22.

school and to the University and have never known what it was to be poor, nor any thwarting of their educational aims or progress, and they would do well to think themselves back into the struggles of the nineteenth century and remember how their educational opportunities were won. During these years, Free Churchmen were not quarrelling over shadows; they wrestled and suffered, as men with convictions, and the whole English speaking world has reason to be grateful for their labours.

The Factory and Education Bill of 1843 is the next stage in the conflict. The Chartist movement and "the depraved morals of the industrial centres" began to alarm the Conservative Government, until a Bill was framed to remedy the shameful conditions of child labour. It was intended to abolish all labour by children under eight years of age: between eight and thirteen years, children were not to work more than six and a half hours a day, but they must also attend school three hours a day; those over thirteen years must not work more than twelve hours daily; and from the wages of each half-timer, one penny in the shilling was to be deducted up to three pence weekly, by his employer, for school fees. The Tory government, however, proposed to build state schools, and allow them virtually to be controlled by the Established Church; for they were to be managed by committees of seven—two church-wardens, four others to be nominated by the magistrates, two of the four were to be mill-owners, with the addition of the clergyman as permanent chairman. The Head master was to be a member of the Anglican church and approved by the Bishop. The schools were to be built and partly maintained out of the rates. These plans stirred the country to indignation, nor did it abate when the Government began to offer several concessions to the Non-Anglican population. Petitions against the Bill contained over four million signatures. "The Bill", said the *Leeds Mercury*, "was an attempt to teach the doctrine of baptismal regeneration . . . apostolical succession and all the Mummery of the Puseyites over the whole of the manufacturing districts at the public expense". The strength of the Free Church resistance to this measure was so successful that the Bill was withdrawn. Persecution, anger against the Church rate which was still being levied, the attempt of the Established Church to direct any State education for ecclesiastical ends, left Free Churchmen no alternative but to continue the struggle for political and religious liberty against an institution which was more concerned for its own preservation than about the conditions of child labour and education for citizenship.

We have further evidence of the baneful effects of children in the mines and factories when the Act of 1844 created the half-time system of schooling and work : again it was education which suffered : after working half the day the children came to school, " dirty and labour soiled, in ragged and scanty clothes, with heavy eyes and worn faces. In the clothing districts, their faces, necks and hands were deeply stained with the blue of the dye used for the cloth. From the spinning mills they came covered with the ' flock ', or as it was termed the ' fluff ' of the yarn, their hair thickly powdered with it, tangled as if no comb could ever penetrate it ".

III. THE VOLUNTARISTS

The Anglicans had resisted the intrusion of the State into the sphere of education on the ground that religious instruction was the prerogative of the Church. The result of the legislation of 1839 and 1843 led to the rise of a Free Church Voluntarist Party— Congregationalists and Baptists of the radical type. Recent legislation had led them to distrust the bias of Parliament, especially that of the Tory High Church leaders ; also, grants of public money for education had seemed to amount to State subsidies to the Established Church. Other problems arose over the Trusts Deeds of the schools partly erected by grants. Kay-Shuttleworth's range of vision included not only pauper and workhouse children but the child population of the whole country, the urgency of large building schemes, the necessity of teachers and training colleges, grants to encourage pupil teachers and pensions for teachers who had retired ; but he deplored " the difficulties with which all progress in these subjects is obstructed on account of religious division ". Concerning the Trusts and management clauses of these new buildings, Kay-Shuttleworth " feared above all else ", says his biographer, " the complete clerical control of the schools . . . and he took steps to secure a system of local management which would secure adequate representation of the laity and ultimate control by the Committee of Council through its inspectors ".[1] But the more he sought to safeguard the rights of the laity and the public the more personal abuse and opposition he received from the High Church party : " We feel it necessary to say that, by the term Education, we mean training for time and eternity, and that, according to our beliefs, the Church of England is the divinely appointed teacher of the English nation " ; " the clergy have a divine commission to teach the children " : " I believe that their principle is vicious—the principle of entrusting the effective control of a Church school to a committee of management ". Such were the claims in the Address to the Queen, and at the annual meeting of the National Society, the demand was nothing less than the exclusive use of schools partly built by the State, complete control over teachers and curricula, also the use of the buildings as Sunday schools. " There was more religious strife in Manchester or Bradford " says Hammond, " in the forties than in the Roman Empire under Augustus ".

The Free Church Voluntarists, in view of such strife, decided to build and manage their own schools. At the Congregational Union Assembly at Leeds in 1843, Edward Bain led the movement. He reasoned that the Government should make and administer laws, but it was not the province of the State to train the mind and morals of the people ; that the ultimate consequence of State grants would be fatal to civil and religious liberty. The Assembly resolved " that the religious education of the people of England must be chiefly provided and conducted by the voluntary efforts of the various denominations of Christians ". As late as 1859 the Congregational Union Assembly maintained this attitude. On the other hand, Dr. Vaughan of Lancashire College, and Henry Rogers of Spring Hill College, stood for State education.

The Voluntarists made heroic sacrifices to build schools and maintain them, but the need was utterly beyond their resources. Admirable as was the voluntary principle in education, it was, in reality, a contraction out of a national responsibility. As British citizens, the Voluntarists were under an obligation to

[1] *The Life of Sir James Kay-Shuttleworth*, by Frank Smith, p. 164.

face the facts, to accept the antagonism of the clergy, and to educate the nation of which they were a part to fulfil its responsibility to the children. It was Dale of Birmingham who grasped the nation-wide issue and began to challenge the attitude of the Voluntarists. As Dale came to know more of the working classes he saw that they were suffering from lack of educational opportunities. By 1866 he was convinced that the State ought to be responsible for the education of its children. A census in Birmingham in 1867 revealed that only half the children between the ages of three and twelve were at school : ten per cent. were at work and forty per cent. were neither at work nor at school. These figures stirred Dale to action and he became the Free Church protagonist of national and compulsory education, and as he saw no possible way of meeting the Anglican demands he affirmed that secular education should be undertaken by the State and religious education by the churches.

In 1869 about 1,300,000 children were attending State-aided schools, another million or so were in uninspected and unsatisfactory schools, but two million were in no school at all. The Liberal Government could no longer ignore the tragic situation revealed by these statistics and resolved to end the scandal.

IV

1870

The Education Act of 1870 marked a new era, making elementary education compulsory for every child and compelling local authorities to provide a State school were necessary. The original Bill proposed to divide the country into areas ; to discover the school accommodation in each area ; to allow a period of twelve months to the denominational schools to meet any deficiency of accommodation ; if within the year the needs of the area had not been met a School Board should be elected with authority to build and maintain schools out of the rates. If the Boards agreed to make grants out of the rates to denominational schools they could do so. A conscience clause was inserted in the Bill, and any parent desiring to withdraw his child from the school when religious instruction was given could do so by stating his objection in writing. These clauses led to the fiercest religious controversy in the nineteenth century. A Liberal Government had been elected mainly by Free Church votes : there was scarcely a member of the Cabinet but owed his seat to such voters. Gladstone was Prime Minister. Forster, who represented a Liberal constituency in Bradford, was in charge of the Bill. Free Churchmen had anticipated a Measure which would make the State responsible for national education and show neither fear of, nor favour to, any religious section of the people. When Forster introduced his Bill it caused consternation among the Nonconformists. Within a week Dale realised the seriousness of the situation. He explained how the Bill would favour Church schools out of the rates ; that the conscience clause was no adequate safeguard ; that School Boards could subsidise church schools out of the rates ; that the period of twelve months' delay in establishing School Boards would enable the Church to put in plans to build new schools with grants of public money : which thing happened. " What we ask for is education, the best education possible, and at any cost, for every child in England. But not even at the bidding of a Liberal Ministry will we consent to any proposition which, under cover of an educational measure, empowers one religious denomination to levy a rate for teaching its creed and maintaining its worship. On this point compromise or concession is impossible. We respect Mr. Forster, we honour Mr. Gladstone, but we are determined that England shall not again be cursed with the bitterness and strife from which we hoped we had for ever escaped by the abolition of the Church rate ".[1] Petitions were presented to Parliament, delegations met Gladstone and Forster, large meetings of protest throughout the country were held to demand amendments. But such amendments were half-hearted. The famous Cowper Temple Clause was carried by the votes of 121 Liberals and 132 Tories, 133 Liberals abstained from voting.

John Bright had reluctantly joined Gladstone's Cabinet, but in 1870 he was a broken man, too ill to attend its meetings : his absence from such critical discussions was an incalculable

[1] *Life of Dale*, p. 275.

loss to the Free Churches. He wrote to Gladstone in November, 1871 : " The Education Bill has done a tremendous mischief to the party, and I am not sure that the exasperation felt by earnest Dissenters will not bear evil fruit. There seems much force in some of the charges brought by Mr. Dale against the Education Department. He is a man of great influence in Birmingham and among the Independents, and speaks the sentiments of a considerable and growing section of the whole Dissenting Body. The Dissenters feel that somebody in London is working the machine for the Church through the phrase of a denominational system . . . the whole misfortune and the magnitude of it cannot yet be measured . . . and has arisen from the error of making the new Act instrumental in preserving and extending indefinitely the system of Denominational schools—it will, I fear, break up the Government and destroy, for a time, the political party which has done so much and from which so much was expected ". Mr. Gladstone soon found, says Trevelyan, " that he had alienated his real friends in order to satisfy implacable enemies ".[1] The Bill was passed by Tory votes. Dale led the Nonconformist revolt against it : he addressed crowded meetings wherever he went. There were ten thousand applications for his meeting in the Manchester Free Trade Hall. The revolt split the Liberal Party. At the General Election in 1874 Gladstone was defeated and resigned the Liberal leadership and the Bradford Liberal Association refused to invite Forster to be their candidate. Later in life, John Bright said it was the worst Education Act by any Liberal Parliament since 1832.

What is known as the Dual System was established by the 1870 Act : henceforth there were to be two types of schools. First : Church schools, known as unprovided or voluntary, were to receive grants from the State, to be controlled by the clergy, and children were to be taught the doctrines of the Established Church ; but as the Church school would often be the only one in rural areas, and numbers of Free Church children would be compelled by the Act to attend such a rural school, a conscience clause was inserted in the Bill, permitting the withdrawal of children by parents who objected to the Catechism, an action which was likely to prejudice Free Church children and parents, and did so, in parishes where priestly arrogance and control

[1] *Life of John Bright*, p. 408.

were exercised in more spheres than education. Second : the Bill divided the country into districts in which School Boards were elected to provide schools, where necessary, out of the rates. The Board schools were new buildings, well lighted, large, healthy ; they were managed by a Board elected by the rate-payers of the area : teachers were appointed without religious tests : the religious education was Biblical : the Cowper-Temple clause of the Act stated that " no religious catechism or formulary which is distinctive of any particular denomination shall be taught ".

The Board schools soon grew in popularity and efficiency, while the Church schools began to decline. The Board school system was working satisfactorily and there was wide public interest in elementary education. The condition of the Church schools, however, had become so serious in the eighteen-nineties that the ecclesiastical party again raised the cry for additional grants. In 1895 the Anglicans presented a memorandum to Lord Salisbury, the Conservative Prime Minister, demanding radical changes in the educational system of the country. Lord Salisbury's reply was : " It is your business to capture the Board Schools, to capture them in the first instance, under the existing law, and then to capture them under a better law which shall place you under no religious disability. That is the aim which we should always keep in our minds. And intermediately we must do all we can to strengthen the voluntary schools and to swell those resources on which they rest. By all means let us get what we can out of increased contributions from the National Exchequer " : further, " there has been expenditure both in the character and in the class for whom it is applied, not intended by those who originally passed the Education Act ". The Archbishop of Canterbury said : " We should prevent what is one of the greatest causes of the present extravagance of School Boards—namely, the constant desire to push elementary education higher and higher, and, as arising from that desire, the necessity of paying very much larger salaries to the masters ". The Bishop of Manchester added : " It is absolutely necessary in any scheme aiming at the assistance of voluntary schools that you should diminish the power now possessed by School Boards ". In these arguments against the success of compulsory elementary education, of higher salaries for teachers, it was thought to help the Established Church. As it was affirmed : " Archbishops and Bishops and Lords, who had enjoyed the privileges of the rich were so short visioned as to try to take away the little chance that the poor had of secondary education ".

The pressure of the Church authorities induced the Conservative Government in 1896 to introduce a new Education Bill, but antagonism in the country was so formidable that the Bill was quickly withdrawn.

V. EDUCATION AND THE KHAKI ELECTION

In 1899 the Boer War broke out and in 1900 there was what came to be known as the Khaki election, when the Conservative Government obtained a large majority " to finish the South African War ". This majority, and full confidence in the House of Lords, provided the Anglican leaders with the opportunity to attack the 1870 Bill. No mention had been made of education in the General Election of 1900, but we have seen how well the ground had been prepared for an assault on the Board schools. In 1902 the Khaki majority pushed through a new Education Bill : the Church schools were further endowed by State grants, the Board school system was destroyed and elementary education was removed from local control and entrusted to the authority of Municipal and County Councils. The Board schools were henceforth to be known as Council schools.

The Act of 1902 contributed to widespread indignation and the reaction of the country contributed to the Liberal Revival of 1906. The Free Church leadership of Dale in 1870 was matched by that of John Clifford in 1902–6. Leading Free Churchmen became passive resisters, their goods were sold, or they went to prison, rather than pay the new education rate which compelled them to contribute to the dogmatic instruction which they believed to be unscriptural and un-Christian. They toiled to convince the nation of the religious injustice of the Act of 1902. When the Liberals were returned to power with the largest Parliamentary majority of the century, one of the first things they did was to introduce the Education Bill of 1906. It was proposed to abolish the Dual system. The democratic principle of public control of public money was incorporated in the Bill. The Cowper-Temple clause was to apply to every school receiving public grants : " no religious catechism or formulary which is distinctive of any particular denomination shall be taught ". The Bill passed the House of Commons by a large majority. But the Bishops had their own plans for defeating the desires of the people. They met at Lambeth, denounced the Bill, used their power in the House of Lords and the Bill was destroyed. The Bishop of Hereford was the only Bishop in the Lords who voted in favour of the measure. Once more the Peers and the Bishops had destroyed the possibility of a national system of education and blocked democratic legislation. The dual system continued.

The Act of 1902 was a false step for a Protestant nation to take. During the controversy Free Churchmen affirmed that the Romanist schools would reap the full results of the Act. And this has happened. Since 1902 the Established Church has lost over 3,200 schools and more than 1,300,000 scholars. Many Anglicans to-day are judging the Dual System as an educational blunder and a barrier to the co-operation of Christian men in the task of religious training in the schools. But at long last the struggle against Dogma and Tradition is being decided within the Church schools. The priest has claimed his divine right to direct education, but there are forces in his own schools which are disintegrating his authority. Large State grants have not enabled the Church to keep her buildings in order, and many are unsuitable for present educational work. But there are more serious internal problems compelling the attention of Church school authorities. I cannot do better than summarise the evidence of Dr. Braley's book, *A Policy in Religious Education*.[1]

The teachers in Church schools are often conscious of their inferior status as compared with the teachers in Council Schools. Few teachers will accept appointments in Church school if they can secure a place on the staff of a Council school. The students who are trained in the Church colleges evade Church schools for Council schools. The day has well nigh passed when teachers in Church schools are expected to play the Church

---

[1] The book was published in 1941. The 1944 Act reclassified the schools, but Dr. Braley's comparisons are still relevant.

organ, or act as choirmaster, or Sunday school superintendent, and the teachers are now resenting the interference of the clergy in the school. Again, the teachers become more reluctant to teach the Catechism knowing that dogmatic instruction is not education; that to cram a child's memory with dogmatic statements which he cannot understand is contrary to all sound psychological methods. Numerous teachers and students have strongly objected to teaching children that they are " born in sin " and are " the children of wrath ", as suggesting a doctrine of original sin which is a wresting of Scripture and which is quite untenable. " Still another reason why some of the members of the teaching profession are reluctant to serve in Church schools is because of the principle involved in the holding of an annual diocesan inspection " : there is much opposition to this examination in theory, if not in fact. Teachers do not object to inspection : " what they do object to is the principle of being inspected by members of another profession " . . . " The teaching profession, numerous, well-trained, and professionally enthusiastic ", said Bishop Hensley Henson, " will not consent to accept any subordination, or suggestion of subordination, to the clergy, such as is traditional in Church schools, and properly inherent in their constitution ". " The result of all these objections is that it is extremely difficult to staff Church schools efficiently and most bodies of managers will readily concur with this statement ".

Further, the diverse theological parties in the Established Church are creating problems. In the new Church senior schools authorised under the Act of 1936 " another difficulty is that the children are drawn from parishes of different shades of Churchmanship—high, low, moderate. Will it be possible for the incumbents of the various parishes to agree to the type of churchmanship to be taught in the senior schools " ?

In view of these problems Dr. Braley concluded that the Church should be prepared to end the Dual System, " to offer all her elementary schools to the State on condition (1) that religion shall be taught as an integral part of the curriculum of every educational institution which receives grants from the Board of Education ; (2) that it shall be taught by people who are able and desirous to do so, and inspected by His Majesty's Inspectors specially appointed for the purpose ". If Dr. Braley's conditions had been endorsed by the Church authorities the Bill of 1944 would have found Free Churchmen prepared to co-operate heartily to make religious education, through the Agreed Syllabuses, the basis of a Christian Society.

VI. THE WAR, THE HOMES, THE SCHOOLS

The war in 1939, unlike all others, opened doors and windows into Britain's homes until the nation was startled by revolting personal and family habits, by dirty houses, dirty clothing, dirty heads and hair, by the ignorance, incompetence and irresponsibility of parents who had brought children into the world and neither fed, nor clothed, nor washed them. The earliest evacuation of children from slum areas struck the cleaner classes with the force of a stunning blow. Later, when the bombs began to fall and when it was urgent to evacuate women and children from devastated districts, there were still louder protests against dirt, ignorance and degradation : it was alarming, and it brought a sense of shame to the nation that there were women who appeared incapable of caring for themselves or their children. I am passing no judgment on these women, for many were to be pitied rather than judged. I am stating facts which staggered the middle and upper classes. On the other hand, no tribute is adequate to the women of Britain who opened their homes to such evacuees, who washed other people's children, bought new clothes and darned old ones, who, by example, toil and sacrifice, bore the burdens of these homeless families.

There were many other evils which lay at the root of the dirt and ignorance which were exposed by evacuation, but concerning these root evils little or nothing was said. So much, however, was said and written at the time by protesting clerics that we seemed in peril of a ramp and racket type of legislation ; fortunately such peril passed. It was argued with some heat that the evils revealed by evacuation were due to the lack of religious education, or the wrong type of religious instruction, and it was openly stated that such a pagan generation had grown up as the offspring of our " godless Council schools ". Paganism, so often associated with moral and physical dirt, is an

ancient and modern bogey, and so paganism and its Council
school sources were marked down by clerical denunciation.
Little or nothing was said of poverty, economic injustice and
other glaring social evils ; no reference was made to the paganism
which was smart and Pharisaic but knew the value of soap and
water. But these poor children who attended slum and black-
listed schools, badly lighted, insanitary, unhealthy buildings,
with one privy for forty scholars, Church schools which for
years had been a crying disgrace to clergymen and managers,
schools where dogmatic teaching was more important than
health of mind and body—these evacuees who never attended
a school where they learned the simplest habits of physical
cleanliness, were exploited as the specimens of undenominational
teaching in the Council schools. The charge commonly made
against Biblical teaching in the State schools was that of Un-
denominationalism, an ugly word, and interpreted to mean Free
Churchism. " It is perhaps worth pointing out ", says Bishop
Hensley Henson, " that the rather uncouth word ' undenominational ' has been largely misunderstood. Polemical zeal has
transformed ' undenominational teaching ' into ' a moral monster '
by reading into it a meaning which its advocates would generally
disavow. If indeed it meant, what its hostile critics affirm, viz.
such residuum of Christian Faith as remains after every challenged belief has been abstracted, it would need little argument
to show that such teaching would be both intellectually contemptible and morally worthless. But when ordinary English
folks speak of ' undenominational teaching ' they mean that
fundamental truth which is held in common by all orthodox
Christians, Anglican as well as Dissenting ".[1] This is a welcome
change of view from the declaration of the Anglo-Catholic
Union in the attack on the Board schools, where undenomina-
tionalism was " the biggest humbug the wit of man ever devised "
and " a nasty, ugly, misshapen beast ". Any evidence of the
change of the Anglo-Catholic attitude would mean considerable
progress towards a new orientation of religious education in
the schools.

It was grievous that the devastations of war should have
been necessary to arouse the British people to the urgency of
educational reform. But it was significant that an Education

[1] Henson, *The Church of England*, p. 202.

Bill should have been presented to Parliament in 1944 when the nation was fighting for its own survival. Mr. R. A. Butler's patience was inexhaustible as he paved the way for the Bill through the House of Commons : to a remarkable degree he succeeded in reconciling conflicting religious interests before which his predecessors had often stumbled and failed. His conferences with representatives of the churches and the teachers : his readiness to receive deputations representing every possible interest in education, prepared the ground carefully for the triumph which he achieved. His Parliamentary Secretary, Mr. Chuter Ede, out of his practical experience as teacher and administrator, and his sympathetic attitude towards deputations, also contributed much towards the success of the Bill through the House of Commons. As the Measure of a Coalition Government the Bill had a smoother passage through the Commons, and a more tolerant reception from the House of Lords, than otherwise might have been the case.

The Bill was a religious compromise. No Church received all its requests, but the Anglican and Roman Churches received more than they were entitled to receive in a democratic State. The Free Church Federal Council, throughout all negotiations, upheld the democratic principle that use of public money should be publicly controlled. The Free Church representatives never consented to the financial clauses which handed over re-conditioned properties to the ownership and use of the churches. In 1944 there were about 500 black-listed schools to which reference has been made and Free Churchmen urged that it would be more democratic and more economical in the long run, to build new State schools, especially in single-school areas.

The Act offers the managers of Church schools two options. The first is that of becoming an aided school which means that half the cost of reconstructing the premises according to the demands of the Ministry of Education, will be met by the Government, leaving the managers to find the other half of the cost, but retaining full control of the school and the teachers. The second option is that of becoming a controlled school, which means that the reconstruction of the premises and the whole maintenance of the school will be a charge on public funds : two church representatives will be retained on the management committee, and a portion of the teaching staff will be retained to give dogmatic instruction under specified conditions two morning each week.

In all schools, every day, religious teaching is now made statutory : in all except aided schools such teaching will be based on an Agreed Syllabus. As there were about four hundred local education authorities using these syllabuses before the Bill was passed, there is convincing evidence of their quality, and acceptability to the teaching profession. As the Act makes Scripture an optional subject in the examination for the Teacher's Certificate, those who wish to teach it will receive lectures in the Training Colleges as preparation for such work. The crux of the matter is to secure that religious teaching shall be given by well-equipped teachers—such as desire to give it. The children of the nation need to learn the values of character, truth, honour, and service to their fellow men ; to learn how to use leisure, how by their own initiative to find happiness within themselves ; to treat human nature in themselves and in others always as an end and never as a means. I believe it is possible to teach Scripture by sound historical and psychological methods, until a child at school is able to understand more of his own instinctive urges, and how to control them, in the light of the noblest moral ideals.

This review of educational controversy extending over a century has not been a pleasant task, but it is history. Anglicans and Free Churchmen have contended for their ideals. If the Church of England had won, what kind of an educational system would there have been ? If Free Churchmen had refused conflict for their principles, what would have happened ? It must be remembered that such dispute over education was only one aspect of a far wider battlefield. What has history to say of education in those States where it has been controlled by the priestly class ? The answer is illiteracy, superstition, civil wars and bloody revolutions. England has had no civil war for the last three hundred years, during which period the struggle for religious and political and economic freedom has been accompanied by the advancing knowledge of a maturing democracy. Free Churchmen have been educationists, and without their liberal educational ideal there would have been no disciplined democracy such as England has known. It is a pleasure to say that many barriers between the Churches have been removed : we hope much from the 1944 Act : that through co-operation we may build a better Christian Society on the foundation of the Word of God.

CHAPTER XV

THE RISE OF DEMOCRACY

I

THE convulsions of the twentieth century, which have shaken so many institutions, " as of things which have been made ", are compelling Christian thinkers to adjust their ideas on the relation of Christianity to the State. The survival of the Christian religion and the freedom to proclaim it in our generation, are being threatened by the rise of atheistic police States. We have been accustomed to assume the Church and State as two institutions existing side by side and establishing relations with each other : an alliance which was made because the State looked for any spiritual support the Church could give, and the Church needed such financial maintenance as the State alone could guarantee. But during the present century States have arisen which have made war on the Church, and have repudiated the central truths and ethical standards of the Christian religion. Instead of an understanding between Church and State, or any relation between them, we appear to be entering on the period when the Church must challenge the atheistic foundations of the State, and be prepared to suffer loss for the Faith. The battle between the Lamb and the Beast, described in the Apocalypse, may yet be prophetic of the present century.

The schoolmen regarded the Church and State as a supernatural alliance ; both were divinely instituted and their separation was unthinkable. The idea that the Church should ever be free from official relation with the State never occurred to the schoolmen. The Pope and the Emperor might quarrel, but the alliance of Church and State was the foundation on which life and religion rested. There were strong groups which revolted against the authority of the mediæval church ; but only in England did the Free Church idea and movement become powerful enough to defy the mediæval conception of the divine right of kings and priests, and finally win freedom of worship and witness from State control. But while Nonconformists were winning freedom for the Church they were also slowly disintegrating the mediæval idea of the State : they were changing the attitude of the State towards the groups which constituted the whole nation. It was well into the nineteenth century before Nonconformists' rights, as Englishmen, were recognised by the Church and State. When it is asserted that Free Churchmen have no doctrine of the State—as it sometimes is—it is a remark which fails to explain the transformation of the idea of the State in the thought of the English-speaking peoples. It was due to the pressure of Free Church life and institutions that the mediæval idea of the State became outmoded, and that the political structures of the British people began to take new form.

The intellectual anarchy of Rousseau and the Encyclopædists led to social anarchy which destroyed the French State : attacks were made on the abuses of the French Church, as they were made in England on the abuses in the Anglican Church ; but the brilliant declamations of the French revolutionaries were made by men lacking the spiritual loyalties and moral discipline of Free Churchmen in England. Between the violent methods which destroyed the French State, and the spiritual life creating a new type of Church and State in England, the contrasts are startling. The evolution of political democracy in Britain was a new emergent in history : the Christian value of man created a new idea of his social and political relationships. Neither Plato's Ideal Republic nor the conception of man in the republics of the Greek City States, can compare with the Christian values which led to political democracy in England. The idea and experience of freedom which gave birth to the Free Church gave birth also to the Free State. It may be difficult for those who are not Free Churchmen to understand our claims ; but the experience of freedom came to the men of whom we are writing, in their personal relation with God through Christ : it was the New Testament which taught these men not only their own value in the sight of God, but that all men had equal value before God : not equal in capacities or possessions, but equal in the sense that they ought to be treated justly by the State. The earliest Free Churches were self-governing communities :

in their Church Meetings they learned the great principles of tolerance and self-government—the control of emotion, the discipline of speech, the adjustment of different points of view, and the unity of purpose. By extending these two basic principles into the realm of the State the Free Churches taught the nation to solve its differences by reason rather than by force : they taught Britain democracy. " The inspirers of democracy in seventeenth-century England were the Anabaptists and the Independents and finally the Quakers. This, not simply because they had taken more literally and centrally than others the doctrine of the priesthood of all believers, but because they had insisted on the self-governing congregation. That meant that they had practical and indeed daily experience of a fellowship united in a common purpose beyond themselves, to which purpose each and every member was found to have something to contribute. Democracy therefore was for them a mystical institution from the practical experience in which it realised itself ".[1] The Tudors, the Stuarts, the Act of Uniformity, tried to compel all men to think alike and worship alike—such is authoritarianism in Church and State : such was Nazism and Fascism. Through the seventeenth and eighteenth centuries Free Churchmen resisted and finally broke the authoritarianism based on the divine right of rulers and priests. " The English history of Freedom is different . . . freedom here has its origin chiefly in the claim of Dissenters from the Established Church to worship God as their consciences might direct. It was rooted in faith . . . and the self-government of the local chapel has been a fruitful school of democratic procedure ".[2]

Between the two wars and well into the early years of the struggle of 1939–45, a group of Neo-Catholic apologists made alarming attacks on Liberal democracy in England : it ran true to papal political policy during the same period, setting forth the preference for Mussolini's Fascist State against Parliamentary political democracy. All I am claiming at the present is that the Free Churches challenged and broke the authoritarian State and that English democracy had a spiritual basis. I am not concerned for the moment with the problem that democracy has dropped the spiritual pilot. I will refer to economic democracy

[1] *The Churches and Democracy.* A. D. Lindsay, p. 24.
[2] *Christianity and the Social Order.* W. Temple, p. 49 f.

later. But it is a shocking fact that men should have claimed to write from the Christian standpoint and should have declared that Fascism was nearer to the Christian Ideal than Democracy. To Christopher Dawson, British democracy is a " sham " ; writing between the two wars, when Mussolini was at the height of his power, he argued that Fascism was the model for all future States, the alternative to Communism on the one hand and Parliamentary democracy on the other ; that Britain was doomed because " democracy has swelled itself out with hot air and high phrases until it has burst like the frog in the fable ". There is no hope, said Dawson, for the unity of Europe, except on the Roman Catholic basis. Maritain, the French Jesuit, agreed : " Liberalism is not merely false in theory ; it is finished in fact : bankrupt by the turn of events ". He was not thinking of the Liberal Party of the early decades of the nineteenth century, but of those liberal and emancipating ideas which were the Free Church contribution to the democratic State. Michael de la Bedoyere, editor of the *Catholic Herald*, writing in 1940, when Fascism and Nazism seemed to be marching to victory, carries the contempt for democracy to the length of saying that the world of 1914–18 was the climax of the Liberalism of the nine- teenth century ; " A world war, in fact, exactly suited the mentality of the ' Dawnists ' (Liberals). Sub-consciously aware that their noble ideals are in fact far removed from the day-to- day nature of man, and, still more, of society as it works in practice, and sub-consciously doubtful of the practicability of a peaceful evolution of man to angel, they welcome an explosion from which, like the conjuror, they hope to bring out a marvellous surprise that in the ordinary course of things cannot be reached. Violence, whether of internal revolution or external war (though not consciously desired and generally reprobated in words), is not unwelcome . . . this world war, then, was greeted as a gigantic bonfire in which once and for all could be consumed all the evil men, all the evil forces, and all the litter left over from the ancient regime which stood in the path of progress ".[1] Here are fair samples of the hatred of democracy such as we find in recent Roman Catholic apologists. In the view of these writers the only hope of the world is somehow to get civilisation back on the mediæval basis ; to use force to compel all men

[1] *Christian Crisis*, p. 53.

to think alike and worship alike. " The Christian West has not failed to appreciate that even in relation to spiritual ends the sword and material means may be used, within the limits of justice. Even St. Augustine admitted in the end that against the destruction wrought by heretics the Church might appeal to the material power of the secular arm. The church again, being a perfect society, is entitled in her own sphere to exercise a certain measure of coercion ".[1] In such terms does Maritain veil the apology for persecution and the destruction of religious freedom. The silence of these writers since the fall and shame of Mussolini is not surprising.

II. FREE CHURCH CONCEPTION OF THE STATE

It is unnecessary to enter into a long discussion of various theories of the State, but I must indicate the principle of historic Free Churchmanship concerning the State. From Plato to More, theories of the State have been Utopian ; and the real States have been far removed from the Ideal Commonwealth of philosophers and dreamers. In his Republic, Plato made it clear that the ideal State must aim at Justice, a noble though an abstract idea, which had profound influence during the Middle Ages. Without justice, said Cicero, there can be no Commonwealth, no *res republica*. But long before the rise of Greek republics, and contemporary with Oriental despotic empires, the Biblical doctrine of the State presented a striking contrast— a theocracy in which the will of God was sovereign. The Bible ascribes absolute authority to the transcendent Law-Giver, Who revealed to Moses, the prophets, and finally through Jesus of Nazareth, the ethical standards of righteousness and love. In the New Testament Jesus Christ is Lord—a term signifying His unique ethical authority over His followers. For His disciple, whether in the Church or as citizen of the State, Christ's ethical standard is absolute. For the individual Christian and for the Church, which is constituted of no one but Christians, loyalty to Christ is decisive for character and destiny.

The attitude of Jesus to the State is the fulfilment of His own

[1] Maritain, *Freedom in the Modern World*, p. 177.

principle of loyalty to God. In His Galilean teaching he is more concerned with the rule of God in the hearts and lives of men than with the rulers of the State. When he was compelled to reckon with the governments of His day, whether that of Herod, or the Jews, or Rome, His attitude was the same. His kingdom, or Theocratic State, was different from the governments of the world ; but as citizens of earthly States His followers should obey authority except when it clashed with loyalty to Himself. Of earthly States His disciples were to be as the light, and as salt, never hiding their light of divine truth and wisdom, and ever acting as an antiseptic against immoral corruption. His most direct reference to Cæsar is that he was entitled to the taxes due to him. If an unjust tax was exacted Jesus does not indicate what attitude the taxpayer should adopt. At the same time Jesus never referred to Cæsar as a ruler by divine right, nor did He pass judgment on Cæsar's character. He made no comments on the Roman Senate. The universalism of His ethical demands transcended those of the Jewish Church and the Roman Empire. If the disciple found himself in conflict with the Church or the State, the guide of his conscience and the test of action was loyalty to His Lord.

We must differentiate between the Kingdom of God, the Church and the State. The Church was in the world, existed under the conditions of the Empire, and during the reign of Constantine the official relations between the Church and the Empire began. What was this step but the alliance of the Church and the World ? The New Testament conception of the " Church " and the " World " admits of no other meaning. It was a false step for the Church to take. For the World entered the Church as it had never done for three hundred years ; and ever since the fourth century its presence in the Church has been the bane of the Christian religion. It was, and is still, a departure from the spiritual independence of the Church. The Church is the bride of Christ who is the Bridegroom ; and between the bride and Christ Who bought the bride with His own blood, the World in the form of the State, has been the great intruder. When it has suited their mutual interests, mostly financial and entirely worldly, the Church and State have flirted with each other, and both have suffered ; the betrayal of Christ and the Gospel lies at the Church's door, and such betrayal cannot be divorced from the demonic forces which have swept over the world in these latter days.

History abounds in examples of the despotic State and of persecuting Churches allied with each other. Is it ever right for Christian men to resort to force to overthrow them? The mistaken exegesis of Romans xiii has been used in the interest of Churches and States to secure submission. On the other hand, the history of the Free Churches bears witness to the claim to resist tyrannical rulers in Church and State. The classic illustrations are the Civil Wars and the Revolution of 1688. Neither of these events would have occurred on political grounds alone. The religious forces were decisive in the Civil War; apart from the fighting quality of the New Model, Charles I would almost certainly have outwitted his enemies. The religious forces of Protestantism (and Free Churchmen were as active as any) initiated and maintained the rule of William III in 1688; afterwards, when the Hanoverian succession was imperilled in 1715 and 1745, and Tory High Churchmen were plotting the return of the Jacobites, Free Churchmen again prepared to resist the possibility of any return of the Stuarts.

Within the Church of England itself the relation of Church and State became a burning question in 1688. Sancroft, Archbishop of Canterbury, with five suffragan bishops and about four hundred clergy (they were known as the Non-Jurors) resigned their livings rather than take the oath of allegiance to William and Mary.[1] They had pledged their loyalty to James II and affirmed that nothing in heaven or on earth could justify the annulment of their oath. James had taken the oath to maintain the Constitution and the Protestant Religion of England. When he appointed Roman Catholics to civil offices and was undermining the Protestant foundation of the State, the Non-Jurors stood by him on the ground that he was King of England by hereditary divine right; according to Romans xiii, they said he was the Lord's Anointed. William III was elected by Parliament and was declared to be no lawful monarch; it was schism to take the oath to him and maintain his rule. But the Non-Jurors had not only vowed their loyalty to James; they had also subscribed to the Thirty-Nine Articles which

[1] cf. p. 123.

upheld a Protestant State. The issue was between the hereditary succession and divine right, or the right of Parliament to elect a King who would maintain the Protestant religion. Protestants judged their responsibilities to the State in the light of the religious principle. When contrasted with the French Revolution it was well for England that they did so. L. M. Hawkins thinks the Non-Jurors were contending for the spiritual independence of the Church : " they were helping to win freedom of conscience for the individual no less than that freedom which is so vitally necessary to the existence of associations within the State ". H. L. Laski's judgment is otherwise, and Sykes agrees with him : " The real interest of the non-juring schism was political rather than religious, and its roots go out to vital events in the past ".[1]

We surely discern that the spiritual independence of the Church is the indispensable condition of her highest service to the State. The Church is the divine society in the world, with ministry and organisation ; the Kingdom of God is the rule of God in the lives of men, and the work of the Church is to extend that rule, to inspire the thoughts, emotions and motives of men. The State makes the laws, must administer justice and restrict evil doers. The function of the Church is to preach the gospel in the State, to leaven society and to educate the people in Christian principles, until they elect men to rule who will make laws approximating to the Christian ethical ideal. Training the people for citizenship, promoting tolerance and self-government, affecting the social and political structures of the nation for good—such is the Free Church conception of its function in the State.

III. NATIONAL CHURCHES AND NATIONAL RELIGION

The Archbishop of York[2] is the protagonist of the movement to secure the spiritual independence of the Church of England ; but he would not agree with the complete independence of the Church for which we plead. He desires to retain alliance with

[1] Sykes, p. 286.
[2] cf. chapter XVI, iv.

the State. But does the Church need alliance with the State ? The Archbishop and many others answer the question according to custom, testifying how deeply rooted the Church-State relation is in the history of nations. The alliance has been taken for granted, and a custom which has persisted for sixteen hundred years is not easily broken. Yet the Christian Church made notable progress in the first three centuries of its history, when independent, and even persecuted by the State ; it " out-thought, outlived and out-died " the pagan religions of the Roman Empire. So successfully was the Church leavening the State that Constantine saw the wisdom of coming to terms with it. If the Church could make such a profound impression on the ancient world when it was independent of the State, it is arguable that State control is neither desirable nor necessary. The rise of the Free Churches in England, their expansion in North America and throughout the British Commonwealth is modern evidence that Christianity does not need alliance with the State. There is no Episcopal State Church in Canada, Australia or New Zealand.

The *Essential Ministry*, or Priestly Hierarchies, ruling National Churches in alliance with the State, have been responsible for the most tragic distortions of the Gospel. Such National Churches in the twentieth century are an anachronism : they belong to the period when religion had not advanced beyond the national stage of evolution. A National Church is a contradiction of itself. Christianity is a universal religion and it is impossible to enshrine the universal in a national institution. The universality of the Christian religion has been cabined, cribbed and confined by national prejudices and by racial interests ; these barriers have checked its sweeping progress. National Churches have arrested the universal ideas of the New Testament, and have thereby de-christianised the idea of God which was revealed by Jesus. The revelation of God as the Father of all men has been cast into national moulds. For example, God has been conceived as a national deity, a fighting God in war, a convenience in days of crisis and rarely remembered at any other time. When Jahweh was the national God of the Hebrews the people afflicted their souls before Him. Not so in the present century. Moreover, as National Churches have de-christianised the idea of God they have de-humanised the idea of man, using him as the tool of national policy in war and in economic slavery. National Churches have gambled in human lives. As we shall see, the de-humanised feudal system was largely the responsibility of National Churches. The Universal Church of God was meant to transcend national boundaries. If we think of God or man or human rights and values—the universalism of the Gospel has been narrowed down to the limits of National Churches. Instead of liberating, reconciling and healing the nations, the universal mercies, compassions, and human values of the Gospel have been smothered by National Churches, controlled by worldly rulers and priestly castes, fighting for privilege and national prestige.

The evolution of religion has moved in three well-defined stages : the primitive and tribal stage, the national, and the universal. The development of Biblical religion is true to these three stages. The primitive and tribal stage in the Old Testament covers well nigh a thousand years, from Abraham to Moses ; the period of national religion is that between Moses and the eighth century ; the universal stage begins with the great prophets—Amos, Micah, Hosea, Isaiah, with whom Jesus of Nazareth is in the true line of God's final motive. Priestly-State churches in Christendom have remained mainly at the national religious stage ; most of them are still at this stage. The Roman Church claims to be universal, and by reason of having asserted itself infallible, and by counting the heads of the population, it has deceived people by the semblance of internationality. In reality, by such alliances as those with Mussolini and Franco, it thinks and acts in the terms of ecclesiastico-political policy and after the manner of national religion.

CHAPTER XVI

THE UTILITY THEORY AND THE DILEMMA OF THE STATE CHURCH IN ENGLAND

I

FREEDOM of worship is the primary need of the religious consciousness, and the early Separatists were expressing this need when they demanded the right to worship God according to their own conscience. When the Church and State under the Tudors and James I denied them these spiritual rights they sailed to Holland. But it had not occurred to them that the Church of England could exist apart from relation to the State. After the civil wars, Cromwell's Triers represented a compromise between freedom of worship and a National Church. Cromwell refused to abolish tithes lest the stipends of ministers should be inadequate. The Levellers were more radical and urged the abolition of tithes, freedom of worship, and the right of the churches to elect their own ministers. It was during the eighteenth century, especially the latter half, that it became necessary to justify the relation of Church and State in England.

The revolution settlement of 1688 was only carried through successfully by the co-operation of the Nonconformists. They had become sufficiently powerful to demand guarantees for their own security and freedom under the new government. William and Mary had consented " to grant a full liberty " to them, but William was thwarted from fulfilling his promise. As a reward for rejecting the enticements of James II and suffering any penalties in the meantime, Bishops and Statesmen vied with each other in their promise of future recompense; they would do better than words could express. Burnet, who later became a bishop, admitted the error of the persecution policy of the

Church: " the wise and generous behaviour of the main body of Dissenters had given them so just a title to our friendship, that we must resolve to set all the world against us if we can ever forget it, and if we do not make them all the return of ease and favour, when it is in our power to do it ".[1] Burnet and others meant sincerely all they promised, but when the Protestant Succession and Establishment of the Church had been secured, the Nonconformists were unrewarded beyond the grudging relief of the Toleration Act of 1689. We have recorded how the Tory and High Church party resumed attacks on Nonconformist places of worship, and by sinister method got the Schism Act through Parliament. The Nonconformists had trusted the Whigs, but Walpole used Hoadly, whose sympathy was with Free Churchmen, to persuade them that the time was inopportune to press for their full liberties. Pitt opposed the repeal of the Test Act because it would imperil the safety of the Church of England: " If you grant this (demand) they will soon come to you to grant more ": it was on this occasion that he referred to the fact that some Dissenters were opposed to all establishments of religion. Priestley was in the gallery of the House of Commons when Pitt uttered these words and answered the speech in a letter: he declared himself as belonging to the class of Dissenters who were enemies of all ecclesiastical establishments. " I have no doubt, that when Christianity shall have recovered its pristine purity, and its pristine vigour, it will entirely disengage itself from the unnatural alliance which it is at present fettered with, and that our posterity will even look back with astonishment at the infatuation of their ancestors in imagining that things so wholly different from each other as Christianity and civil power had any material connection ".[2]

As the Methodist societies multiplied they could not escape the issues of their relation to the Established Church. John Wesley lived and died a member of the Church of England. While he rejected the theory of Apostolic Succession and the divine right of Episcopacy, and was opposed by many of the clergy whose parishes he visited, he remained a loyal member of the Church. But as early as 1744, at the first Conference,

[1] Skeats and Miall, p. 73.
[2] ibid., p. 393.

it was agreed that Methodist societies should not secede from the Church : at the same time they affirmed that they were not Dissenters. Later in 1755 the Conference agreed " whether lawful or not, it was not expedient to separate from the Church ". " It was for Wesley ", says Brash, " a problem of two loyalties. He cherished a loyalty to the Church of England . . . but his dominant loyalty was created by the crying needs of his age. He saw which way Methodism was moving ; and although he had done things to hasten the severance, fought with a rare tenacity to restrain his people from leaving the Church of England. . . . John Wesley's letters from 1784 onwards tell that he foresaw the possibility of separation, although he strove to do all in his power to prevent it . . . we believe that although Wesley delayed the breaking away of the Methodists from the Church of England, he was responsible for it ".[1]

The continuing controversy over the principles of the Non-Jurors kept alive the issues involved in the Establishment, and provoked angry strife in the Church of England itself. Hoadly, a Broad Churchman, maintained that James II was legally deposed, so were Sancroft and his followers who refused to take the oath to William III. Hoadly began to defend the right of private judgment, denounced the penal laws which limited the civil rights of Christian men, declared that religious tests were a scandal to religion and that human laws and penalties could never protect the Church as a spiritual institution. But it was in May, 1717, when Hoadly, as Bishop of Bangor, preached before the King from the text, " My Kingdom is not of this world ", that excitement flared up over the nature of the Church, and its relation to the State. Hoadly declared " that Christ was the only and absolute authority in His Church ; that the Kingdom of Christ was different from the kingdoms of this world in that Christ left behind Him no visible human authority, no viceregents who can be said properly to supply His place . . . no judges over the consciences or religion of His people ".[2] In this militant sermon, Hoadly rejected Apostolic Succession, the divine right of Episcopacy, and the policy of the State Church towards the Nonconformists : but in doing so, he kindled the vehement " Bangorian Controversy " which

[1] W. Bardsley Brash, *Methodism*, p. 155 f.
[2] Sykes, p. 292 f.

produced over a hundred pamphlets. If Hoadly had understood the Church as a divine society, and known the New Testament doctrine of the Holy Spirit indwelling the Church, he would have been far less vulnerable to the attacks of his opponents, especially the answer of William Law : and his views of the relation of Church and State would have gained more weight accordingly.

II. THE UTILITY OF THE ESTABLISHMENT

The unredressed grievances of the Nonconformists, the rise of the Methodist Societies, the Non-Juror debates, and the Bangorian battle of pamphlets, compelled several apologists to justify the existence of the Establishment. Kettlewell reasoned that " although the State has no power either to give or to deprive the ministers of Christ of their mere spiritual powers, yet it has a direct authority to grant and deprive them of their temporal powers ".[1] Whatever secular gifts or privileges the State bestows on the Church, the State can in its wisdom take away. In 1736 Warburton published his volume on *The Alliance Between Church and State*. He wrote to vindicate the Establishment and the necessity of a Test Law, such as would safeguard it and maintain the authority of the Church. Warburton reasoned that Religion had an essential function in any society which aimed at stability : the Church was such a Society, whose officers and members must function to bring men to God ; it must, therefore, have Articles of Faith, or a Creed, as the test of membership ; the Church must have authority over its members, deciding who shall be admitted to fellowship, who shall be refused, and who shall be excommunicated. The authority of the Church, however, must be spiritual, and must concede freedom of conscience and worship for all. The State must not inflict penalties on those who refuse to conform to the Establishment. The authority of the Church, and the State, is valid, each in its respective sphere, but they both need each other and need a relation which is advantageous to both, " such then is the nature of that famous union which produces a Church

[1] ibid., p. 289.

Established, and which is indeed no other than a political league and alliance for mutual support and defence ".[1] Warburton used the contract theory of the State to explain the Establishment. The relation was that of a contract between two sovereign powers ; but he admitted that the Church surrendered her own independence by serving the State and contributing spiritual support to civil administrators and institutions. But in return, the Church received endowments from the State, the presence of the Bishop in the House of Lords, and the advantage of civil power to enforce the decisions of the ecclesiastical courts. Having surrendered its independence to the State the Church receives complete protection from the State. Hence the Test Law was necessary to prevent members from other religious societies from entering Parliament " lest they should inflict harm on the Established Church ". Here then was Warburton's theory of the Establishment : it was due to a contract between Church and State " on the practical basis of utility ": It was a remarkable, even a revolutionary change, for Warburton to reject the accepted theory of the divine right of the Establishment, and substitute public utility as the nature of its claim upon the nation.

Paley would have no dealings with the contract theory of Church and State, but he extended and popularised the principle of public utility. In his Moral Philosophy (1785) he acknowledged his debt to his predecessors who had applied the idea of utility to theology and to Christian ethics. Jeremy Bentham had even influenced theologians to reduce morality to the one principle of utility—that actions were good and right as they promoted happiness, and wrong as they promoted unhappiness, and every man's ethical ideal should be to secure the greatest happiness of the greatest number. Paley could write, " virtue was doing good to mankind, in obedience to the Will of God, and for the sake of everlasting happiness ". Within the scope of such a principle Paley justified the Establishment : it was an Institution which existed for the good of mankind and for the sake of everlasting happiness. " A religious establishment ", he said, " is no part of Christianity . . . the authority of a Church establishment is founded in its utility ". Christ " left the laws of His Church so open and indeterminate that whilst

[1] Sykes, p. 320.

the ends of religious communion were sufficiently declared, the form of the society might be assimilated to the civil constitution of each country, to which it should always communicate strength and support in return for the protection it received. If there be any truth in these observations, they lead to this temperate and charitable conclusion, ' that Christianity may be professed under any form of Church government '." Paley included the order of bishops, priests and deacons as functioning according to the utility principle : a theory far removed from Dr. Kirk's claims for the *Essential Ministry*. The endowments and revenues guarantee clerical incomes, and the kind of security which redeems preaching from becoming " a mode of begging " ; apart from the security assured by the State the Christian ministry would become " degraded, would soon fall into the lowest hands for it would be found impossible to engage men of worth and ability in so precarious and humiliating a position ".[1] There was wider tolerance and charity in Paley's conception of utility. He rejected Warburton's Test Law : apart from Quakers whom he excluded on the ground that they refused military service to the State, he thought there was " no reason why men of different religious persuasions might not sit on the same bench, deliberate in the same council ". Again, in Paley, we notice the distance he had travelled from the claim that the Establishment existed in virtue of its divine right—it existed because it was useful.

III. THE PRESENT ATTITUDE TO
DISESTABLISHMENT

This defence of the Establishment on the grounds of Utility has persisted to this day, and we must examine it. It is the defence of the Commission of Church and State which was published in 1935. After reviewing several reasons advanced in favour of Disestablishment and rejecting them out of hand, the Commission stated the following pragmatic reasons for the

[1] Sykes, p. 327 ff. Sykes says, " a characteristic mark of Paley's defence of the establishment was its homespun common sense ".

continuance of the Establishment. The Commission was " impressed " by the evidence from the Free Churches ; also from the Irish and Welsh Churches which have been disestablished : " We should misrepresent the impression made upon our minds if we did not make clear our conviction that the case for Disestablishment is strong. Some of us deliberately consider that Disestablishment should be preferred to an indefinite continuance of the present relationship between Church and State ".[1] But separation between Church and State would be injurious to both : " the Establishment is the symbol of the official acceptance of Christianity as the national religion ". If England were to seem to become neutral in the battle between Christianity and secularism the whole world would suffer. The national recognition of the Christian religion is expressed " in the coronation of the Sovereign, in the daily prayers in both Houses of Parliament, in the part traditionally taken by representatives of the Church in all State functions, by the attendance of the Judge of Assize at divine service ". If the value of these national recognitions of the Christian religion was lost it was claimed that Christianity would count for less in the national and civic life of England.[2]

Here, then, we have the latest considered official statement of the matter : the main appeal for the continuance of the Establishment is made on the grounds of Utility. The Establishment has served a useful purpose in the past, and the nation should keep it, or desire to keep it for its future usefulness. There is a curious assumption in this special pleading—that what was useful once in keeping the nation loyal to the Christian religion is useful now for the same purpose, that what " worked " under the Tudors will " work " in the twentieth century ; as though an institution which was useful under the supremacy of the reigning sovereign must also be useful under Parliamentary democratic structures. But the whole argument from Free Church history is a protest against the complacency of the principle of the utility of the Establishment. Hooker's shade is somewhere lurking in these recent utility suggestions. The Anglican leaders may assume that the Establishment, with its privileges and endowments, is useful to the nation, but they

[1] *Report*, p. 48 f.
[2] cf. p. 279 on the public recognition of Religion in America.

ought to take steps to ascertain the judgment of the nation on such a matter. For it is the mind of the nation, and not simply the views of Free Churchmen, which should be considered.

It will be admitted that Utility is not the surest ground on which to judge this issue : nor will the principle of utility commend itself as a substitute for theological and ethical principles. For example, the theological divisions in the Anglican Church raise serious objections against these claims of utility in the present day. When the nation, through its representatives in Parliament, had the latest opportunity of expressing judgment on the utility of the revised Prayer Book in 1927 and 1928 the decision was against the claims and the theology of the *Essential Ministry*. And since Anglo-Catholic bishops are still appointed to vacant sees, and in turn appoint Anglo-Catholic priests to vacant livings, the situation has become more serious during the last twenty years. I believe Parliament would reject again the utility of the revised Prayer Book, and would almost certainly rebuke, in the name of the nation, the defiance of the Anglo-Catholic clergy in perpetuating lawlessness in the State Church. Why do Anglican leaders refuse to face squarely this issue ? The British people have a sense of justice and they resent Anglo-Catholic propaganda and practice under a Protestant settlement. The decision of Parliament in 1928 was to the effect that the Prayer Book of 1662 had more utility for the nation—because it maintained Protestant principles. Can an institution in a theological and ecclesiastical impasse substantiate its claim to speak for the nation ?

The pragmatists have always claimed that a thing is true if it works : at any rate, true for those who think it works. We must beware of " using " God when we ought to know Him as He has revealed Himself in Christ and the Scriptures. The national idea of God " worked " during the period of national religion, but it does not " work " now ; it does not serve the universalism of the Gospel. The church has " used " the State, and the State has " used " the Church, and it has been easy for those who are interested to conclude that the relation of church and state " works " for the spread of the Christian religion—an illogical and a dangerous conclusion : one which European history denies and discredits. The Church feared that religious freedom would lead to the destruction of the State ; the State feared that political freedom would lead to the destruction of the Church : so they " used " each other to resist religious and political freedom : they would have continued to use each other to maintain their own interests unless Free Churchmen had challenged the principle of utility in the Church-State relationship. In resisting such ecclesiastical statecraft Free Churchmen created a new type of church and a new type of State : they built up a new political structure on the inherent spiritual values of human personality : and this kind of State has survived in Britain the strains and stresses which have broken states and churches in other lands during the twentieth century. But while in Britain the constitution of the State has been radically changed, the establishment has become an anachronism.

If the history of the Established Church during the past three centuries is estimated in the terms of utility, whose utility has it been ? And on such a principle, how must we estimate the conflicts of Nonconformists who won solid spiritual gains for the Church of God and the nation ? Are the Puritans to be dismissed as wrestling with shadows ? I believe they were spiritually and morally right : which means that the policy of persecution on the part of the Church of England, and the theological basis on which it rested, were spiritually and morally wrong. Were the Nonconformists who suffered for religious freedom misguided men, who failed to understand the " utility " of the establishment in Britain ? The answer is that they regarded the alliance of Church and State as a betrayal of the Gospel and a hindrance to the spiritual growth of the nation. John Wesley's estimate of the establishment did not restrain him from breaking the rules, and setting forth to preach the Gospel to the masses who were neglected by the Church. I have no desire to deny that the Church of England has been useful, and is useful still, to those who use it : I pay tribute to its saints, scholars and preachers, but the fact remains that the great majority of the English people to-day do not use it. With its vast financial resources and its privileges, has it christianised the nation and stood for righteousness and freedom ? I believe it could have achieved far greater results in the past, and could accomplish these ends in the present, if it had been, and were to-day, independent of the State. But the dread of the loss of endowments keeps the Church in bondage to the State: the proposals for her independence confirm this statement.

IV. THE ARCHBISHOP OF YORK SEEKS SELF-GOVERNMENT OF THE CHURCH

On repeated occasions Dr. Garbett, Archbishop of York, has voiced the demand of the Anglican Church for the freedom of self-government. No one agrees with this request more heartily than Free Churchmen; every argument used by Dr. Garbett for the spiritual freedom of the Church of England is a vindication of Free Church principles. But when he considers the means of obtaining it he is confronted by the relation of the Church with the State. If Free Churchmen have any criticism to offer on the methods of reaching his goal, it is not through lack of understanding, for with a great price we have obtained our own freedom. With admirable candour the Archbishop discusses the situation in the chapter on Church and State in his volume, *The Claims of the Church of England.*[1] He rather protests too much that the Church of England " has in practice freedom which is hardly equalled by any other church or sect ",[1] for he then proceeds to admit that the Church cannot legally determine its worship without reference to Parliament; " the control of the State over the Church is considerable; the Crown appoints bishops, deans, and to many benefices; the consent of Parliament is necessary for changes in statement of doctrine or in forms of worship, and for any change in the legal, constitutional and administrative fabric of the Church which is at the present time regulated by Statute law ".[2] The Report of the Commission of 1935 was compelled " to recognise that Parliament might insist on some measure, at least, of Disendowment as the concomitant of Disestablishment. We do not think that the fear of Disendowment should be allowed to play any great

[1] p. 182.
[2] p. 191f.

part in shaping the policy of the Church. Yet the possibility of Disendowment remains ; and no one who values the work of the Church can make light of that possibility ". Dr. Garbett is not at present able " to ask for Disestablishment, though he is prepared to accept it without opposition if the State demands it ".[1] In the meantime he sets forth the proposals which are those of the Commission : " We recommend that Parliament should be asked to pass an Act authorising " the following procedure. Any measure passed by the Church Assembly in accordance with its own Constitution, as to which, " the Archbishops of Canterbury and York and the Lord Chancellor and the Speaker of the House of Commons shall certify their unanimous opinion that it relates substantially to the spiritual concerns of the Church of England, and that any civil or secular interests affected may be regarded as negligible " ; and that such Measure, in the opinion of the two Archbishops, " is neither contrary to, nor indicative of, any departure from the fundamental doctrines and principles of the Church of England, as set forth in the Thirty-Nine Articles and the Book of Common Prayer, may forthwith be presented to His Majesty for the Royal Assent ". And " on the Royal Assent being signified to any Measure . . . it shall have the force and effect of an Act of Parliament ". " If, however ", says Dr. Garbett, " the Church cannot agree to these reforms, or if Parliament after due consideration refuses to accept them, then Disestablishment and Disendowment will be unavoidable . . . if spiritual freedom can be obtained in no other way it will be necessary to pay a heavy price of Disendowment. But the Church must have genuine freedom and retain its cathedrals and ancient churches ".[2]

These ingenious proposals are evidence that Anglican leaders are resolved to avoid another rebuff from the House of Commons ; they recognise that another full-dress debate in Parliament involving the Communion Service and the rejection of the book which the Bishops unlawfully authorised after 1928 would be both unseemly and disastrous. But Dr. Garbett all but despairs of the above proposals receiving the assent of the Church Assembly : " unhappily by some strange error of judgment, the Commission placed in the forefront of its proposals the

[1] p. 198.
[2] p. 197.

request that the Archbishops, by ' summoning a Round Table Conference or otherwise ', should seek to secure agreement on permissible deviation from the Order of Holy Communion and on the use and limits of Reservation.   This was a fatal proposal ; at once it raised again the old controversies : it gave opportunities for those who were opposed to the other recommendations to obstruct progress by refusing this preliminary agreement, and it aroused suspicion as to the purpose of all the other proposals.   This preliminary condition for agreement, on the Order of Communion and Reservation, doomed from the outset the Report to failure.   Various meetings and conversations were held, but there was no likelihood of substantial progress or agreement when further proceedings were interrupted by the outbreak of war ".[1]

Dr. Garbett's frankness has placed before us all the fears, hopes and aspects of the problems confronting the Church in relation to the State.   It is recognised that Disestablishment would involve delicate legal and financial adjustments, but no one desires to impoverish the Church in her work, certainly not Free Churchmen.   It is not likely that the nation would be mean concerning endowments.   The precedents of the Irish and Welsh Disestablishment Acts were generous regarding endowments and property.   Gladstone was loyal to the Church of England, but as Prime Minister, in 1869, he introduced the Bill for the Disestablishment of the Irish Church.

I have two comments to make on these proposals to obtain self-government.   First : the Lord Chancellor and the Speaker of the House of Commons may not be confessing Christian men ; to place responsibility upon them to say what relates " substantially to the spiritual concerns of the church " is somewhat anomalous ; in any case, " substantially " is a very specious term.   Second : it is revolutionary in a democratic State to appeal over the head of the House of Commons to the Crown. Such procedure may possibly draw the Crown into a most unfortunate national controversy—a possibility we should all do our utmost to avoid.   To attempt to gain self-government by circumventing Parliament would, I believe, rouse the nation's anger against the Church.

[1] p. 195.

213

V. MR. T. S. ELIOT'S IDEA OF A CHRISTIAN
SOCIETY

Is a State Church essential to educate or create and stabilise a Christian nation ?   Not a nation of confessing Christians, but a nation which orders its life and culture on Christian principles ? In his book, *The Idea of a Christian Society*, Mr. T. S. Eliot examines this question and insists that a Christian society, a nation which thinks and acts in the light of Christian truth, is only possible in and through an Established Church. He reasons that in order to keep England a Christian country we should need to establish the Church unless it was already established. The lectures which constitute his book were delivered in March, 1939, a date which may have influenced their form, but does not greatly affect his conclusions. He confesses his debt to the books of Christopher Dawson and Jacques Maritain, whom we have noticed as men preferring Mussolini's Corporative State rather than British democracy. Mr. Eliot is severely critical of nine-teenth-century Liberalism—especially what seems to him the impotence of Liberalism to control its own tendencies. His diagnosis of Liberalism is a warning to all of us, and I shall return to it later. He thinks " totalitarianism can retain the terms ' freedom ' and ' democracy ' and give them its own meaning ;[1] and its right to them is not so easily disproved as minds inflamed by passion suppose. We are in danger of find-ing ourselves with nothing to stand for except a dislike of everything maintained by Germany and/or Russia . . . you have only to examine the mass of newspaper leading articles, the mass of political exhortation, to appreciate the fact that good prose cannot be written by a people without convictions. The funda-mental objection to fascist doctrine, the one which we conceal from ourselves because it might condemn ourselves as well, is that . . . we sometimes use the word ' pagan ' and in the same context refer to ourselves as ' Christian '. But we always dodge the real issue. Our newspapers have done all they could with the red herring of the ' German national religion ', and eccen-tricity which is after all no odder than some cults held in Anglo-

[1] p. 19 ff.

Saxon countries ". He says we delude and comfort ourselves that we have a Christian civilisation.

Mr. Eliot has two guarantees of the Christian society. He asks, first, how can we be sure that any government will legislate according to Christian principles ? He answers, only when public opinion has been educated and religious practice has become a habit, will statesmen pass legislation within the framework of Christian ideals. The second guarantee of a Christian society in England is through the Anglican Church as by law established ; he is so sure that his judgment is true that it is useless for him to appeal to those who do not agree with it. " The goal of the Christian society will be reached when the majority of the sheep belong to one fold ". The Church of Mr. Eliot's dream must have a priestly organisation in direct and official relation to the State . . . " and finally it must have in the persons of its more intellectual, scholarly and devout officers, its masters of ascetic theology and its men of wider interests, a relation to the Community of Christians. In matters of dogma, matters of faith and morals, it will speak as the final authority within the nation ".[1]

This revival of the medieval synthesis, for such it is, is utterly out of question in the twentieth century. The medieval unity and Christian society never existed in the sense in which neo-Catholic writers exploit it ; and it is a claim which a Christian ethical test exposes to the severest judgment. The Reformation struck Mr. Eliot's idea a blow from which it has never recovered and never will, for the Reformation brought back the laity into the Church. And into the hands of the laity the Free Churches have put the torch of truth and freedom. Mr. Eliot has no place for the Free Churches in his guarantees of a Christian society. They are dismissed as marginal dissentients, " tending only to make marginal contributions " ; they have only been able to flourish against the background of Anglican orthodoxy. An absurd judgment lacking historical foundation. As for America, there can be no positive culture because there is no State Church.[2] Unfortunately, the dissentients are in the vast majority, and they still represent the progressive spiritual and moral forces of the world. Mr. Eliot looks backward, but he

[1] p. 47.
[2] p. 46.

does not seem to understand that the State Churches of Russia and of the Latin bloc of nations have bred atheists, Communists, cruel revolutionaries, and anything but Christian societies. The Church must take the forward way to complete self-government —which is disestablishment.

CHAPTER XVII

FREE CHURCH OPTIMISM

I

DIFFERENT conceptions of the nature of the Church and of the Christian Ministry explain the rise of conflicting political parties in England. The nation became divided socially and politically as men owned allegiance to Anglicanism or Nonconformity. In no other country were Nonconformists numerous and strong enough to challenge the State-Church and develop political action as they did in England. It is this religio-political tension, running through the latter part of the sixteenth to the nineteenth centuries which distinguishes Britain from other European nations ; the religious aspect of this tension, even in the days of the civil war, saved England from the godless revolutions which laid other nations waste. This Tory Church *versus* Nonconformists and Whig dissension became more acute as Free Churchmen became more politically conscious during the nineteenth century. The Free Churches had learned by hard experience the necessity of united political action. The repeal of the Corporation and Test Acts had been too long delayed through lack of united attack. From Walpole onwards, while Whigs were put into power by Nonconformist votes, they did nothing to remove the injustices under which their numerous supporters suffered. An example of the policy of " letting things alone " was the refusal to removed Church rates before 1868.

There were two main reasons which accounted for this lack of unity and political frustration. First: there was the decline of Presbyterianism in England. During the civil war, when the Independents and Baptists, under Cromwell and Milton, had taken the leadership against the Stuarts, the Presbyterians began to lose their power; after 1646 their influence waned. Apart from London and Lancashire, a definite " organisation of Presbyterian Churches ceased to exist in England ". It is true that Presbyterian leaders took considerable responsibility for the recall of Charles II ; but after 1660 the movement towards Liberal theological views led to dissension. After the Revolution in 1688, out of some eight hundred congregations only about seventy remained, says Miall, in the early years of the eighteenth century. " Until about 1836, well into the nineteenth century ", said Mr. Justice Kekewich, in his judgment in the Tooting case, " the Presbyterians had no active life as a body ; there appears to have been no returns of their chapels, and no other evidence of their identity. It is impossible to suppose that, after such prominent success as they had had in the earlier years, and the faith being still strong in Scotland, there were no Presbyterians here and there yearning after the return of what they called the ' good old ways ' but they dropped out as a body ".[1]

Second : the Methodists held aloof from political action during the early decades of their history. Their primary calling was the evangelisation of the nation. Their roots were not in the turbulent period of the seventeenth century. No one has been more generous than Dale in his appreciation of the blessings of the Evangelical Revival ; the sermon preached in the City Road Chapel on 4th March, 1891, in connection with the centenary of Wesley's death was Dale's noble tribute to John Wesley and his Methodist preachers : " Assembled for this sacred commemoration, the hearts of millions of men in many lands are drawn to you . . . we are encompassed by a great cloud of witnesses. In their presence, in God's presence, over the very ashes of your founder whose death we commemorate, but who lives for evermore in the light of the Eternal, I call upon you to resolve, with all the solemnities of an oath, that you will stand fast until you die, in your fidelity to the truths which have given to Methodism its power and glory ".[2] But Dale thought " the Evangelical Revival was defective in two directions—ecclesiastically and ethically ".[3] In this defection

[1] Skeats and Miall, p. 714.
[2] Dale, *Fellowship with Christ*, p. 245.
[3] *Life of Dale*, p. 348 ff.

Dale included the political neutrality of official Methodism well into the nineteenth century. Wesley was adamant in his attitude to the political side of evangelism. In his view, such action would divert his societies from the divinely appointed task of preaching the Gospel. With a strong hand Wesley insisted on " No politics " among his preachers, though he himself was a decided Tory. Methodists were scandalised by the French Revolution and therefore by the radical Free Churchmen who welcomed it. Under the Stuarts, Nonconformists had paid dearly for freedom of worship, and they had not hesitated to draw the sword and enter the political arena to obtain it. The Toleration Act of 1689 had been placed on the Statute Book, the Protestant Succession had survived the Jacobite plot of 1715, and such gains had prepared the ground for Wesley's mighty work. If the older Nonconformists seemed to him too politically minded, it is relevant to ask what would have happened to Wesley and his societies under the Tudors and the Stuarts. " It would be unjust to say that the Dissenters have been equally as interested in politics as in religion, but in the eighteenth century they had become deeply involved politically. Methodist politics were an incidental outcome of conditions ; Dissenting politics were almost inseparably bound up with their own church life. It was indeed the realisation of the fate which had befallen the sects, who had exhausted their spiritual life in the struggle for freedom, both ecclesiastical and political, that made Wesley and his successors so careful to warn their people against participation in politics, and which at least in part explains the ' no politics ' attitude which the Methodist Conference adopted in the nineteenth century ".[1] Still, the census of 1851 gives the older Nonconformists a majority of worshippers over all Methodists. It is scarcely surprising, however, that the continuous battles for religious freedom had taxed the political resources of the Nonconformists. For a hundred and fifty years they had fought the good fight of faith ; they had subdued and broken the tyranny of kings and priests and wrought righteousness ; they had won inestimable gains for the nation such as gave Wesley freedom to do his work, unmolested by penal legislation which had brought blood and tears, prison and exile, to the older Nonconformists. When Wesley appeared

[1] Taylor, *Methodism and Politics*, p. 29.

on the English scene, surely raised up of God at that particular time, there was freedom for his genius to create his societies and organise their connexional activities for evangelism. The firm government which he exercised over his converts can only be explained by the love they bore him. Even so, there were more than murmurings against his autocracy. " As long as I live ", he wrote to John Mason in 1790, the year before his death, " the people shall have no share in choosing either stewards or leaders among the Methodists. We have not, and never had, any such custom ; we are no republicans and never intend to be. It would be better for those who are so minded to go quietly away. I have been uniform both in doctrine and discipline for above these fifty years, and it is a little too late for me to turn into a new path now I am grey-headed ". When Wesley was accused of shackling free-born Englishmen and denied the request for a Conference where the majority should rule, he replied, " All talk of this kind is highly injurious to me who bear this burden merely for your sakes. And it is exceed-ingly mischievous to the people, tending to confound their understandings and to fill their hearts with evil surmisings and unkind tempers towards me, to whom they really owe more, for taking all this load upon me—for exercising this very power —for shackling myself in this manner—than for all my preaching put together. Because preaching twice or thrice a day is no burden to me at all ; but the care of all the preachers and all the people is a burden indeed ".[1]

Six years after Wesley's death the political ideas of the French Revolution and the hard lessons of the Industrial Revolution, stirred democratic ideals in the Methodist Societies ; the Metho-dist people were more politically progressive than the leaders. Kilham was tried and expelled from Conference and the Methodist New Connexion came into existence as a protest against a " clerical Conference ". As Jabez Bunting became the strong leader he sought to guide and restrain Methodists according to the tradition of Wesley ; he insisted on the rule of " no politics ", though he spoke and acted as a Tory till he won for himself the title of the " Pope of Methodism ". Bunting supported Tory candidates, drawing upon himself the criticism that while he gagged others, " he said and did as he liked ". So pronounced

[1] Taylor, p. 47.

was his political consciousness he said, " Methodism hates democracy as much as it hates sin ".[1] The revolt against Bunting's official autocracy came in the deplorable crisis of 1849, when " he lived to see the Methodist Church rent from top to bottom and ' Pastoral Supremacy ' anathematised by 100,000 Methodist ' exiles '. His policy destroyed the very unity it was intended to bring to the Church ".[2] When the Reform Bill was passing through Parliament, *The Christian Advocate*, edited by John Stephens, attacked Bunting, who had voted at Liverpool for Lord Sandon, a Tory and a slave-owner. The Conference censured Stephens and Bunting felt " deeply and eternally obliged ". When, in 1833, Stephen's brother had spoken in favour of Disestablishment he was rebuked by Conference and compelled to resign. During the debate Bunting declared : " If I went from the Methodists I would go to Church rather than to Dissent. I would not go to fierce formal Dissent. We cannot be friendly to Dissent. One of its first principles is, Every man shall choose his own minister. Can you be friendly to that "?[3] Bunting's idea of choosing a minister in the old dissenting churches was, of course, a caricature of the solemn proceeding of the Church meeting, seeking the guidance of the Holy Spirit in the appointment of a pastor.[4] It is a long story from Jabez Bunting's rule and official Methodist policy to Hugh Price Hughes and his Presidency of the National Free Church Council in 1892 ; there was no political neutrality in the ministry of Hugh Price Hughes. He was a loyal son of the Evangelical Revival and kept the flame in his heart, but no one hit political injustice and social evils harder blows than this winner of souls. But in the middle of the nineteenth century, when Nonconformity was growing conscious of its power, its application of evangelical principles to political and social problems would have been far more fruitful in the life of the nation if official Methodism had thrown its weight into the struggle for religious equality.

[1] Taylor, p. 133.
[2] ibid., p. 139.
[3] Redfern, *Modern Developments in Methodism*, p. 116.
[4] cf. p. 66 : 4.

II. DISESTABLISHMENT BECOMES A POLICY

In 1844 the " Anti-State Church Society " was founded, but the name was changed in 1853 to " The Society for the Liberation of Religion from State Patronage and Control ". The change of name was due to the fact that several members were using the society for their own ends. But the origin of the society marked the beginning of direct political action to achieve the disestablishment of the Anglican Church. It owed its origin to Free Church leaders who were deeply sensitive to the social and political evils for which State Churches were responsible. The first Conference announced that no attack would be made on the Church apart from its relation with the State ; it was " out of a deep sense of obligation to Christ, the sole head of the Church, that the society resolved to persevere in its opposition to the principles of State-establishment in religion ; that the existence of State Churches lacked scriptural authority ; that the society stood for the complete independence of the Church of Christ, which could only be secured by spiritual freedom and self-government according to the sanctions of the New Testament ". The motives of the Society were purely spiritual, but the separation of Church and State necessitated political action. In 1844 Anglicans and many Nonconformists took the Establishment for granted and considered the Society as attempting the impossible. During the debates on the Reform Bill in 1832 there had been vigorous denunciation of the policy of the Bishops and the Church. It was in one of those debates that Lord Grey uttered his oft-quoted warning to the Bishops " to set their house in order ". The comprehensive ecclesiastical reforms which followed the Act of 1832, largely due to the effect of the *Black Book*, seem to have diverted wide public interests from the Establishment to more urgent economic problems. It would appear from these facts that in 1844 the question of disestablishment made no appeal to the masses ; they were campaigning with Cobden and Bright for the repeal of the Corn Laws, which was achieved in 1846 ; they were also swelling the ranks of the Chartists. The Establishment was accepted as an essential part of the British Constitution, so that it seemed inconceivable to the average Member of Parliament that the State could exist apart from the Church. So little understood was the idea of religious equality. Edward Miall's opponent in the election at Halifax in 1847 was Sir Charles Wood (afterwards Lord Halifax), a Whig Statesman, who put the question to Miall : " Can any man tell me what he means by the separation of Church and State " ? Here was a Whig States-man who could not imagine an intelligible answer to his question. How few of the Whigs understood the spiritual realm of Free Churchmanship !

It was this lack of understanding and indifference which led the Liberation Society to take the long view and prepare to educate the country in Free Church principles. It was no negative programme which was outlined ; the campaign laid primary emphasis on the inherent spiritual nature of the Church and the ways in which patronage and State control subverted its inherent divine right of self-government. On the platform, in the Press, the Society propagated its principles and soon stimulated public interest in its objective ; several of its members were in Parliament during the nineteenth century : great Free Church leaders, including Dale, Guiness Rogers, Spurgeon, McLaren and John Clifford became its sturdy supporters, and many ministers organised its work in their own local areas. The Liberation Society has been in existence since 1844 and is still loyal to the ideals of its founders, still helping to remove grievances from which Free Churchmen suffer at the present time. The Society has quickened public opinion, prompted Nonconformists and others in Parliament to political action and the passing of the following Acts—all removing religious or civil injustice to the benefit of the nation.

1844 Roman Catholic Relief Act.
1845 Jewish Relief Act.
1854 Oxford University Act removing certain religious tests.
1856 Cambridge University Act removing similar tests.
1857 Act removing jurisdiction of Ecclesiastical Courts over Wills.
1860 Endowed Schools Act providing for admission of Non-conformists.
1863 Statute Revision Act finally removing the provisions of the Test Act of 1673.
1868 Compulsory Church-Rates abolished.

1869 Church of Ireland disestablished.

1870 Education Act establishing School Boards.

1871 The Universities Tests Act threw open to Nonconformists lay academical degrees and lay offices.

1880 Burial Laws Amendment Act permitting burial in church-yards without Anglican rites.

1888 Oaths Act permitted persons elected to Parliament to be admitted by affirmation instead of by oath.

1889 Welsh Intermediate Education Act establishing High Schools under popular control.

1898 Nonconformist Marriage Act dispensing with the necessity for the presence of the Registrar.

University of London Act allowing the University to confer degrees in divinity.

1900 Burial Act making further reforms in cemetery law.

1914 Church in Wales—Disestablishment Act passed.

After forty years of educational work, in 1884, there were expectations that the objective of the Society would be reached : " on all sides there are indications that the close of the great struggle for religious equality is drawing near. It will not come immediately, but it is hardly possible that it should be much longer delayed. The enfranchisement of the borough house-holders in 1867, led at once to the disestablishment of the Church in Ireland ; and one of the earliest results of the extension of the suffrage in the counties is not unlikely to be the downfall of the existing establishments in Scotland, and in England and Wales ". What were the reasons in 1884 for what has proved to be such misplaced optimism ?

III.   THE GROUND OF NONCONFORMIST OPTIMISM IN 1884

The first explanation of this optimism was the widespread unpopularity of the Church of England. The cup of indignation was overflowing in the eighteen seventies and eighties. It was a time of huge public meetings when English political oratory was in its prime, and when the influence of the Non-conformist pulpit was at its zenith. Cobden, Bright and the Chartists had taught the multitudes who never went to school to do their own thinking. Throughout the country the Church was denounced for its Tory Alliance and its political reaction. The votes of the Bishops in the House of Lords were placarded and chalked on pavements for the populace to read. Further, radical politicians, inside and outside Parliament, not primarily on the ground of religious interests, but for the sake of political righteousness, were scathing in their criticism of the Church and the clergy. The modern reader will never understand the situation unless the facts are given and reference is made to contemporary speeches.

In 1873, John Morley asked his hearers and readers to study the verdict of history on the political offences of the Anglican Church. " Putting all the polemics of theology and ecclesiastical discipline aside, which of the two parties has done most for freedom and good government and equal laws in England ? Apart from the present issue,[1] is the political tradition of Nonconformity, or the political tradition of the State-Church, the wiser, the nobler, the more enlightened, the more beneficent ? Let History answer. Its voice is clear and beyond mistake. There is not a single crisis in the growth of English liberties in which the State-Church has not been the champion of retrogression and obstruction. Yes, there was one. In 1688, when her own purse and privilege were threatened, she did for a short space enlist under the flag which the Nonconformists had raised in older and harder days, and immediately after, when with their aid and on their principles the oppressor had been driven out, she reverted by a sure instinct to her own base principles of passive obedience and persecuting orthodoxy.

" Yet this is the brightest episode in her political history. In every other great crisis she has made herself the ally of tyranny, the organ of social oppression, the champion of intellectual bondage. In the sixteenth century, the bishops of the State-Church became the joyful instrument of Elizabeth's persecution, and in their courts the patriotic loyalty of the Puritan was rewarded with the pillory, the prison, the branding iron, the gallows. In the seventeenth century the State-Church made her cause one with the cause of the Star Chamber and the Court of High Commission, with prerogative and benevolences, with absolutism and Divine right. The Nonconformists shed their blood for law and ordered freedom. The Church, when she

[1] Morley's pamphlet, *The Struggle for National Education.*

returned to ' exalt her mitred front in Court and Parliament ',
retaliated on them for their services in the great cause which she
has always persecuted when she could, and always denounced
when she could not persecute, and bitterly suspected, when she
had been unable to persecute and ashamed to denounce, by urging
on the most vindictive legislation that defaced the English
statute-book even in those evil days of Restoration.   She
preached passive obedience with an industry that would have
been apostolic, if only its goal had been the elevation instead of
the debasement of human nature.   When that doctrine became
inconvenient, she put it aside for a while, but, as we have seen,
she speedily relapsed into the maxims of absolute non-resistance
when power and privilege once more seemed safe.   The Revolution was no sooner accomplished than the State clergy turned
Jacobite, deliberately repudiated the principles of the Revolution
which they had helped to make, and did their best to render the
Hanoverian succession impossible before it came to pass, and
unpopular after.   The evil thread of this monotonous tale has
been unbroken down to the last General Election.   That election turned upon the removal of an odious and futile badge of
ascendancy from the Irish nation.   The Dissenters were, to a
man, on one side, and the dignitaries of the Church, almost to a
man, on the other.   All this, it may be said, is an old story.   It
is so ; but if we are told that the present struggle for national
education is only a repetition of an old battle, it is worth while to
steady our judgment by reminding ourselves what that old battle
has been about.   The story may be trite, but the moral is not
yet out of date.

" Nobody pretends that the State-Church alone is answerable
for all the iniquities and follies of legislation and policy in which
she has taken a leading part during the three centuries of her
existence.   The majority of the nation must share the responsibilities of the laws of the Restoration, of such outbreaks as the
Sacheverell riots, of the war against freedom in America, and
the war against freedom in France.   The active leaders of the
State-Church had no monopoly of intolerance or coarseness, or
ferocity, or hatred of light.   No one asserts anything so extrava-
gant as this.   What is true, and a very important truth, is that
the State-Church has never resisted or moderated these coarse,
ferocious, intolerant, and obstructive political impulses in the

nation ; that, on the contrary, she has stimulated and encouraged them, and, where she could, has most unflinchingly turned them to her own profit. The clergy have not been the only enemies that freedom and light have had in our country ; but the enemies of freedom and light have always found the clergy eager to lend unction to their own bad causes, and dress up obscurantism and servility in preachers' phrases and Bible precedents. Nor, again, does anyone pretend that either high forms of spiritual life, or noble sons, have been wanting to the Anglican establishment. Human nature is a generous soil, even in the baleful climate of a State-Church. But it is her noblest sons, from Jeremy Taylor down to Maurice, who have ever found their Church the most cheerless of step-mothers. It is not they who have shared her power or shaped her policy, or exalted 'a mitred front in Court and Parliament'. They have ever been inside the Church what the Nonconformists have been outside. Alas ! they have been too few and too weak. Their names are rightly held in honour among men of all persuasions ; but they have been neither numerous enough nor powerful enough to turn aside the verdict of the impartial student that the political history of our episcopal establishments, alike in England, in Scotland, and in Ireland, has been one long and unvarying course of resolute enmity to justice, enlightenment, and freedom ".

The Times of 9th October, 1876, has its own unsparing indictment : " The ' Church of England ' was in favour of the alliance of continental absolutists against constitutional government : it was against the amelioration of the criminal code, and in favour of the principles of vengeance and prevention as against that of reformation ; it was in favour of hanging for almost any offence a man is now fined for at the assizes ; it was in favour of the slave trade, and afterwards of slavery ; it was against the repeal of the Test and Corporations Acts ; it was against Catholic emancipation ; it was against Parliamentary reform and municipal reform ; it was against the commutation of tithes, though it has since had to acknowledge the Act a great benefit ; it was against the repeal of the corn laws and navigation laws ; it was against free trade generally ; it was against all education beyond the simplest elements, and even religious instruction ; it was against public cemeteries and extramural interment ; it was against the division of parishes. Indeed it is hard to say what it has not been against in the way of improvement. In all these cases it was a worldly clerical oligarchy, combined for mutual advancement, and working for high preferment, that took the name of the Church, and lent the name of the Church of England to leaders of party. The Church of England all this time was helpless because misrepresented, duped, and betrayed by that which called itself the Church party ".

In confirmation of the unpopularity of the Church I append a catalogue of the Bishops' votes :

	BISHOPS' VOTES	
	For	*Against*
Bill to abolish capital punishment for stealing from shops property of the value of five shillings 1810 - - - - - -	0	7
Roman Catholic Disabilities Bill 1821 - -	2	25
,, ,, ,, ,, 1822 - -	1	23
,, ,, ,, ,, 1829 - -	10	19
(Ireland then on verge of civil war)		
Reform Bill 1831 - - - - - -	2	21
,, ,, 1832 - - - - - -	12	15
Jews' Disabilities Repeal Bill, 1833. The Archbishop of Canterbury, Dr. Howley, in moving the rejection of this Bill, urged that the " moral and intellectual capacity of the Jews was not such as to entitle them to any share in the Legislature ". - - - - - - -	3	20
Jews' Disabilities Repeal Bill 1858 when the Bill passed - - - - - - -	7	11
Admission of Dissenters to Universities 1834 -	2	22
University Tests Abolition Bill 1867 - -	2	4
,, ,, ,, ,, 1869 - -	0	3
Church Rate Abolition Bill 1858 - - -	0	24
,, ,, ,, ,, 1860 - - -	0	16
,, ,, ,, ,, 1867 - - -	0	7
Qualification for Offices Abolition Bill. This was the Bill to make it possible for all Englishmen to obtain civil employment without taking the sacrament at the Church of England. 1860	0	2
,, ,, ,, 1861	0	4
,, ,, ,, 1862	1	12
,, ,, ,, 1863	0	8
,, ,, ,, 1865	1	10

	Bishops' Votes	
	For	Against
Irish Church Bill 1869 - - - - -	1	13
Burials question. Lord Granville's motion to permit "Christian and orderly" services other than that of the Church of England in Church-yards 1876 - - - - - -	1	16
Similar motion 1877 - - - - - -	1	15
,, ,, later in session 1877 - - -	3	11
,, ,, ,, ,, 1877 - -	4	8
Burials Act 1880 - - - - - -	10	6
Marriage with Deceased Wife's Sister 1883 -	0	22
,, ,, ,, ,, ,, 1883 -	0	17

The House of Commons adopted the following resolution in March, 1641 : "The Legislative power of the Bishops in the House of Peers is a great hindrance to the discharge of their spiritual functions, prejudicial to the Commonwealth, and fit to be taken away by Bill " : a resolution supported by Cromwell, Hampden, Vane, Selden and Hyde. The resolution was enforced and the Bishops were expelled. Nearly two hundred and fifty years afterwards, on 21st March, 1884, the above identical resolution was moved in the House of Commons and was defeated by only eleven votes.

Lord Quickswood's judgment on the presence of the Bishops in the House of Lords in our own day is significant : as a loyal member of the Church of England his verdict impresses Free Churchmen and confirms their attitude. "I began my political life as an ardent defender of the Establishment; and I greatly valued the presence of the bishops in the House of Lords, and even (with the optimism of youth) hoped that their membership might be at some time extended to include all diocesan bishops. But now, though I could not in conscience support Disestablishment, because it would imply the withdrawal of a formal recognition by the State of the truth of Christianity, yet if it were forced upon us from outside, I should feel resignation and, perhaps, even rejoicing, for I should hope that it would make the leadership of the church more spiritual and less worldly; certainly I should be glad if the bishops could be withdrawn from the House of Lords. I remember saying to Sir Austen Chamberlain, who warmly welcomed the statement, that I thought the House of Lords did more harm to the bishops than the bishops did good to the House of Lords. Indeed, it is precisely the atmosphere of the House of Lords—an atmosphere of course to be found not only there, but in many places—that seems to me to have such a demoralising effect upon episcopal rule in the Church of England. It is an atmosphere of respectable good sense, full of the pagan virtues, but not full of those virtues and beliefs by which Christianity is sharply separated from pagan opinion. It is, in short, the atmosphere of the world—not of a very wicked world—but of a world that is not now, whatever it may have been centuries ago, predominantly Christian ".[1]

IV. THE GOLDEN AGE OF FREE CHURCH LEADERSHIP

The second ground for optimism that Disestablishment was near at hand in 1884 was the spiritual and political leadership of outstanding Free Church ministers and laymen—men whose names and work were known and honoured throughout the country. It was the golden age of Free Church preaching; of evangelical preaching related to political and social reform. Most large towns and cities had their Free Church leaders who quickened the forces of progress. It is impossible to do justice in a few paragraphs to men whose ministries were national or world-wide. I select, however, the ministry of R. W. Dale of Birmingham, as relevant to my purpose; it illustrates the genius—and in retrospect there is no other word to describe it— also the constructive quality of the Free Church ministry on the highest levels. Dale was saint and seer, evangelist and theologian, the crusading reformer, both municipal and national.

Dale (1829–95) was the minister of Carr's Lane Church, Birmingham, for forty years, his only pastorate; he was a man of strong convictions but also tender, kindly, and gracious. " For years ", said A. M. Fairbairn, " he was to me much more than a friend, for he acted more like an objectified and embodied conscience than a friend is wont to do. When one was tempted

[1] From *Church Quarterly*.

to say or do a mean thing, he was instinctively thought of, and his eyes always looked silent reproof into the soul. A friend in high academic position in the United States, who knew every British theologian, including the Bishops most distinguished for public and theological spirit, and who had entertained all who visited the University where he was settled—once said to me that he held Dale to be the foremost Englishman he knew, the man with the most statesmanship in him, whether of a civil, an ecclesiastical, or a theological kind. The American friend was not alone in his judgment; with him, all who really knew Dale, though not of his own, or, indeed, of any Christian communion, could not but agree . . . Dale was a faithful, yet not a credulous man; he was indeed, a born mystic, but strenuous as all our great mystics have been, ambitious to see the will of God perfectly obeyed on earth, in order to its more adequate realisation. He was a great democrat, though for reasons that concerned God rather than the demos. He thought that the Maker had fashioned man with a nature that needed freedom; to be free was to realise the good in him, whether as promise or as fulfilment. He was under no illusions; he did not think all men fit to be free; yet he thought that freedom was what each man needed for his perfecting and that he must achieve it, in order to become the best that he was capable of. But while a democrat he was no individualist, for he conceived man as essentially social, so made that he could only be his best when he lived in society, yet he was bound so to live there as not to allow society to dwarf or stunt him. The society for which man was made was the society that did most justice to his freedom, as also most justice to the nature it was charged to form, and be a home for. We can say, therefore, that what Dale loved was a freedom rooted in his conception of God, though realised in man; not, indeed, that he loved freedom for its own sake, or as an end in itself, but as the condition for the realisation of all the excellencies latent in men.

" Now, this ideal determined his idea of the Church. When he came to the front, the State had so extended the franchise as to make any tyranny of individuals impossible; and so he became the exponent at once of political and social ideals, first for his town, then for his community, and, finally, for the State and the people of England. We can, therefore, describe him as a great Free Churchman, the emphasis being double, both on " Free " and on " Church ". I have often heard him mourn sincerely that the High Church party had no idea of the Church ; and for this reason, that they had no idea either of freedom or of man, whether as outside or as inside society. The party may have striven to realise a traditional polity ; but it was as traditional rather than as ideal, a polity that had suited a time long past, but that could make no headway or progress in the society now present. What he termed " the fair ideal of the Church " was the Church conceived as " a Christian brotherhood ", or " a society of saints, illuminated by the Holy Ghost ", or " a community of men sharing the life and the power, and the glory of Christ, and having immediate access to the Father because of their union with the Eternal Son ". What he feared and disliked, in opposition to this ideal, was an institution in which the authority of the Church rulers made the ambition possible which devised instruments of tyranny, where the defence and maintenance of the Christian faith was entrusted to official hands, and where a human priesthood was the channel of Divine Grace. He disliked the idea which the Catholic Church represented, for this, if for no other reason, that it conflicted with his notion of God, on the one hand, and man, on the other. The God who had made man to be social made him also to be free. The freest society was the best ; and this freedom Dale thought could be better found in free communities which believed in freedom rather than in the authority of the officials who, making its laws and administering the laws they made, held a community in bondage ".[1]

Fairbairn knew Dale the man, and the books he had written : it is wiser to use such an illuminating description of Dale's character and controlling ideas from a learned contemporary, than to attempt any synthesis of my own from his biography and books. Dale's ideas of the freedom of the Church and the freedom of man have influenced me from my student days : that is, from the beginning of the twentieth century when I began to treasure his books. I have vivid memories still of my first visit to Birmingham when I went to the Art Gallery to see his statue. For I owe more to Dale than to any other Free Church thinker.

[1] From Fairbairn's review of Dale's *History of English Congregationalism* in *The Nation*, 2nd March, 1907.

Before discussing Dale's views on Church and State, it will be useful to recall the attitude of the Voluntarists and of the Congregational Union of England and Wales towards the State and education; it was Dale who convinced his brethren (and Free Churchmen) of a truer function of the State. The Church of England had used the State to uphold its privileges and to safeguard its exclusive claims to teach the nation its own principles; it had humiliated Nonconformists by manipulating Parliament in its own interests; but that such manœuvring should lead Congregationalists to adopt a negative policy towards the State was a departure from Christian principles. In the late eighteen sixties, Dale had reached a positive attitude to the State as an institution ordained of God; it was not something inherently evil, the incarnation of the world, the flesh and the devil; on the other hand, it was an institution which, under God, the Christian conscience should shape until it served the ends of political and social justice. In his sermon at West-bourne Park Chapel in April, 1893, Dale confessed that fifty years previously Evangelical Christians had regarded the State as no more than an instrument to suppress violence and fraud; that others had retained a belief in Hobbs' social contract theory of the State: "many of us, I suppose, owed our emancipation from that theory, partly to John Stuart Mill, whose authority was at its zenith in 1850; partly to Edmund Burke, who taught us that the State is a great historical growth, a partnership in all science, in all art, in every virtue, in all perfection. To Frederick Denison Maurice, probably more than to any other man, many of us owe the original impulse which started us on another line of thought. I think that I am not in error when I say that many Evangelical Nonconformists had come to have a vague impression—it was not inherited from their greatest ecclesiastical ancestors—that political activity lies beyond the true province of the Christian life. When I was a young man I believe that that impression was a very general one. Edward Miall had already done something to dissipate it, but it had not disappeared. The State, with all its affairs, was regarded by large numbers of Christian people as belonging in an evil sense to this world, and to be political was to be worldly. They went to the polling booth, many of them, no doubt; but they went as many Christian people now go to the theatre, feeling that they were hardly in their right place. Maurice insisted that the State was a Divine institution—like the Family, like the Church; many of us, I say, probably owe to him more than to any other man the original impulse which started our thought in that direction. But as soon as we began to look seriously into the New Testament we found it there, and we were astonished that we had not found it before. . . . It is our belief that the Church and State, though both of them are Divine institutions, are Divine institutions of such a different description, and with such different immediate objectives, that any organic alliance between them is certain in the long run to be injurious to both. The State is primarily the visible respresentative and defender of the Divine justice in the temporal order; the Church is primarily the visible representative of the Divine mercy and the Divine redemption in the eternal order. The State has other functions, the Church has other functions, but there is that deep distinction between them ".[1] Dale knew how Maurice, the Anglican thinker who was moved with compassion towards the Chartists in the " hungry forties " had condemned from his pulpit at Lincoln's Inn the social system which drove Ludlow and the atheistic leaders of the April revolt in 1848 to march on London ; knew how Maurice had stretched out friendly hands to Ludlow when they met ; that Kingsley and Maurice had sat late into the night drafting a poster for a placard in the streets the following morning assuring the working classes that " all men who have heads and hearts " sympathised with their wrongs, but urging the revolutionaries not to put their trust in the Charter alone to set things right. " The Almighty God and Jesus Christ, the poor man who died for poor men, will bring freedom to you, though all the Mammonites on earth were against you ".[2] " It is the first manifesto of the Church of England ", says Raven in his study of *Christian Socialism,* " her first public act of atonement for a half-century of apostasy, of class prejudice and political sychophancy. And as such . . . it may fairly be described as epoch-making ".

The Disestablishment issue began to assume lively political significance after Dale enunciated the positive doctrine of the State ; and particularly after the disillusionment of Free

[1] *Fellowship with Christ,* p. 200 ff.
[2] Higham, *F. D. Maurice,* p. 59 f. (S.C.M.)

Churchmen over the Education Act of 1870. Dale had joined the
Liberation Society about 1860 and had addressed its meetings ;
but after 1862 he became deeply involved in other work and somewhat critical of a few speakers who had not pleaded for Disestablishment from the highest motives. A large Free Church
Conference met in 1872 of which Dale was one of the secretaries.
When Miall wished the Conference to undertake a campaign in
the country against the alliance of Church and State, Dale was
reluctant to share in it for the above reason. He had his own
approach to this religio-political controversy ; finally an agreement was made between Dale and his friend Guiness Rogers
to conduct a campaign under their own management. During
the winter of 1875 and that of the following year, they addressed
immense audiences in the big towns and cities ; at several centres
they encountered opposition which had been worked up by
opponents, but which had the effect of stimulating public interest
in their visits. The success of their itinerary was obvious from
the enthusiasm created for Disestablishment.

The comprehensive and thorough treatment of the subject
by Dale produced a profound impression. With a consummate
mastery of his theme he lifted argument and persuasion to the
highest level. In a series of articles in 1863 and his speeches
of 1875 he advanced his lofty spiritual reasons for Disestablishment—and they are the most relevant reasons still, after the space
of eighty years. His aim was never to score off opponents,
neither to complain for himself and others, but to contend for
the freedom of God's grace and all that it meant for personal
redemption and the purity of the Church.

He examined the theory of Hooker and Burke, that to be
an Englishman was thereby to be a member of the Church of
Christ : a theory which " destroys Christian Churches, and
replaces them by nominally Christian nations ". " The Churches
founded by Apostles were societies constituted of persons who
by their free and voluntary act entered into religious fellowship
with each other ; a nation is a society constituted of persons who,
only by a fiction constructed for the sake of a theory, can be said
to have entered it, or to remain in it of their own free will. The
churches founded by Apostles were established for strictly
spiritual purposes ; a nation has a thousand inferior objects to
secure, and its entire organisation is constructed with a view to

these inferior ends. The churches founded by Apostles exercised no secular and political power in maintaining the authority of spiritual law; but a nation cannot divest its acts of a secular and political character. The churches founded by Apostles derived their pecuniary support from the voluntary liberality of their members; a nation must derive its revenues from the forced contributions of all its subjects.

" If in any society, membership ceases to be voluntary and becomes compulsory; if the original objects of the society are so extended and multiplied as to include very many which are essentially different from those for which it was first founded; if the sanctions on which its laws originally rested are changed for sanctions of a fundamentally different character; if its funds which were first derived from love, are now exacted by force—you have not modified the original institution; you have destroyed it altogether.

" Have we any right thus to annihilate the visible churches of Christ? Have we any right to constitute in their place and to call by their name a society composed not of voluntary adherents, but of all the members of a commonwealth; a society existing not merely to sustain the worship of God and to save the souls of men, but to protect the lives, the wealth and the secular greatness of a people; a society relying for its peace and for its safety, not on the reverence of its members for the august authority of the throne of Christ, but on the prison and the gallows, the truncheon of the policeman and the bayonet of the soldier; a society which dares not trust to the love of its members for the revenues it requires, but compels the contributions of the reluctant giver?

" By the change in the terms of membership you change the relations of individual members to each other and to the whole community; by the change in the objects of the society you change its entire constitution; by the change in the principles and sanctions of its government you change the whole genius and spirit of its public life; by the change in the source of its pecuniary strength you change an act of religious homage into a tax paid to a political power. Change the membership of a society, change its objects, change its government, and, though you may preserve its name, you have lost everything besides. . . . It does not follow that the authorities in whom political power is vested are fit to be entrusted with spiritual power also. The organisation of the State has been framed for other ends. Men rise to authority by other than spiritual gifts ; they may owe their advancement to their vices rather than their virtues. They may reach the summit of power without any faith in God, and without any apprehension of the laws which govern the right development of the spiritual life of a community ".[1]

Dale next examines the idea of the nation as a corporate personality, as set forth by Gladstone in his treatise *The State in its Relations with the Church* ; that it was the duty of the Government to establish the Church, to provide and maintain churches, that every individual might worship and be instructed. As the individual ought to confess and practise the Christian faith, so Gladstone said it was the duty of the nation to confess and practise it. Dale's analysis of Gladstone's thesis is a warning to us in a day when the State is doing too much thinking for the individual and relieving him from far too much personal responsibility : " There are some particulars in which a nation in the unity of its action and responsibilities resembles a person ; there are many other particulars in which it does not. A nation corresponds to a person in the unity of its acts, but not in the unity of its inward life. The acts of a nation are like the acts of an individual, but there the analogy ceases. In the same national act different individuals may concur under the control of opposite motives and at the impulse of opposite affections. One statesman may engage in a war to promote the cause of freedom ; another may engage in the same war to baffle the schemes of a political opponent ; another to vent his hatred against a foreign nation ; another because he may suppose that the kindling of military ardour among the people may destroy the mutual animosities and suspicions which may have arisen between different ranks and orders in the State, by inspiring all with the same passions, subjecting all to a common danger, and covering all with a common glory. The external act of a nation has a certain moral unity ; but even if all the people concur in the act, there are, I repeat, infinite diversities in the motives which impel them to it. And it is precisely where the outward act ceases that religious responsibility begins. It is not against a nation as such that we denounce the everlasting

[1] *Life of Dale*, p. 371 ff.

penalties of wrong-doing; and a nation as such cannot trust in Christ, and so obtain eternal life. A State, as distinguished from the individuals composing it, cannot repent of sin, cannot be renewed by the Holy Ghost, cannot hold communion with the Father, cannot be mystically united with Christ; but the capacity for all these things is essential to religious life and religious responsibility.

" I believe, indeed, in the possibility of a nation becoming Christian, as I believe in the possibility of railway companies becoming Christian. Let all ranks in the State discharge their secular duties under the influence of the spirit and law of Christ; let commerce, let social habits, let those mutual relations of the different classes of the community which civil legislators cannot regulate, all be moulded and penetrated by the principles of the Divine law enthroned in individual consciences, and the spirit of the Gospel diffused through individual hearts; let statesmen come from the sanctity of private communion with God to the great tasks of legislation and of diplomacy, and without any formal profession of a national faith the national acts will be harmonious with the will of God. Since a nation must act as an individual, those Christian men who conduct its affairs will endeavour to regulate national acts by Christian law; but since it cannot believe or worship as an individual, they will not require from it the profession of a faith which is the expression of individual conviction, or the observance of forms which are the expression of individual devoutness ".[1]

In his speeches Dale dismissed with contempt the social grievances, both for those who inflicted them and Nonconformists who allowed themselves to be offended: " It is very silly of Churchmen to plume themselves on their social superiority; it is very silly of Dissenters to care for it ". At the same time he denounced these social divisions in the nation as a serious evil. " The strength of a nation comes from the unity of the people; anything that tends to split it and to sever it is hurtful. As matters now stand, there are some who are conscious that they are privileged, others who are conscious that they are wronged; and the two parties are necessarily separated by the policy of the State. For the State takes sides in the conflict of churches. It has ceased indeed to sustain the

[1] ibid., p. 375 f.

Established Church by the methods of the past—by the in-fliction of pains and penalties on those who dissent from it. But though the method has been modified the policy remains. The State, as the late Bishop Wilberforce insisted, confers an exceptional authority on the Anglican Church as com-pared with other religious bodies and treats it as a favoured faith."[1]

" By the providence of God this much is certain, and must be admitted by everyone, that the Church of England, as treated at present by the State and the nation, is the religious teacher of the people. Mark you that this is so. There has been given, and I think very properly given, perfect liberty to all other religious bodies—and I for one would not see that liberty infringed upon by prerogative or other legislation in the least degree. But that is not in the least degree giving up the claim that the Church of England is the teacher of the people. It is saying : We provide what we believe to be the properly constituted system of teaching, but if others think differently, we do not enforce upon their con-sciences that which they condemn, but leave them to provide another for themselves if their conscience dictate to them to do so ".[2]

This quotation represents with exceptional accuracy the policy against which Dale contended. " The Church of England claims to be ' the teacher of the English people '. The Con-stitution treats it as such. Its bishops sit by right in the legis-lature ; its clergy represent the State in the ceremony of marriage. Their other privileges, arising by prescription out of this position of authority, though curtailed of late, are still considerable. Although the people are openly divided in religious opinion, the State, the country through, takes sides with one community against the rest, and clothes its ministers with the moral authority derived from the special sanction of law. It meets the Unitarian with its doctrine of the Trinity ; the Baptist with its theory of baptismal regeneration ; the Presbyterian with its system of Episcopacy. Against each and all it asserts its claim to be the only authoritative teacher recognised by the State in matters of religious belief. The authority of the State is so exerted as

[1] ibid., p. 380.
[2] Quotation from *Wilberforce*, p. 380.

to obstruct and discourage the free growth of religious conviction ".[1]

In his speech at Liverpool Dale dealt with the static forms of doctrine and worship which are inevitable when they are embodied in Acts of Parliament. For the State to bind the Church to certain doctrinal expressions or to verbal limitations in prayer and the conduct of the Communion Service, is a repetitive verbal bondage which is not conducive to progressive thought and life. " Let us see how the perpetuating of certain theological definitions by Act of Parliament has affected the theological life and thought of the English Church. You all remember what an outburst of indignation there was forty years ago, when John Henry Newman wrote Tract Ninety in order to prove that the articles of the Church of England did not condemn certain doctrines which nearly every one before had supposed that they did condemn. I am not going to say whether I think that Dr. Newman's ingenuity was legitimate or not, but it seems to me that if the articles really do not express the faith which nine Englishmen out of ten have supposed they do express, it is time so to change the articles as to make them express that faith. You remember, too, how, again and again, the Evangelical party in the Church of England has been charged with disloyalty because it has not accepted the High Church theory concerning baptismal regeneration. If the Church were free to discuss these questions in a convocation in which its clergy and laity were fairly represented, and if Parliament had nothing to do either with its articles or its offices, theologians, instead of having to resort to a thousand ingenious devices which are alien to the habits of Englishmen in order to show that their opinions are in harmony with the authentic documents of the Church, would simply endeavour to convince the mind of the Church of the truth of their opinions, and the Church would be able to define afresh in what sense it held the articles and what meaning it attached to the offices. You all know perfectly well that there is not the slighest chance of Parliament discussing the question of baptismal regeneration in order to readjust, if necessary, the baptismal office. There is not the slightest possibility of Parliament investigating Ritualist doctrines in order to readjust, if necessary, the Thirty-Nine Articles. The articles

[1] p. 381.

and offices are bound upon the Church by the Act of Uniformity, and there can be no possible revision of either until the affairs of the Church are administered by Parliament no longer, but by a free assembly representing the faith and the piety of the English Church. No matter what changes may pass upon the faith and the religious life of the adherents of the English Church, they can make no change in the articles or in the prayers in which that faith and life ought to receive a perfect expression, and the reason of this is that the articles and prayers are in the schedule of an Act of Parliament ".[1]

" The system leaves no liberty to the working of the Spirit ; it perpetuates that which should be temporary, and fetters that which should be left free. The same evil—obstruction of the natural course of development and the play of activity—makes itself felt in other ways also, less hurtful, perhaps, to the religious life of the Church, but not less real ". These words, uttered in 1875, express the yearnings of our hearts to-day. We desire freedom and self-government for the Anglican Church. Our motive is the same as Dale's—that the Church of Christ cannot fulfil the purpose of God amongst us while in bondage to the State. We magnify the Divine motive that the Church, united and free, should be set for the conversion of England. There are problems which will try the patience of political and ecclesiastical statesmanship, but they can be grasped and solved to the permanent good of the British nation.

The Act for the Disestablishment of the Church in Wales was passed in 1914. The evidence before the Commission, given by Mr. Frank Morgan, secretary of the Governing Body of the Church in Wales was most reassuring of the spiritual and financial results : " There can be little doubt that since 1920 the corporate life of the Church in Wales is more fully realised and that its members do feel a real responsibility for its welfare and influence. The effect of the Disestablishment campaign which had been going on for twenty years was to educate our people a great deal and to improve the corporate life of the Church. It brought us together and taught us much of the history and principles of the Church. It created a feeling of interest in the Church. This is illustrated by the attendance at the meetings of the Governing Body, which is always very good,

[1] *Life of Dale*, p. 382 f.

and by the attendances at Vestry Meetings, which have improved very much since Disestablishment ".[1]

Question : Do the laity contribute a great deal more than before to the finances of the Church both in parish and diocese?

Answer : The laity undoubtedly contribute more than prior to 1920 to the finances of both parish and diocese. The appended figures illustrate this.

TOTAL VOLUNTARY CONTRIBUTIONS RAISED IN THE PARISHES.

	1906 £	1923 £	1930 £
St. Asaph - - - -	52,876	65,339	85,389
Bangor - - - - -	44,257	38,567	48,049
St. David's - - - -	93,195	114,806	75,178
Llandaff - - - - -	108,653	103,426	109,578
Monmouth - - - -	—	54,314	52,746
Swansea and Brecon - -	—	—	64,809
	£298,981	£376,452	£435,749

The year 1906 is taken because the figures for that year were official, given before the original Welsh Church Commission. The figures for 1930 are from the Year Book returns checked in the Representative Body Office.

V.   THE PRAYER BOOK CONTROVERSY—THE PLAN TO AVOID THE VETO OF PARLIAMENT

In 1884 it was thought by responsible Free Churchmen that Disestablishment could not be long delayed. We have referred to the unpopularity of the Church, and the rise of Nonconformist leaders who quickened the expectation of their own people and many others, that Disestablishment in England must soon follow that of the Irish Church in 1869 ; but the political scene was also set for other objectives than Disestablishment. After Glad-

[1] Commissioner's Report on Church and State, 1935 ; evidence, and answers by Mr. Morgan.

stone's return to power in 1885 and his " determination to force
Home Rule to the front ", the Liberal party was split. Any
hope of a Disestablishment Bill was shattered by this tragic
event. Further, the forces of progress were so disrupted that
the radical programme of social reform was also foiled—until
the Liberals returned to power with the huge majority of 1906.
Strange to say, the majority of Nonconformists agreed with
Gladstone, who would almost certainly have resisted Disestablishment and would not have welcomed too much radical reform ;
yet it is not so strange if we remember that Free Churchmen
have always trusted men of moral and political integrity, and
have turned away only when they found their idol had feet of
clay. It has been one of the inexplicable accidents of English
history during the last sixty years that the Liberal Party has
come to blows with itself to the incalculable loss of the nation.
Dale used all his powers of persuasion and mediation—his
correspondence with Gladstone and Morley confirm this—to
prevent the split of the party in Birmingham, and after it occurred
he refused to be identified with either the Liberal Party or the
Liberal-Unionists ; he gave himself with characteristic devotion
to his spirital work. The political hostility between Anglicans
and Free Churchmen continued over the Education Bills of
1902 and 1906 ; but during the 1914–18 war relations improved
until there is now more kindliness and willingness than ever
before to co-operate in the service of the nation. To refer again
to Manning's evidence before the Commission on Church and
State in 1935 : if Free Churchmen " are increasingly unwilling
to fight for ecclesiastical rights, to the scandal of unbelievers ",
it does not mean that Disestablishment has disappeared beyond
the horizon of religious controversy ; it means the ground has
shifted from political conflict to controversy within the Anglican
Church itself ; it means, further, that we hope the Church will
seek Disestablishment to fulfil more effectively its divine ends.

To indicate how Anglicans and Free Churchmen view the
contemporary situation, I turn to the two Commissions which
have presented Reports during the present century—the Royal
Commission of 1904–6 " to inquire into the alleged prevalence
of breaches or neglect of the Law relating to the conduct of
Divine Service in the Church of England and to the ornaments
and fittings of Churches " ; also the Commission on Church

and State which reported in 1935. A brief review of the Anglican and Free Church standpoints will intimate the facts which have created theological and ecclesiastical unrest and raised the issue of Disestablishment in its present form.

It is a painful matter that the trouble centred, and centres still, in the Lord's Supper. The Prayer Book of 1662 forbids the Roman Catholic belief in, and practice of, the reservation and adoration of the Sacramental bread and wine. Such practices, however, had become sufficiently common that the Bishops met at Lambeth in 1898 and issued their declaration : " All reservation of the Holy Sacrament is distinctly forbidden by the Prayer Book ; it must therefore be wholly discontinued ". The answer to the Bishops was a meeting in January, 1899, at Holborn Town Hall, when two hundred and twenty clergy resolved that : " The right to such reservation and ceremonial use of incense cannot and must not be abandoned ", a clear defiance of the authority of the Bishops. Moreover, in pamphlets and manuals such priests were teaching the worship of the Virgin Mary, Transsubstantiation, Purgatory, the Mass and Invocation of Saints.

" O God, who by the resurrection of Thy Son our Lord Jesus Christ, didst vouchsafe to give joy to the world ; grant we beseech Thee, that by His Mother, the Virgin Mary, we may obtain the joys of everlasting life ; through the same Christ our Lord. Amen ".

It would seem from evidence before the Commission in 1904 that there were about fifty churches where these prayers and practices existed. At the Church Assembly in February, 1928, the Archbishop announced that Reservation was practised in about seven hundred churches. After the defiance in 1899 of the Pastoral Letter of the Bishops, it was obvious that something should be done, and on November 4th, 1902, the Bishop of London requested the Rev. H. M. M. Evans, Vicar of St. Michael, Shoreditch, to cease the use of the Rosary, of Invocation of Saints, of prayers to the Virgin Mary, and of Benediction with the reserved sacrament : unless he ceased the Bishop said he would prosecute him under the Church Discipline Regulation Act of 1840. Mr. Evans at first refused the Bishop's request ; later he resigned and joined the Church of Rome. His successor, however, continued the practices ; the Mass and the corresponding ritual of changing vestments, incense, lights, sacring bell, genuflections and the elevation of a wafer with the words "Behold the Lamb of God that taketh away the sin of the world".

Mr. Evans wrote a pamphlet, *Why I Left St. Michael's,* an extraordinary account of the methods of training men for the priesthood. When he was ordained and instituted at St. Michael's, he assented to the Thirty-Nine Articles "without any serious misgivings as to the rightfulness of my action ". He had read Newman, and Bishop Forbes' book on the Articles and implicitly trusted the views of these writers. "I did not make any serious study of the matter at first-hand myself, but pinned my faith to Bishop Forbes and to other teachers . . . I believe I was only doing what ninety-nine out of every hundred of the High Church clergy of the Church of England have done before me. Not one in a hundred has ever taken the trouble to look into the question in any serious way in the original authorities ". When Mr. Evans began to examine the dogmas which he had accepted on the authority of others, and had regarded as impregnable, he found they were "a mere *ex-parte* statement ". The particular aspect of this confession, which at once impresses a Free Churchman, is the nature of the *ad hoc* training of the priesthood ; as though Biblical Languages and Theology, and the foundation truths of the Gospel, and the New Testament idea of the Church, were unnecessary or secondary to the training to repeat the Liturgy and conduct Divine worship decently and in order.

But the High Church clergy were in no mood to submit to the Pastoral Letter of the Bishops ; they grew, until in 1922 three thousand, seven hundred and fifteen, through the English Church Union, handed a Declaration of Faith to the Patriarch of Constantinople ; it affirmed Apostolic succession, ordination as a Sacrament, the sacrificial character of the Eucharist "which may be offered both for the living and the dead ", Absolution, the Transubstantiation of the bread and wine in the Eucharist, by Consecration, into the Body and Blood of Christ, worship of the virgin. "We account the Thirty-Nine Articles of Religion as a document of secondary importance concerned with local controversies in the sixteenth century ".[1] This was the answer to the "Appeal to all Christian People " sent out by the Lambeth Conference in 1920.

[1] Schaefer, *The Catholic Regeneration of the Church of England,* p. 189.

Here was lawlessness indeed ! I know how sincerity may be driven to revolt against law ; but here were " the ten specific illegalities " which the Commission of 1904 said should be promptly made to cease ; now it was the year 1922, and over three thousand priests believing, and ready to practise, more than the ten illegalities. The Convocations had commenced revision of the Prayer-Book in 1907 but the war of 1914–18 delayed procedure : not until 1927 was the Revised Book presented to Parliament. In the House of Lords it was accepted by 241 votes to 88 ; in the House of Commons on the following day it was rejected by 238 votes to 205. It was presented a second time to Parliament in 1928 and rejected by the House of Commons by 266 votes to 220.

The clash between Parliament and the Church Assembly which had approved the Revised Book was serious ; legal authority rested with Parliament and rejection of the Revised Book should have led to its disuse in divine worship ; but after 1928 the Bishops took the responsibility of condoning the use of the Revised Book ; and that is the accepted situation at the present time. In 1898 the Bishops said certain illegalities should cease : in 1928 they give moral sanction to these illegalities. As the Bishops could not, or would not, stop the illegalities, a measure was submitted to Parliament in the hope that such illegalities would be made legal. When Parliament refused to do this, the Bishops defied Parliament and gave permission to the clergy to use the illegal book. Hence the appointment of the Commission on the relations of Church and State which reported in 1935.

The evidence of the Church Association before this Commission has relevance to matters which have been mentioned, that while revision of the Prayer-Book " dragged along " for twenty years some of its most objectionable features were not considered, or were rejected ; that the attempt " to bear down opposition to the revised book by weight of the mere names of the Bishops failed because it deserved to fail " : that the Bishops were not sufficiently informed " on the matters under discussion to be able to express an opinion to carry weight with students " ; nor had they " special and accurate knowledge of the subjects under discussion ".

The evidence of the change in the Episcopate indicates how

High Churchmen had been appointed Bishops by Prime Ministers " acting under high ecclesiastical advice. Unfortunately the result has been to saddle the Church of England with a majority of Bishops who are quite openly out of sympathy with the traditional Anglican standards of doctrine and worship ". Out of forty-three diocesan bishops in 1927, thirty-two had been appointed since 1919 and thirty of these were supporters of the policy of the revisers of the Prayer-Book. " As time went on it became more and more evident to increasing numbers that the proposed revision of the Prayer-Book was affecting vital issues of doctrine. We repeat our protest against change of doctrine without so much as an attempt to appeal to the Word of God in justification ".[1]

Was the House of Commons justified in rejecting the revised book ? Considerable resentment was expressed because Free Churchmen, and Scottish and Welsh members, had voted for the rejection of the book which concerned the Church of England. As Manning points out, the Church of England has accepted many privileges and advantages from Parliament, a body which is not a part of the Church of Christ, but as soon as Parliament refused to legalise what it regarded as Roman Catholic doctrine, there is an outcry against " interference ". Archbishop David-son rebuked this resentment against the House of Commons : " we hear words, which I think windy and even foolish, to the effect that this is not really a matter for Parliament, that the Church has spoken its own voice decidedly and that the duty of Parliament is to endorse what the Church has said. I dissent altogether from that view and dissociate myself from those statements ".[2] As the way out of all the complications raised by these matters Dr. Garbett asks for the self-government of the Church of England.

The Commission invited three representative Free Churchmen to submit their evidence. Carnegie Simpson wished to know the limits of the freedom of self-government. A limit there must be for the Church of England to remain the National Church : " it may pretty confidently be said that the British Parliament and the British people have not the smallest intention of granting

[1] Report of Commission, vol. II, p. 59.
[2] p. 55.

to the National Church of England an unrestricted freedom under which—to take two extreme but not inconceivable instances—on the one hand, the essential Christian faith could be eliminated, or on the other hand, the Roman Missal could be substituted for the Prayer-Book and the Tridentine Decrees for the Thirty-Nine Articles ". Again, Parliament at present safeguards the rights of the laity of the Church and the nation. If the veto of Parliament goes, what will be the measure of freedom guaranteed to the laity? Is the self-government for which Dr. Garbett pleads to be freedom for the ecclesiastical rulers? " Spiritual freedom is not a clerical privilege but is a birthright of Christ's Church . . . the Church's freedom is compatible with and indeed includes the fullest recognition of the place of the laity, as well as the clergy ". There are those who fear that increased liberty for self-government " will mean increased liberty for tendencies in the Church which they distrust and resist ". Concerning disestablishment and disendowment a great deal of over-tragic language is used. " The case of Wales shows the exaggeration of much of it. In 1843 a great part of the Church of Scotland disestablished and disendowed itself with unquestionable gain to the religious life of the country ". If Disestablishment came in England it would be a challenge to faith, courage and liberality ; only if the Church refused the challenge would Disestablishment " be a blow to religion and an injury to the country ".

Dr. M. E. Aubrey assured the Commission of the goodwill of Free Churchmen towards the Church of England : " we have no desire to see her humiliated or hindered in the performance of her spiritual functions, but rather we wish that with her history and her treasures of experience and human material she would give that spiritual leadership in our country which her prestige and numerical strength ought to make possible. . . . For these reasons, as it seems to me, it would not be possible to stir up at the present time a vigorous Nonconformist campaign for Disestablishment and Disendowment unless it were precipitated by pressure on the part of the Church of England along the lines of the proposed campaign of the Church Self-Government League, to seek freedom from State control without Disestablishment. That would be a challenge which the Free Churches could not but accept ".

Dr. Aubrey said that the Establishment is an insuperable barrier to Christian Unity, for the Free Churches have not weakened in the conviction that State establishment of a Church is wrong. The question has been raised regarding the " good taste " of Free Churchmen in Parliament speaking and voting against the Revised Prayer Book. The answer is " that they had a very special and sacred duty to represent the views of that section of the nation to which religiously they belong, because the character of the National Church was involved ".

" Free Churchmen hope that Disestablishment will come about not by an agitation outside the borders of the Church of England, but as a fine act of renunciation on the Church's part, mainly for the sake of spiritual freedom, but also (as we should like to think) because to a great Christian community it might appear unjust and unfair to claim a first place and privilege to the exclusion of other parts of Christ's Body ". Voluntary Disestablishment would not diminish but increase the moral authority of the Church. Compulsory Disestablishment would be a defeat. Nor would Disestablishment mean any necessary loss of the national recognition of religion.[1]

Bernard Lord Manning argued that the Puritans " had the misfortune to be defeated politically " but ecclesiastically had every right to the privileges and even endowments which had been appropriated by the Church of England ; that Establishment affected the Crown rights of Christ within His Church, and that this is the most important aspect of the matter from the Free Church point of view. His evidence of the effect of social, or financial privilege, or a policy of persecution on the part of the State-Churches towards the non-Christian section of the population, has overwhelming historical confirmation. The tragedy is that State Churches have been too blind to see it until it has been too late ! " In so far as any section of society is non-Christian or anti-Christian, an Established Church gives to some citizens reason for a sense of injustice. If the section outside the Established Church is small, the sense of injustice may be negligible. But if the sense of injustice caused by an Established Church is not negligible, there is accumulating (it may be very slowly and silently) a store of ill-will and a desire for revenge. What this ill-will and desire can mean we have seen in the

[1] p. 279.

infamous treatment of the Church in Russia and Mexico, and doubtless we shall soon see the same infamous treatment in Spain. From our own experience of political and educational and social repression we Free Churchmen know how bitter and how lamentable this sense of injustice can be, how it can poison the springs of life, even in their own life. We dread, therefore, very greatly the effects of this sense of injustice in those who hate the Church and Faith and make no effort to rid themselves of the worse effects of their own passion. We fear an Established Church in a modern State for this reason. We think that it is asking very much of our non-Christian and anti-Christian population to have any sort of Established Church. . . . Free Churchmen consider anti-clericalism one of the most hideous phenomena of modern life, and take no small credit to themselves for the comparative immunity of England from it ".

" I have said little about disendowment. The better instructed among us, since we were admitted to the universities and have had a chance to learn better, do not base our notions on myths about the State presenting tithes to the Church. But our view of old endowments is the same as our view of old buildings. They were given for the whole Church of Christ in this kingdom. We agree with the Anglicans that the Roman claim to these things is ludicrous ; we agree in dismissing the Roman claim to exclusive continuity with the medieval and ancient Church as historical humbug. But, with respect, we deem your exclusive claim (or your claim if it admits the Romans only to share with it) equally ludicrous ; and for the same reasons. Nothing is further from our minds than a wrangle about money if ever a day of reckoning comes. You will find that whatever we think of justice we think more of generosity ; and since the stronger party has shown little disposition to be generous, we shall usurp that privilege for ourselves. About the treatment of ancient buildings by bishops and the Ecclesiastical Commission those of us who have had intimate dealings feel far less satisfied. The case of the Lincoln churches is at the moment much in the mind of a Lincolnshire man like myself.

" If the Commission asks me, Do you personally wish to see the Episcopal Church disestablished ? I can only answer ' I do not know ', though I know that most Free Churchmen would not hesitate for a moment ". Manning hesitated on the ground that disestablishment might mean an interval of unrestrained episcopal government. Such a result he feared. He thought, at present, " that Parliament was a check on episcopal government ".

This chapter makes it clear that the religious situation in England is serious to Anglicans and Free Churchmen alike. The tension in the Church of England does not contribute to the conversion of England : the Church cannot continue to drift and Dr. Garbett's urgent plea for self-government is an attempt to grasp and control the situation. But Anglicans are divided : a large and powerful section looks Romewards regarding faith and order. Recently Dr. Fisher requested a statement by Anglo-Catholics which would help him in his conferences with Free Churchmen on inter-Communion. In response, several writers have expressed their own views and offered criticism of other views, in a booklet, *Catholicity*. I quote their tribute to the religious and political services of the Papacy : " If such an institution as the ' Universal Church ' is to exist as more than a sentiment and an ideal—as a concrete substantial reality within human history in our highly organised modern society—then some such central institution would seem to be more than just a convenience. It is at least a pragmatic necessity, as is shown by the obvious temptation of the modern ' œcumenical movement ' to try to provide a substitute for it. To cast away so lightly an institution with such deep roots in Christian history, and with such universal claims on European gratitude and veneration, was to prove oneself blind to the profounder realities of what is meant by the ' universal Church'. Further, above all, it (the Papacy) has never wavered in its adherence to the central Christian truths", and " it is at once the strongest single bulwark of the historic tradition of Christian civilisation in Europe ". These words make the direction of Anglo-Catholic vision clear enough. To lead England Romewards in faith and worship and ethics, this large group would welcome Disestablishment but fears disendowment. On the other hand, the strong Evangelical and Protestant group in the Church of England desires to retain the Establishment as a check on Anglo-Catholic propaganda and progress.

Against this drift of Anglicanism, Free Churchmen hold firmly the conviction that the only authority or control in and over the

Church, derives from Christ Himself; that Christ's authority extends over the whole membership of the Church; that priestly rule and State control subvert the Crown Rights of the Redeemer. For over three centuries Free Churchmen have contended for these great principles which are rooted in the New Testament. Their victory constitutes their claim on all men who believe the New Testament as the revealed will of God in Christ; it is no less their claim upon all who value religious freedom, as the source of all other freedoms.

CHAPTER XVIII

ACTIVISM AND ECONOMICS

I

THE tendencies of the Protestant spirit came to fulfilment in the Nonconformist conception and use of freedom; in ideas and initiative which magnified the New Testament doctrine of God as free and active : " My Father worketh hitherto and I work ", said Jesus. The Free Churchman believed in the mighty works of God : he rejected the idea of the passivity of God, also the submissiveness of man to an ecclesiastical institution and priesthood : he thought of the Christian life in the terms of intellectual and spiritual effort; it was a good fight; it was activity; it was " good works ", not to accumulate merit, but as a man's reasonable service to His Redeemer. And when he had put forth his utmost exertions he knew he was an unprofitable servant. This use of freedom found its expression in Christian vitalism and activism. Worship was no longer a formal repetition of creeds, nor a routine attendance at the Sacrament. To the Free Churchman worship was praise and adoration, but through the preaching of the Word it was also a means of grace and education, bringing new insights into the character of God and His redeeming purpose. Worship, public and private, quickened the conscience and prompted responsibility and activity in Christian service. The Lord's Supper was worship, an experience of communion with Christ which was creative of Christian ethical values. This spiritual vitalism was a return to the New Testament experience of the Holy Spirit indwelling the believer and moving his will; an experience in startling contrast to the medieval idea of the Christian life as submissive and passive.

When the utmost has been written in praise of asceticism and monasticism, the fact remains that they were a misrepresentation of New Testament Christianity. They were based on the Greek idea of God as a purely Contemplative Being ; a God who was " The Alone ", unapproachable and passive. " None of the poets ", said Aristotle, " has represented Zeus as Himself singing or striking the lyre " ; he meant that God was inactive, neither exerting His will nor striving towards a goal. Any reference to the Will of God was bad philosophy and psychology. He was pure Intelligence and eternally contemplative. It was from such teaching, not from the New Testament, that asceticism and monasticism took their rise. And as the contemplative life of God excluded all emotion and moral activity, it followed that the contemplative life of the cloister and the cell was the highest virtue for the man who desired to save his own soul. One effect of such flight into the cloister was that the Church was robbed of many of her finest and choicest spirits. It was a serious loss when the monasteries drained the Church of the flower of her membership and the moral energy of her idealists. We must distinguish ascetics and monks, who were laymen, from the priesthood. The former withdrew from the church, as they withdrew from the world : they made no attempt to reform the Church ; they left it to save their own souls.

When the idea of God as Pure Intelligence was wedded to the Oriental-Greek theory of the human body as incurably evil, the lure of asceticism and monasticism became irresistible to many laymen whose aim was to win merit in the sight of God. Believing the body was evil, and must at all costs be crucified, the most incredible methods and instruments of self-torture were devised. The anchorite and the hermit vied with each other in the mutilation of the body and the starvation of the natural instincts. The sex instinct was always the great obsession. Renunciation and repression were also the methods of the monastic communities. The vows of chastity, poverty, and obedience, a violation of human instincts, exacted a dreadful revenge on many who entered the monasteries. When the monk had fled from the Church and the world he found he was unable to flee from himself. The tortures of repressing the sex instinct prompted volumes of nauseating introspection. While sex repression and the rule of poverty obsessed the monk, other passions grew and corrupted community life. I am not unmindful of the contributions to learning ; it is impossible to do other than appreciate Pachomius and his Rule, or Basil's care for the sick and aged. Benedict understood human nature and saw that lazy asceticism was no safeguard against the flesh and the devil. But the rise and fall, the reforms and the reactions of the monastic orders, are a dreary repetition of corruption, immorality. luxury and decay.

Monasticism was harmful in that it set up a double standard of the Christian life—one for the monk and the other for the ordinary member of the Church. The attainment of the perfect Christian life was only possible in the cloister and the cell. The common people were taught that their Christian devotion was less meritorious in the sight of God. The marriage relationship, the life of the family, the daily worker in the shop and the field, the merchant in the market-place, were spiritually inferior to the monk. This double standard of morality had disastrous effects from the second century to the period of the Reformation : and it still prevails. That the celibate state is higher than the married state is still taught by the Roman Church and believed by the people. But the verdict of history on this matter is decisive. With rare exceptions, men do not win their moral victories by repression of their instincts, but only as they sublimate and consecrate their instinctive urges to the highest spiritual ends : and they do this as the love of Christ sanctifies the marriage relation, creates the Christian home, and moralises social institutions.

II. LEFT-WING PROTESTANTISM

Through reading the New Testament, Luther was led out of his cell into the experience of forgiveness and freedom by faith in Christ ; he knew then the futility of his efforts to save his own soul, knew also how false was the claim of the superiority of the monk over humble Christian peasants. Luther restored the layman to his rights in the Church and affirmed the priesthood of all believers. But when these laymen began to apply the principle of religious freedom to political and economic problems, Luther was resolute in his opposition. Passivity and submissiveness to rulers was the advice he offered. A confession of such passivity was made by Niemoller in April, 1946, when he was rebuking the tendency of the Germans to shift the blame for Nazi crimes, until the only men responsible seemed to be Hitler and Himmler : "I used to think I was free from blame, but I no longer think so. If the fourteen thousand Protestant pastors had, from 1933 onwards, condemned from the pulpit the Nazi régime there might have been fourteen thousand additional martyrs, but later events might have been avoided ". He added that about thirty-five million people had been killed or suffered wounds since the rise of Nazism in 1933. This passivity of the Lutheran Church to the rule of Kaisers and dictators has had tragic results in our own day.

John Calvin was never a monk. He had lived in cities, had studied at universities and knew the ways of the common people. Rejecting the submissiveness of medieval Christianity, the chief end of man, according to Calvin, was to consecrate his active will in the service of his Master. Calvin reformed theology and ethical ideals by compelling men to think of their personal responsibility in the light of the majesty and sovereignty of God. Under the profound conviction of God's personal demands upon their time and labour, the followers of Calvin conceived their duty in the terms of activity and exertion ; a call to establish righteousness in the earth and to overthrow the strongholds of wickedness. This theology which gave men steady and iron nerve, this relentless logic of the divine sovereignty, led Carlyle to say that Calvinism had created all the heroes. Even so, both Luther and Calvin retained medieval ideas which arrested the ecclesiastical, political and economic aspects of the Reformation. The Anabaptists and the peasants were far more radical in these matters, but these left-wing groups of the Reformation were maligned and misrepresented by the great Reformers themselves ; only in recent years have their ideas, their martyrdoms and numbers received anything like justice.

The sixteenth-century struggle between the right and left wings of Protestantism was a portent of what occurred in England during the next three centuries. I must survey the battle-ground, if only to arrive at a sound historical judgment concerning Max Weber's charges that most of the tragedies of the modern world derive from the evils of the Industrial Revolution in England ; and the further accusation that the Industrial Revolution owes its rise to the Protestant Ethic and Spirit of Capitalism.

It is curious that English Baptists should have been so reluctant to do justice to the ideas of the Anabaptist radicals of the sixteenth century, the explanation being a lack of interest and appreciation of the political and economic aspects of the Anabaptist movement. It is justly claimed by the Master of Balliol that they were the pioneers of modern democracy.[1] The madness of the Münster fanatics had repelled Baptist as well as other Church historians. It is also admitted that there is no historical link showing that modern Baptists emerged from Anabaptist communities. A few Anabaptists in England were put to death under the Tudors; but as Baptists were often classified as Anabaptists—as late as the Civil War Baxter frequently made this mistake—it may be that a few Baptists were put to death under Henry VIII and Elizabeth because of the crazy men of Münster. The word means one who was baptized as a child, and later re-baptized as a believer; it is this emphasis of believing in Christ as Lord and Saviour which must receive consideration. In an age when infant baptism was the accepted tradition of the medieval Church, also of the reformers, it was revolutionary theology and practice, to declare that belief in Christ and confession of such belief in baptism, was the teaching of the New Testament; when it was insisted that such baptized believers alone constituted the membership of the Church, provocation was more acute. Such doctrine implied a new quality in the individualism taught by the Reformers; it emphasised the new birth from above, that Christian experience began in a personal relationship with God through faith in Christ, and that such faith gave a new ethical dynamic to individual responsibility. Herein lies the explanation of the radical political and economic programme of the Anabaptists. Unfortunately the clash with the Reformers came over the nature of the Church and its relation to the State. The Anabaptists said the Church was a community of believers, regenerated by the Holy Spirit and entered by personal confession of faith and baptism. For the Reformers the Church included the regenerate and the unregenerate in one visible communion. This gulf between the right and left wings of Protestantism was not only unbridgable, it became wider. At first Luther reasoned the matter, but later talked reason out of court. In 1527 he was tolerant and

[1] cf., *The Churches and Democracy*, p. 24.

regretted the persecution of the Anabaptists : "it is not right, and it fills me with pity that such wretched people are so murdered, miserably burned, and cruelly done to death. Everyone ought to be allowed to believe what he will. If his belief is wrong, he will suffer punishment enough in the eternal fires of hell. Why will men persist in martyring such people in this life as long as they err only in matters of faith and do not, in addition, preach rebellion or otherwise resist the civil power ? With the Scriptures, the Word of God alone, we should oppose and resist the erring. With fire we can affect little ".[1] By 1532 he accuses the Anabaptists of being "sneaks and hedge-preachers"; they went into the fields and the forests as well as the cities, and their numbers vastly increased; they became so numerous as to rival the Lutheran Church in Germany :[2] "If they were God's messengers they would first of all consult and prove their credentials to the pastors, to whom is committed the office of preaching the Word and administering the sacraments, instead of prowling about and stealthily alienating the people from them. In this nefarious propaganda they are thieves and murderers of souls, enemies of Christ and His Church, and seditious disturbers of public order ".[3] At last Luther urged the princes to destroy the Anabaptists : "I, Luther, approve. Although it seems cruel to punish them with the sword, it is still more cruel to damn the ministry of the Word, to propagate false doctrine and spurn the truth, and in addition to seek to overthrow the kingdoms of this world ".[4]

In contrast to the Reformers the Anabaptists affirmed freedom of the will and complete moral responsibility; the individual interpretation of Scriptures; that the State was ordained of God and ought to be obeyed unless its laws offended the conscience; they denied its supremacy in religious matters; they were Separatists and rejected the State establishment of the Church; they affirmed universal toleration. Hubmaier, a scholarly representative of their views and practice, gave clear expression of these views. They were passivists. In Moravia they had large communal settlements, but many did not favour

[1] Mackinnon, *Luther and the Reformation*, IV, p. 60.
[2] IV, p. 74.
[3] IV, p. 65.
[4] IV, p. 69.

such settlements and taught that wealth and property were a
personal stewardship to be rendered to God. They opposed
usury and lent money without interest. The Reformers and
Romanist priests and princes were merciless to these radicals.
They were slaughtered. By 1531 there were over 2,000 martyrs
in Bavaria alone. They were forbidden to remain in Zürich
on pain of death by drowning. Hubmaier was first imprisoned
and later burnt as a heretic; his wife was thrown into the
Danube and drowned. In these years the Anabaptist martyrs
were far more numerous than right-wing Protestant martyrs.
It is the darkest chapter in the story of the Reformation. " Protestant tradition ", says Professor Paterson, "judged Anabaptism
by its worst examples, ignored the ethical idealism which entered
into its dreams . . . it is indeed one of the tragedies of history
that men like Hubmaier and Denck and a great company of
victims who followed them to the slaughter should have been
involved in the same condemnation with Münzer and John of
Leyden ".[1] " The researches of recent years ", says Harnack,
" have presented us with splendid Christian leaders from among
the Anabaptists. They were noble characters and many of them
come nearer to us than the figures of an heroic Luther or an
iron Calvin ". He says the whole history of Europe would have
been transformed had the Reformation followed the ideals
of the Anabaptists rather than the Lutheran and Reformed
Churches.[2]

III. FEUDAL LORDS AND RADICAL PEASANTS

The Protestant left-wing movement towards political and
economic reform presents an equally painful story of Luther's
prejudice and inconsistency. His preaching had brought
strength of purpose and hope to the discontented peasants ;
but while Luther had claimed the right of religious freedom for
the individual, the peasants began to assert their rights for political
and economic justice. The answer and attitude of Luther to
such extensions of religious liberty will indicate his doctrine of
passivity to the State. He had resented the attempts of the

[1] Paterson, *The Rule of Faith*, p. 89.
[2] *History of Dogma*, VII, p. 125 f.

German princes to intermeddle with the spiritual rights of the people. In his address to the Nobility (1522) he affirmed the spiritual freedom of the believer against all such civil control. Luther knew the rising anger of the common people against their rulers in Church and State, and he seized the opportunity to warn the oppressors of their peril and the certainty of divine judgment. The princes of the Church and State " are a set of blind fools and tyrants . . . who are steering straight for destruction. . . . From the beginning of the world a wise prince has been a rare bird, a pious one still rarer. They are usually the greatest fools, the worst scoundrels on the earth . . . make your account with this fact, my dear princes and lords. God will no longer put up with your tyranny. The world is no longer the world of old days, when you could hunt and harass the people like game ".[1] The feudal system under the Church and the landlords was incredibly cruel. The peasants had risen against their masters in England in the fourteenth century : assembling on Blackheath, they had marched on London, beheaded Archbishop Sudury and others, and compelled the king to grant charters of freedom and a fixed rent for land. The revolt, however, was crushed and ended in tragic slaughter. Wicklif and his preachers in the fourteenth century had stimulated indirectly these movements in England as Luther did in the sixteenth century in Germany. In both countries and both centuries the risings had political and economic objectives ; they were not primarily religious, but the application of the religious principle to the State and to human values. John Ball, " the mad priest of Kent ", inflamed the serfs in England in 1381 : " Why do they hold us in serfage ? . . . They are clothed in velvet and warm in their furs and ermines, while we are covered with rags. They have wine and spices and fine bread ; we oatcake and straw, and water to drink. They have leisure and fine houses ; we have pain and labour, the rain and wind in the fields. And yet it is of us and of our toil that these men support their pomp. We are called slaves, and if we do nor perform our services we are beaten ". Tithes and the mortuary system, by which the landlord and the Church enriched themselves at the expense of the widows and the children of the deceased bread-winners, kept the peasants in perpetual poverty and

[1] Mackinnon, *Luther and the Reformation*, III, p. 173 f.

bondage. In the light of such conditions the merry England theory of the Middle Ages will not bear scrutiny. G. G. Coulton's work has destroyed all such religious romancing. They were the ages when the " Priests of Prey ", says Coulton, devoured the poor and all the fruits of their toil ; the medieval church " justified servitude in theory and practice. . . . Aquinas expressly defended it as economically expedient. Servitude was recognised and enforced by Canon Law. Monks especially were always among the richest holders of serfs ".[1] " Liberty in the Middle Ages ", says Lord Acton, " depended on property, and as the serf had no property he had no liberty ; when Monasticism was at its height half the population was in bondage ".

Long before Luther walked out of his cell the storm in Germany had been brewing. The peasants had lacked leaders who could voice their grievances, but with the rise of Luther it seemed that he had been sent to deliver them from feudal bondage. True, he was no political revolutionary, but he had attacked the landlords, the Church and the wealthy merchant class, until the peasants were encouraged to submit to him their programme of reform. The Twelve Articles of the peasants of Upper Swabia indicate the reasonableness of their demands : it is said that Hubmaier contributed to the form of these articles which were : the right to choose their own pastors ; they will pay the tithe of corn for the support of the preacher of the pure gospel, but they refuse to pay the tithe of a head of cattle any longer ; they will no longer submit to villainage which is incompatible with the Gospel ; they demand their share of fish and game on the estate ; they ask for the restoration of the woods which the landlords had stolen and enclosed ; they insist on a reduction of oppressive service ; they ask for reasonable wages, a fair rent ; the abolition of unjust punishment ; the restoration of common land which unless granted they will take back from the landlords ; the abolition of death duties as a merciless oppression of widows and orphans ; the last article agrees to forego any of the above demands which cannot be reconciled with God's Word.

These Articles are moderate and clearly derive from Luther's teaching. The peasants were ready to reason with their masters

[1] See G. G. Coulton, *Social Life in Britain from the Conquest to the Reformation,* section VIII.

and submit their demands to arbitration ; they disclaimed the use of force except as the last resort of resolute men. As the movement spread to other areas the aims became more revolutionary even to the threat of establishing a republic. When their demands were rejected by the princes and the Church, the peasants began in 1525 to burn churches, sack monasteries, and attack the castles of the rulers and the bishops : " Hatred of the Church and its degenerate hierarchy is, in fact, a notable feature of the rising ".[1]

Several of Luther's former friends and fellow-workers had shown sympathy with the aims of the peasants ; but when the latter consulted Luther and hoped to win his support and leadership, he wrote his *Exhortation to Peace in Response to the Twelve Articles of the Peasants in Swabia*. Again he blamed " the blind bishops and mad priests and monks " who raged against the Reformation, the day of wrath had dawned upon them ; but he also denounced his former friends who were becoming more alienated from him and who had urged the peasants to revolt ; at the same time he rebuked the violence of the peasants as a defiance of the law of God. However tortuous their existence might be, they must submit to wicked as to beneficent rulers : " suffering, suffering, cross, cross—this is the Christian's right and no other ". The Gospel, he said, had nothing to do with temporal things nor did it condone such methods as they had adopted to abolish their feudal miseries : had not Abraham, the patriarch, practised slavery ? Had not Paul taught slaves to be obedient to their masters ? It is not surprising that the peasants began to despise Luther. If their feudal lords were avaricious and inhuman, why should they passively submit ? At one and the same time Luther was countenancing tyranny and advising a fatalistic submission to it. Hence the peasants were ready to follow the advice of Luther's former friends and fight it out to a finish. To such a decision Luther's answer was his outburst : *Against the Robber and Murdering Bands of the Peasants*. He now charged them with doing the devil's work, amd he urged the German princes " to strike, throttle, stab, secretly or openly, whoever can, and remember that there is nothing more poisonous, more hurtful, more devilish than a rebellious man. . . . I believe there is no longer a devil in hell.

[1] Mackinnon, *Luther and the Reformation*, III, p. 197.

They have all taken possession of the peasants ".[1] Luther advised the princes " to wield the sword without mercy ". He had previously denounced the princes as scoundrels ; now they are ministers of God and martyrs if they are slain by the rebels. By such means was the rising crushed. " Over 100,000 at the lowest computation had lost their lives during the Rising and in the retribution that followed it " ; and the last condition of the peasants was worse than the first. Luther accepted the responsibility for the shocking loss of life : " It was I, Martin Luther, who slew all the peasants during the Rising, for I commanded them to be slaughtered. All their blood is on my head. But I throw the responsibility on our Lord God Who instructed me to give this order ".[2] It is easily understood how untrained and undisciplined mobs were slain by the regular soldiery. The religious consequences were disastrous. The hosts melted away from the Lutheran Churches and the Roman Church was one of the greatest gainers. The left wings of the Protestant movement were thus martyred through the blind stupidity of right-wing leaders. The loss to the religious, political and economic progress of Europe has been incalculable. The Anabaptists had leaders like Hubmaier, who could think and preach, but refused to take up arms, who hated war and refused to shed the blood of others, but were ready to suffer the loss of their own life. The peasants were a mob, without military leaders, or without the material resources of war. The ancient institutions of Church and State, as so often, knew how to use the weapons of privilege and wealth to secure their own survival.

IV. THE DISCOVERIES AND INDUSTRIAL EXPANSION

The Anabaptist and Peasant movements were apparently stamped out : the ideas of these radicals, however, were living forces which heralded the doom of church-civilisation. Likewise the Church-State of Geneva was to prove no pattern of the city of God on the earth. The Reformers had vigorously

[1] ibid., III, p. 204.
[2] ibid., III, p. 208.

resisted the Anabaptist idea of the separation of Church and State, in such a separation they could see no guarantee against political anarchy. But while the Reformers repressed these revolutionaries, dreading the disruption of church-civilisation, they were unaware of other forces which were already disintegrating the economic ideas and institutions of the sixteenth century. Calvin himself did not, could not, visualise that the medieval element in his own church-state at Geneva was passing away ; nor could he foresee the rise of the economic man, who would be largely the creation of his own genius, and who would find a powerful ally in the religious man, whom the Reformation had liberated. Religious and economic freedom together were to be the disintegrating forces of the medieval structure and the integrating forces of western civilisation. It is unfortunate that so many historians of the Reformation have treated their theme as religious and political. But the soul of man inhabits a body which must be fed and clothed and sheltered. For the poor and the dispossessed, the religious experience and the means of a livelihood, are too intimate to be ignored. Religious experience cannot be divorced from the earthly conditions which are its setting. While the Reformers were liberating the soul of man, the world was showing signs of an economic irruption which was to change its face. It is beyond the scope of this book, or my ability, to do more than indicate the economic pressures which were re-shaping European civilisation before and after the sixteenth century—an indication, however, which is relevant to Puritan and Free Church activism and the direction which it gave to the making of the modern world. Until this task has been more fully discharged the confusion of medieval and modern economic theories will exist. Catholics will continue to attribute all the evils of modern trade and industry to the rise of Protestantism ; and Protestants will continue to think of the Reformation as a religious movement divorced from other mighty forces which were also contributing to the new world.

" The discovery of America and that of a passage to the East Indies by the Cape of Good Hope " said Adam Smith, " are the two greatest and most important events recorded in the history of mankind ". Whether we agree or not with Adam Smith, both these events, which occurred before the Reformation, gave to Europeans far wider horizons and trade expansion.

These discoveries led to the intercourse of nations and quickened individual ambition and initiative. The centre of European commerce began to shift from Italy to Antwerp and slowly to London. Landlordism had hitherto been the main conception of wealth ; now the merchant class began to compete with feudal masters. The lure of riches urged men across oceans on adventurous expeditions which removed barriers between classes and nations. The rise of the merchant class and the expansion of industry, created an economic individualism ; and when the larger opportunities of business came to men who were convinced of the "calling" of God in the whole of their activity, England, in particular, began to step out of the Middle Ages, and towards the end of the eighteenth century had become the workshop of the world. The discoveries and the inventions had changed the whole conception of Capital and Capitalism. But while medievalists denounce Capitalism as the private ownership of property, whether land or mills or mines or ships, they seem unaware that feudal lords, and the Church as owner of land, were Capitalists ; they think Capitalism is something which came into existence through and after the Reformation, and which is identical with economic individualism and modern industry.

V. THE PROTESTANT ETHIC AND THE SPIRIT OF CAPITALISM[1]

Neglect of the evidence of Capitalism and commercial activity in Europe prior to the Reformation has led to a pitiable religious controversy which shows no signs of abating. The historical mistake has been made, and as it has been used to serve a popular ecclesiastical appeal, patience and education will be necessary to correct it. In 1904-5, Max Weber wrote two essays on *The Protestant Ethic and the Spirit of Capitalism* ; he initiated in these essays what has proved to be an extremely subtle attack on Calvin and the English Puritans, particularly on the Free Churches, the left wing of the Protestant movement. It is strange how far Protestants themselves have been influenced by Weber. I do not know any Free Church writer who has challenged his thesis. I have heard Free Church ministers repeat

[1] cf. Troeltsch, *Social Teaching of the Christian Churches*, II, p. 576 ff.

it. Dr. H. M. Robertson[1] replied to Weber and exposed his inaccuracies ; he pointed out his neglect of social organisation which developed in the late medieval period. Professor Tawney's lectures on *Religion and the Rise of Capitalism* do not deal with Weber's arguments as analytically as Robertson's book ; they have been quoted in support of Weber by one Bishop. Tawney says, however, that Weber deals with economic and social theory,[2] whereas his conclusions relate to social and economic organisation ; that his statements are unhistorical ; that he ignores intellectual and economic movements which had slight relation to religion ; that Machiavelli's cynical doctrine of the State, and his policy of what is expedient is right, was disintegrating moral and religious sanctions before Calvin. Tawney pointed out that Calvin's discipline at Geneva was so rigid that he would have been horrified at the individualism of English Puritanism—all valuable criticism of Essays which treated a complex subject too simply and without historical accuracy. But Hilaire Belloc, G. K. Chesterton, Christopher Dawson, Maritain, Fanfani, and other neo-catholic apologists, have seized on Weber's thesis and used it to attack Liberal ideas, British democracy, and all the economic evils which are said to be the legacy of Calvin's teaching. Accepting Weber's thesis the above writers trace our political, social and economic miseries to Calvin as their source. Protestantism is said to be responsible for religious individualism, which begat in turn the greed, avarice and lust of money such as is expressed in modern Capitalism.

It is not difficult to use such an argument to prove to Catholics and the working classes that the worst forms of Industrialism are the curse for which Protestantism is responsible. Other factors are ignored and omitted. Between the two world wars when there was large scale unemployment and suffering, the above writers were unceasing in their efforts to convince the working classes that they were the victims of a wicked capitalism which grew out of the political and religious individualism of the Reformation. The subtlety of such appeals was mostly linked with the exaltation of Mussolini who had not found it necessary to strike at the Church in Italy, as the Bolshevists did in Russia,

[1] *Aspects of the Rise of Economic Individualism.*
[2] p. 319.

and the Nazis in Germany. On the other hand the Duce regarded " the church rather as an ally to be conciliated ". Fascism as a State form, said Maritain, the French Jesuit,[1] " is so strictly in line with the needs of our time that under different names and in the service of different ideals it has already come into being in Soviet Russia and in Fascist Italy. In the City of our imagination that we conjure up in order hypothetically to illustrate our principles—a City which is conceivable only after the dissolution of capitalist society—the economic and political order of civil society would embody distinct and compact social groups, be they called corporations or guilds or what you will. But each of these lesser unities in the social order would have its own spontaneous life not derived from the State ".

Maritain says the most extreme form of Liberalism is the Puritan type of civilisation—the ethical system which " began to flourish in the sixteenth century and of which the world has had enough to make it sick and tired—the time would seem to have come for Christianity to draw its full consequences from the fact that the world which issued from the Renaissance and the Reformation has completed its process of separation from Christ. For Christianity can own no fellowship with the principles of putrefaction which are at work in a world that one may fairly take to be the corpse of medieval Christendom ".[2] When Mussolini, " the man sent by Providence " according to the papal benediction, was despising democracy and all its political structures, and when the above writers were warming their hearts at the imminent fall of the democratic States, it was possible to be exuberant. The Democracies had not, however, built their civilisation on such sandy foundations as did the Latin bloc of nations. Democracy has enough troubles of its own in these years ; it lacks discipline from men who think freedom is license ; but the storms of the last thirty years have not broken it ; even yet, they may purify it.

We must ask, however, whether capitalism existed before the rise of the Protestant spirit. It is this serious question which Weber and others have ignored. The Cloth Hall at Ypres, rebuilt in the thirteenth century, is evidence of the extent of the Flemish cloth trade. Wool was exported from England to

[1] *Freedom in the Modern World*, p. 56 f.
[2] ibid., p. 101.

Flanders in 1273 ; the Florentine banks were financing commercial enterprise in the thirteenth and fourteenth centuries: they had agents in all the great centres of trade in the fourteenth century. By the sixteenth century, the Florentines had built up a specialised capitalist system. The Roman Church encouraged these banking institutions. The Cistercian Monasteries traded in wool ; the abbeys were mortgage banks. The fact of double-entry book-keeping before the sixteenth century is evidence of Capitalism. " The age of Chaucer ", 1340–1400, says G. M. Trevelyan, was " the great breeding season of English capitalism ".[1] Edward III borrowed money for his wars from the Florentine bankers. The Jesuits were bankers and their maxim was " nothing like business ". " There are no merchants so skilful as the Jesuits ",[2] said a Dominican Missionary Bishop : their foreign missions were not to be distinguished from commercial exploitation. In Seville the Jesuit College became bankrupt through trading losses. The Jesuits used the Confessional to gain experience of business affairs. " What will the Protestant English and German say, who boast of preserving such inviolable faith in their contracts, and of proceeding so sincerely and openly in their commerce ? Of a truth they will deride and mock the Catholic faith ".[2] Thus complained the Bishop of Angelopolis to Pope Innocent the Tenth. The Roman Church, " says Robertson, " was an enormous financial organisation collecting taxation from all parts of the Christian World " through banks and financial agents, all of which had immense influence on the history of Capitalism. Again, the German family of the Fuggers acted as the agents of the Papacy, financing Popes and Emperors who raised armies to fight the Protestants. Mr. Tawney writes that the head of this house died a good Catholic, a Count of the Empire,[3] " having seen his firm pay fifty-four per cent. for the preceding sixteen years ". Dr. Robertson gives a memorable illustration of this Capitalistic spirit.[4] A certain Albrecht was in debt to the extent of 30,000 ducats, the price he had paid to the Pope for his Archbishopric, and which amount he borrowed from the Fuggers. In order to

---

[1] *English Social History*, p. 35.
[2] Robertson, p. 107 ff.
[3] Tawney, *Religion and the Rise of Capitalism*, p. 79.
[4] p. 112.

ensure repayment, the Fuggers suggested that Albrecht should secure the right to sell indulgences ; the Fuggers were to receive all the proceeds of the sales, remitting half to the Pope and keeping the other half in liquidation of the Archbishop's debt. It was this commercialism or Capitalism or Fuggerism as it was called, which led to Luther's fierce denunciations of the sale of Indulgences and the rise of Protestantism. It is astonishing that Weber ignored all such evidence of pre-Reformation Capitalism.

Lest it should be assumed that such catholic commercialism belongs to a past era, an illustration of modern methods will be useful. During the Spanish civil-war, which was a try-out of Mussolini's and Hitler's engines of destruction, a period of tortuous heart-ache for masses of British citizens, John McGovern, a Catholic, an Independent Labour member of Parliament, went to Spain to investigate the situation for himself at first hand. On his return he wrote a pamphlet, *Why the Bishops back Franco*. " The church ", says Mr. McGovern, " has become an institution of Capitalist ownership and exploitation. How ? The Church appointed from an inner circle five men in Catalonia. They held a considerable amount of the stock of the Underground, the trams, buses, railways and the worst slum property in Barcelona. These men held land for the Church, and the poverty of the peasants on the land was the worst in the world. The Church paid the peasants two pesetas a day or five shillings weekly in English money. The Church controlled the greatest amount of stock in telephones, banks, engineering, cinemas, cafés, hotels and even the bull ring. Every time the bull was stabbed to death, the Jesuits drew a profit ". A Swedish company erected electricity works in Catalonia and charged thirty-five centimos a unit. The Church, however, owned electricity works in Spain and undersold the Swedes by charging three centimos a unit. When the Swedish firm had been ruined and compelled to sell out to the Banks owned by the Jesuits, the price of electricity was raised to sixty centimos a unit. There was a cabaret in Saragossa which cost half a million of money and was owned by the clergy. " The least said about that cabaret the better ". " The Church in Spain ", he adds " is allied to the Fascists. The truth is that the Fascist movement, had its birth in the Church ".

VI. "THE CALLING"

There were two aspects of Calvin's teaching and rule in Geneva, said Weber, which accounted for the spirit of capitalism ; the first was his doctrine of the " calling " and the second was his encouragement of capitalism in Geneva where he founded a bank. Weber misunderstood and misinterpreted Calvin on both these matters ; he thinks the doctrine of the " calling " was a direct incentive to amass wealth, whereas it related to the consecration of the whole activity of the Christian man. The " calling " had profound significance for the right and left wings of Protestantism in England and Scotland. The Puritan doctrine of the " calling " meant that God elected men for his service : the doctrine is based on Scripture and explains the consciousness of vocation, apart from which Puritanism assumed that no ministry could be blest. But Calvin's doctrine of the " calling " related to all members of the Church and the whole life and activity of the Christian. So Puritans taught it ; so must we understand the energy and activism, which present a strong contrast to the submissiveness of the medieval and Lutheran Christian types. Against the ethical laxity in the Church, Calvin demanded character and achievement which drew their vitalism from mystical union with the risen Lord. It was a " calling " to moralise all life and activity. Calvin understood " the moral law within, and the starry heavens above ", but he also knew the majesty and mercy of God which gave dynamic to character and conduct—inspiration which was absent from the moral law of Kant and the achievements of his categorical imperative. The Will of God was no abstraction to Calvin : it was revealed in the Word made flesh. And the " calling " was obedience to God's Personal Will in domestic, political, economic and religious activities. Thus it was that truth, purity and righteousness expressed the divine purpose. Laziness was sin whether in the monastery, on the farm, or in the factory.

Calvin's conception of the " calling " could never tolerate compromise ; it cleansed the ecclesiastical and civil courts, gave moral direction to rulers, quickened the slumbering conscience into dynamic conviction. If it created the russet-coated veterans of the New Model Army, it was also readable in Milton and Bunyan.

The earliest idea of the " calling " was that of duty in one's station in life. At this stage Calvin was in agreement with Aquinas. Feudal society was graded as (*a*) rural and agricultural peasants, (*b*) as dwellers in towns, (*c*) as Trade Guilds ; and the medieval church taught that each social grade should render duty to God in its respective sphere. But the idea of a man remaining in his grade, or being content with his lot, was much more in accordance with the doctrine of submission to medieval authority than the Puritan idea of the " calling ". It is true that Calvin and Aquinas based their idea of fulfilling one's station in life on Paul's exhortation : " Let each man abide in that calling wherein he was called. Wast thou called being a bondservant ? Care not for it : nay, even if thou canst become free, use it rather . . . brethren, let each man, wherein he was called, therein abide with God ".[1] The Puritan idea, however, was not submission to tyrants ; nor was it submission to circumstances which could be made more human. The Puritans were sure of their " calling " to put down Charles I from his throne and exalt the nation in righteousness.

Weber interpreted the Puritan " calling " as containing all the potencies which impel men to seek personal gain and wealth —a serious misunderstanding ; he thought Baxter in the seventeenth century taught this view of the " calling ", whereas Baxter thought of it much more in the terms of going about and doing good. Nor did the Puritan boast success in his " calling " as evidence of God's favour. He was diligent in business, but such diligence did not originate capitalism ; what it did was to give a sense of the ultimate end of life and work : " it caused me first to seek God's Kingdom and His righteousness, and most to mind the one thing needful, and to determine first of my Ultimate End ".[2] *The New Whole Duty of Man*, a moral directory which first appeared in the reign of George II and went into twenty-two editions, " dealt quite literally with nothing else than the advantages of honest dealing to a nation of shopkeepers. It delivered a long homily on ' Honesty is the

[1] 1 Cor. vii, 20–24.
[2] Tawney, p. 200 ; quoted from Baxter.

best policy ' ".[1] At this date the early conception of the " calling " as contentment with one's station in life, or as a check on ambition, had been abandoned ; business was now a " calling " and prosperity a worthy goal to pursue, but it must be activity which was honest. From Calvin to the period of George II the doctrine of the " calling " had become modified until " worldly success was of great moment ". *The New Whole Duty of Man* furnished evidence that the " calling " did not exclude capitalism ; howbeit, it was honest capitalism, and to classify such moral guidance for Puritans of the eighteenth century as Prudential Ethics is scarcely less than cynicism. For who would knowingly twice trust a rogue ? The book agreed that diligence and honesty were good business qualities ; a man should use his skill in driving a bargain " within the latitude of lawful gain ", never imposing on a man's ignorance, and such a man's success was a legitimate reward. Moreover, does not God reward and punish men ? Did not the medieval church commercialise sin and forgiveness and death ? Then why decry the rewards of diligence and honesty in business ? As an introduction to his chapter on The Puritan Movement, Tawney quotes Tyndale's translation of Genesis xxxix, 2 : " And the Lorde was with Joseph, and he was a luckie felowe " ; but he proceeds to interpret Tyndale's idea of a " luckie felowe " by an illuminating discussion of " godly discipline and the triumph of the economic virtues " ; as he points out, " it is a strange school that does not teach more than one lesson, and the social reactions of Puritanism, trenchant, permanent and profound, are not to be summarised in the simple formula that it fostered individualism ".

VII.   USURY : THEORY AND PRACTICE

High claims are still made for the medieval theory of usury, and Calvin is still denounced as though he were responsible for its practice in the modern world ; the divorce between medieval theory and practice on this matter is alarming evidence of the formality and expediency of the age. We have furnished historical proofs of the habits of the Jesuits and the Papacy regarding usury. It is baffling when modern writers suggest that medieval

[1] Robertson, p. 22.

practice corresponded to theory, and then proceed to attack the Puritans who charged a reasonable interest on loans. When Calvin was asked to state his rule on usury he knew that he would probably be misinterpreted and misunderstood, but he replied " by no testimony of Scripture am I resolved that usuries are altogether condemned ". He dealt with the subject of usury by the test of equity : what was the difference between the farmer who paid rent to a landlord and the granting of a loan to the farmer on which a fair interest was agreed by both parties ? Was reasonable interest on a loan morally bad while an unreasonable rent was condoned ? Calvin safeguarded his idea of equity by condemning seven abuses of the practice of usury. To claim that the establishment of a State Bank at Geneva in 1538 was a proof of capitalistic tendencies is absurd when we recall how Florentine bankers prior to the Reformation financed the papal scheme of Indulgences.

There is no disputing that the Puritan " calling " in regard to business led to success. When the butcher, the baker, and the bootmaker were diligent and honest and trusted, and when they were thrifty, as well as industrious, thinking of goods and work as a stewardship from God to whom they must render their account, the " calling " was likely to be accompanied by an adequate livelihood and a measure of domestic security. Spendthrifts and prodigals were selfish and wasted their substance in riotous living. To suggest that the " calling " gave license to moral or economic laxity is due to deplorable ignorance. The discoveries, the inventions, the application of steam to shipping and industry brought wealth to good and bad men. It was no unusual thing for reckless landlords to seek loans from the merchants and then rend them with curses for charging interest—according to the theory of the Church. It was this diligence and success in business which began to make the Puritan and the Nonconformist too great an asset to the State to be sent to gaol for their religious individualism ;[1] statesmen began to see that their initiative was better engaged in business at home and abroad than in hatching revolution in the rotten prisons of England. When the Nonconformists were persecuted under the Clarendon Code they were far from submissive in prison : even there they were intellectually and politically

[1] Tawney, p. 204.

active. Hence the objections which began to be made that it was impoverishing the State to persecute these people—their business initiative was better employed in promoting England's prosperity. Weber singles out the Baptists as the greatest offenders who devoted their " calling " to the end of accumulating capital—an idea which is somewhat amusing to those who know their Baptist history. It is true that William Kiffin (1616–1701) was a Baptist who knew how to use his wealth when dealing with Charles II. Twelve Baptists had been arrested in Buckinghamshire as they were worshipping, and they had been condemned to death under the old Act of Elizabeth. Kiffin went to see the king and secured their release. It is reported that at one time Charles had asked Kiffin for a loan of £40,000. The Baptist merchant replied that he was unable to lend him such a large sum, but he would be pleased to make a gift of £10,000 if Charles would accept it. When Kiffin told the story he added that he had saved £30,000 by his generous gift ![1]

[1] Underwood, *A History of English Baptists*, p. 98.

CHAPTER XIX

THE EXPANSION OF FREE CHURCH PRINCIPLES

A. AMERICA

1. THE COLONISTS

THE emigration to America made the expansion of Free Church principles possible on a vaster scale than in Britain. How the main streams of religious thought and life have run through American history is not only a vindication of such principles, but unavoidably leads to comparisons with turbulent religious conflict which we have traced in England. The separation of Church and State is the distinguishing feature of American life. How does the absence of an Established Church affect not only the order of worship and Church institutions, but also the social and political structures which cannot be divorced from religious convictions? When Americans visit England they are profoundly impressed by what is ancient; they read our history as it is written in monuments of stone, our national buildings, the Abbey and cathedrals, and other memorials of antiquity which a new country must of necessity lack; they appear sometimes to identify the Church, as distinct from the churches, with our heritage in stone; they are not as interested in the sites where stood the Clink and other horrible gaols, crowded as they were with Nonconformists and especially Quakers, nor in small white-washed buildings where Free Churchmen met to worship in secret; yet such blood and tears were the liquid history which bore from England the principles of freedom which pulsate in the veins of the American people.

The Pilgrims arrived at New Plymouth in 1620. The journey from Leyden to Southampton and thence across the Atlantic, seeking freedom of worship in a strange land, has ever stirred the imagination of Free Churchmen. They were Congregationalists—only two Baptists accompanied them—and they founded their State on the Congregational principle of Church membership and the franchise—Calvin's conception of Church citizenship being their model. They were blessed in Bradford's leadership ; from 1621 until his death in 1657, with rare exceptions, and at his own request, he was elected governor. He guided the community through its early hardships and initiated social progress beyond anything that was known in England : " such as local self-government based on the township meeting, elective unpaid officials, State registration of births, death and marriages, registration of land transfers, State schools and pensions. The foundation of Harvard University was begun in 1636 by John Harvard, a godly gentleman and a lover of learning who gave one-half of his estate, it being in all about one thousand seven hundred pounds, towards the erecting of a college, and all his library. His foundation was made effective by gifts from New England towns which gave them a voice in the administration of its affairs. The importance of those methods lies not in their local value, but in their having created a type that was imitated far and wide as settlements multiplied and spread over the hinterland behind Plymouth ".[1] To found a university sixteen years after they had landed at New Plymouth and encountered all but insuperable obstacles to progress—a University free from the kind of religious tests which closed Oxford and Cambridge to Free Churchmen until over two hundred years later—was astonishing as well as a sign of the Pilgrims' love of learning. The colony survived until 1691, when it was incorporated in the Massachusetts commonwealth. In 1626 new settlers arrived, mainly Puritans of the Anglican type who adopted the Congregational Church polity. Congregationalism became the legally established religion of Massachusetts ; similar legal establishments of Congregationalism occurred in other settlements.

As the Pilgrims had protested and gone into exile against the persecutions of the Established Church of England, objection has been raised against their establishment of Congregationalism in the colonies. To charge the Pilgrims with palpable incon-

---

[1] Hastings, *Enc. Religion and Ethics*, X, 33.

sistency is to neglect several aspects of the situation in England and America. In England the Pilgrims were separatists, primarily demanding freedom to worship according to conscience ; if such freedom had been granted they would never have gone into exile. It will be recalled that Puritans of the right wing, even as late as the Commonwealth, could not conceive a religious settlement apart from a national church. Moreover, the Pilgrim colony had self-government, and the establishment of Congregationalism was settled in a democratic manner. It is regrettable that the Quakers were persecuted and that Roger Williams was handled somewhat severely. We must, however, admit provocation, and point out that judgment was taken on civil rather than on religious grounds. Bradford confessed that Roger was " godly and zealous . . . but very unsettled in judgemente " —a view which subsequent proceedings justified. Williams, in 1638, founded a new colony at Rhode Island on the basis that the State must be neutral towards all religious faith and worship and organisation ; it was complete religious toleration. But all religious establishments in the colonies were short-lived, nor, as in England, were they the occasion of civil war ; in 1775 the Church was legally established in three colonies ; by 1833 such establishments had passed finally from the American scene. The explanation was that the time had arrived when the colonists could not agree that any one church should be established.

II.   NO RELIGIOUS TESTS

The divergent religious views of the colonists found their ultimate expression on the relation of Church and State in the statute of which Jefferson was the author, and which was passed by the State of Virginia in 1786 : this is claimed to be " the first law ever passed by a popular Assembly giving perfect freedom of conscience ". It is so significant that Englishmen will do well to consider it as a revolt against the statutes under which Free Churchmen suffered injustice for wellnigh three hundred years :

" Well aware that Almighty God hath created the mind free ; that all attempts to influence it by temporal punishments or burdens, or by civil incapacitations, tend only to beget habits of hypocrisy and meanness, and are a departure from the plan of the Holy Author of our religion who . . . chose not to propagate it by coercion . . . that the impious presumption of legislators and rulers, civil as well as ecclesiastical, who being themselves but fallible and uninspired men have assumed dominion over the faith of others . . . hath established and maintained false religions over the greatest part of the world and through all time ; that to compel a man to furnish contributions of money for the propagation of opinions which he disbelieves is sinful and tyrannical . . . that our civil rights have no dependence on our religious opinions . . . that therefore the proscribing of a citizen as unworthy . . . of being called to offices of trust and emolument unless he profess or renounce this or that religious opinion, is depriving him injuriously of those privileges and advantages to which in common with his fellow citizens he has a natural right. . . . Be it therefore enacted by the General Assembly that no man shall be compelled to frequent or support any religious worship, place or ministry whatsoever, nor shall he be enforced, restrained, molested . . . nor shall otherwise suffer on account of his religious opinions ". The sixth Article of the American Constitution affirms : " No religious test shall ever be required as a qualification to any office or public trust under the United States ". Two years after the Constitution had been adopted ten amendments were proposed and the first was : " Congress shall make no law respecting an establishment of religion, or prohibiting the free exercise thereof ". Every clause quoted above has a history behind it and is a condemnation and repudiation of the Tudors, Stuarts, and the Anglican Hierarchy and their oppressive persecutions extending over two hundred years ; further, every clause condemns the political, educational and ecclesiastical injustice continued by the Established Church since 1786. To read Jefferson's Act is to realise poignantly how much suffering has been inflicted through the influence of British ecclesiastics on our legislation.

III. THE PUBLIC RECOGNITION OF RELIGION

Has religious life, or the public recognition of religion, been affected by this separation of Church and State ? American writers who know England say that Christianity has not suffered, but rather expanded through freedom from State control. English visitors who know American Church life and institutions agree with this verdict.   They confirm the view that there is quite as much public recognition of religion in the United States as in England.   It would appear that public recognition of the Christian religion in the United States is far from being as neglected as some Anglican writers suggest ; and it is almost certainly less formal.   One fact is sure—the social distinctions which have been created in England by the Established Church are absent on national occasions and days of prayer in America. Dr. M. E. Aubrey, who knows American religious life, gave evidence before the Commission on Church and State in 1935 : " A fear exists that the abolition of the establishment would lead to the disappearance of religion from some of the acts and ceremonial of the State.   This does not appear to follow.   My own impression is that, in America, religion has a larger and not a smaller place in public life than among us.   Being not " official," it is less formal and more real.   A good deal of the religious value of public ceremonial in this country is nullified by its unrepresentative character, and often by a certain playing for position where the supposed " rights " of a State Church are claimed ".[1]   The separation of Church and State in America is of political significance and is not affected by social distinctions. Equality of all Christians on public occasions, religious or otherwise, is a feature of American life; in England there is often neither recognition nor place of equality.   " On the other hand," says Sweet, " in such countries as the United States, where the law does not attempt to define the specific functions of the Church, or the exact part religion is to play in the life of the nation, the Church will be more inclined to attempt to permeate all of life.   Thus the concept of the part that the Church is to play in society is greatly widened, since it conceives of its task, not simply that

---

[1] Report, vol. II, p. 247.

of maintaining worship, but also that of righting wrongs through influences exerted upon the public conscience, either by direct or indirect means ".[1] And he adds : " By the recognition of equality under the law of all religious bodies in the United States, one of the greatest barriers to cordiality between the Churches has been removed ".[2]

The two houses of the United States Congress, like the State legislatures, have their chaplains, chosen impartially from the major religious communions, and their sessions are formally opened with prayer. In the large Universities, especially those with affiliated theological seminaries, Sunday worship with the sermon is the custom. Sperry's " impression is that chapel-going among American college students in our private universities, though by no means the general practice, is appreciably better than that in Oxford colleges, and at St. Mary's Church as I have seen it in recent years ".[3] In upwards of six hundred " accredited institutions of higher learning " there are more than three hundred church colleges. It is not suggested that the majority of the teaching staffs and students attend worship, but what is true of Harvard may be claimed of other Universities : compulsory attendance at worship was discontinued in 1886, " but there has not been a Sunday or a week-day in term time when morning worship has not been conducted ".[4]

IV.   CHURCH STATISTICS

A census of Denominations, churches and their membership in the United States, is conducted every ten years under Government supervision. The last census in 1936 with figures supplemented by the 1943 edition of the Yearbook of American Churches, will indicate the approximate proportion of Church membership to the whole American population. The inclusive church membership says Sweet numbers nearly seventy-two and a half million, which means " that more than half the total

[1] *The American Churches*, p. 12.
[2] p. 38.
[3] Sperry, *Religion in America*, p. 60.
[4] p. 167 f.

population of the nation are either communicants or nominal members of some religious body. Of these, some forty-four million are Protestants, something over twenty-three million are Roman Catholics, four million six hundred thousand are Jews, and nearly seven hundred thousand are Eastern Orthodox ".[1] The seven largest Protestant denominations are as follows :[2]

Baptist - - - - -	11,400,000
Methodist - - - -	8,400,000
Lutheran - - - -	4,000,000
Presbyterian - - - -	2,800,000
Protestant Episcopal - -	2,100,000
Disciples of Christ - - -	1,700,000
Congregational - - -	1,100,000

The proportion of Church members to the whole population is considerably higher than in Britain. However the above statistics may be explained, the separation of Church and State in America has not led to a forsaking of religious worship on the part of the nation ; it is a legitimate conclusion from the above statistics that such separation has been a stimulus to church life and the expansion of Christianity within the State. Yet, Mr. T. S. Eliot does not think that the United States can " develop a positive culture of their own " apart from an Established Church : just as he thinks " that no Christianisation of England can take place without " the State Church.[3]

V. CHURCH UNION

How does the absence of an Established Church affect the relations of the American denominations ? " Of all the differences between the Old World and the New," says James Bryce, " the separation of Church and State is perhaps the most salient. Half the wars of Europe, half the internal troubles that have

---

[1] p. 28.   [2] Sperry, p. 75
[3] *The Idea of a Christian Society*, p. 46 f.

281

vexed European States " from the fifth century down to the nineteenth, " have arisen from theological differences or from the rival claims of Church and State. This whole vast chapter of debate and strife has remained virtually unopened in the United States. There is no Established Church. All religious bodies are equal before the law . . . so far from suffering from the want of State support religion seems in the United States to stand all the firmer because, standing alone, she is seen to stand by her own strength ".[1] Religious equality in America has rendered such terms as Dissenter and Nonconformist meaningless. Protestantism and Roman Catholicism form the great divide, and American Protestant writers are revealing concern over the political policy of the Vatican in their own country. While the word re-union has little or no meaning in America the tendencies toward closer fellowship, and union, between the Protestant churches is most pronounced. The training of the ministers of the largest Protestant Churches is becoming increasingly inter-denominational. " Churches such as the Lutheran and Episcopalian are the only large denominations which maintain strictly denominational schools. The theological seminaries of the Methodists, Baptists, Presbyterians, Disciples and Congregationalists, are all to a greater or lesser degree inter-denominational. The Divinity School of the University of Chicago, established by the Baptists as a part of the University of Chicago, had, during this last spring quarter, students from twenty-two denominations. For a number of years past, the Methodists have had the largest student attendance of any of the Churches. The same is true of the Yale Divinity School and Union Theological Seminary in New York ".[2] Thus a deeper consciousness of their unity in Christ is growing in the Protestant Churches of America. Concerning prospects of re-union between Protestant, Roman Catholic and Orthodox Churches—the whole idea " carries with it a connotation which is un-American " : such discussions reveal wide divergence of views on the nature of the Church and the Ministry ; and " the whole issue comes to a head over the question of ordination. How is a man made a minister " ?[3] As far as any " return " to the Church of England is concerned,

---

[1] *The American Commonwealth*, vol. II, pp. 763–768.

[2] Sweet, p. 36 ; the book was published in 1946.   [3] Sperry, pp. 241 ff.

" our colonial history and the consequences of the Revolution " make it impracticable.

B. THE BRITISH COMMONWEALTH OF NATIONS

The expansion of Free Church principles has profound historic significance when we recall the contribution made to the founding of the British Commonwealth of Nations. It is safe to say there would never have been a British Empire in the twentieth century under the conditions of government which Englishmen had known in their own land in the seventeenth and eighteenth centuries. As pilgrims and exiles left England there was a pride of race and love of the old country in their hearts ; but there was resentment and a determination to suffer no more tyranny of Church and State : as settlers in new lands they would build their institutions on the democratic principle. It is also safe to add that the Empire would never have endured on any other foundation. In Canada and Australia nothing has stirred my own emotions more than the loyalty of men and women to the British Throne, and how young couples of the second and third generation will save money for years to visit the " home " of their parents in Britain. But they would never sell or barter their freedom. Through the two wars of the present century their loyalties have stood the test and have proved to the world that free political institutions can fight and endure when their freedom is threatened. It was folly and stupid dictatorship which lost us the American colonies : even men of English blood in America in the eighteenth century were resolved never again to submit to the bondage of Church and State such as they had experienced on English soil.

The conditions of the working classes in Britain after the Battle of Waterloo have been outlined, but no reference has been made to the methods of peopling Australia and Canada. Tasman had discovered parts of Australia in 1642, but it was not until 1770 that Captain Cook staked out the coastal areas of Australia and New Zealand as a British possession. But when that had been done it was a perplexing problem for the Government to colonise these distant lands. After 1774 when the American colonies had been lost and were no longer available as a dumping ground for convicts, they were shipped off to Australia under the control of British officers. The main motive for transporting religious and political rebels, and criminals, was " to rid England of such undesirable pests ". In the early 1830's " the labourers of the Southern counties, driven by famine, were marching through the country-side demanding the living wage of half a crown a day. They were cruelly punished at the Assizes, when four hundred and fifty of the rioters were torn from their families and transported to Australia, besides three unjustly executed ".[1] It is relevant to illustrate Trevelyan's statement from the Free Church standpoint. The Tolpuddle Martyrs, in 1834, furnish evidence of the attitude towards these southern farm labourers, partly because they were Methodists, and because they were transported to Australia. The industrial revolution in Lancashire and Yorkshire, and such agitators as Hume, Owen, Cobbet and the Chartists, have received attention, In southern rural areas the farm labourers were unorganised ; dared not organise lest they should be evicted from their cottages and their families become destitute. Six such labourers were arrested at Tolpuddle for attempting to form a union to secure an increase of wages. They were receiving seven shillings weekly and demanded ten. Several masters had promised to pay this amount. But the Tolpuddle men were charged in the local court and committed to gaol for administering unlawful oaths. While in prison, the Anglican chaplain visited them, treated them as criminals, told them they were idle and well paid. " Why should we fear the master ", asked George Loveless their leader and a Methodist lay-preacher, " because we are combining to get a living wage " ? The punishment of dismissal by the masters was not adequate ; they must be kept in gaol and sent for trial to Dorchester Assizes. There, they were accused of holding a meeting of trade unionists and of trying to ruin their masters. When the Methodist minister came to Tolpuddle to inquire of the wife of George Loveless why her husband and the rest were in gaol, she replied : " I don't know what to think, sir, as I tell you. It may be that (asking for more wages). It may be anything else. You know they are always persecuting men in this village for being chapelmen. Perhaps it is because the parson has set the magistrates against them for preaching ".[2]

---

[1] Trevelyan, *British History in the Nineteenth Century and After*, p. 235.
[2] Rattenbury, *Flame of Freedom*, p. 54.

Lord Melbourne, the Prime Minister, sent Judge Williams to deal with the case. It was affirmed in court that no complaint could be made against the quality of the work of the accused men. "Is there anything in their past life", asked the judge, "that points to insubordination ? You say they are Methodists. I suppose they talk about having been converted. Weren't they terrible sinners before they were converted—drunkards and liars and poachers and so on ? I have heard that these Methodists generally have a long tale to tell of the terrible wickedness they used to practise and what a difference their conversion made to them. Don't these men talk in that way " ? " They don't, my Lord ", replied a farmer, " they couldn't, for everybody knows them in the villages round about here ". Counsel agreed that not a single charge had been proved. " Well, then ", said the Judge, " there is only one thing for it. We must proceed " ; and under an Act of George III, for the suppression of mutiny and for administering secret oaths, the Tolpuddle labourers were found guilty. " Not for anything that you have done, or, as I can prove, that you intended to do, but for example to others ", said the Judge, " I consider it my duty to pass the sentence of seven years' penal transportation across His Majesty's high seas to each and every one of you ".[1] Loveless replied for the six men : " we have injured no man's reputation, character, person or property, we were uniting to preserve ourselves, our wives and our children from utter degradation and starvation." Pathetic were the efforts of Jane Davis to secure influential help from Jabez Bunting and others and thus prevent transportation. It was strange, how in City Road, London, she met a procession of 40,000 workers from the North of England, led by Hume and Owen, to secure better wages. And it was characteristic of a sturdy Lancastrian to defy all authority against injustice : " Seven years transportation for what ? Just because they formed a trade union. Why we have thousands of men in unions in Manchester, Bolton and Oldham. Why don't they tackle us and bring us before the judges ? "[2] On May 25th, 1834, these Methodist labourers sailed with a hundred and twenty convicts, thieves and murderers, all in irons. On September 4th they landed at Hobart in Tasmania where Loveless remained,

[1] p. 67.
[2] p. 101.

others went to Australia. How Loveless was bullied and treated as a slave as he worked in the chain gang : how he saw men whipped, and how maggots were taken from suppurating wounds ; how Wakeley spoke for two and a half hours in Parliament and stirred public opinion against the infamy which had sent these Methodist farm labourers as convicts from their wives and families ; how at long last Loveless was released by the order of the British Government and arrived in London in 1837 are matters of history.

On his return Loveless continued to preach : " it is indelibly fixed in my mind that labour is ill-rewarded in consequence of the few tyrannising over the millions ; and that, through their oppression, thousands are now working in chains, on the roads, abused by overseers, sentenced by the comitants and punished by the flagellator ; young, and once strong men, now emaciated and worn almost to skeletons. Is this the plan to reform men ? I say ' no ' ; if they were bad before, they are tenfold more the children of Hell now ".[1] Seeing an Anglican clergyman in his audience, Loveless said he "believed that half the power of the squire, which had sent him and his brother and his friends to serve in durance vile, was due to the clergy ". The Rev. Henry Walter, vicar of Hodsbury Bryant reported this speech to the President of the Wesleyan Conference ; to which action Loveless replied, that as Nonconformist preachers, they would "uphold the free access of the individual soul to God ", denounce the wickedness of the clergy, and above all " their alliance with the squires, grinding down the faces of the poor ".[2]

In 1840 the white population in Australia was 130,000 strong but they were able to persuade the British government to cease the shipment of convicts ; a policy, however, which was revised in later years.

The loss of the American colonies had also significance for the populating of Canada. After the American War about 40,000 English speaking peoples were sifted out by persecution and expelled from the United States. Many settled in Nova Scotia : others pressed inland ; when the clash came with the French they demanded English land laws and institutions. " It is difficult to exaggerate the advantage to the Empire and the

[1] p. 188.
[2] p. 191.

race, of the creation, at this particular juncture, of the pioneer province of Upper Canada, as a place ready made for the reception of the victims of the economic revolution then going on in Great Britain. The Canadian conditions, like those of Australia and New Zealand shortly afterwards, were almost ideal for rehabilitating the self-respect of the bullied and pauperised labourers of the English shires ".[1] "In Canada," wrote one of them, " we can have our liberty and need not be afraid of speaking our rights ". " We have no gamekeepers and more privileges ", wrote another.

In these early settlements of lands now included in the British Commonwealth, Free Churches were founded. In the 1930's in Adelaide, Sydney, Melbourne, centenary celebrations of these churches were held and British Free Church representatives were present. The larger Free Churches have existed long in Canada and make enduring contribution to the life of the Dominion. In 1925, the Congregational, Methodist and Presbyterian Churches (considerable continuing churches contracting out) were constituted the United Church of Canada ; the membership is now well over 700,000. It is a fact of considerable importance that no Established State Church exists in these self-governing nations of the Empire. Moreover, the united membership of the Free Evangelical Churches, in these nations, far exceeds the membership of the Anglican Church.

C. WORLD EVANGELISM

The consciousness of nationhood is intimately associated with the rise of Protestant State Churches in Europe. Until the nineteenth century, the State Church in England was nationalistic in outlook and in the scope of its work. The Church was expected to serve the religious needs of the State, and the Book of Common Prayer was, in England, the directory of worship to this end. But such vision and scope were a limitation of the universalism of the Gospel. The Free Churches had been so long involved in the struggle for their own existence that the command of Christ to go into all the world to preach the Gospel

[1] Trevelyan, *British History in the Nineteenth Century and After*, p. 59.

did not awaken vision or quicken their conscience until the eighteenth century was drawing to its close. Any religious movements abroad had been those of the Separatists and the Pilgrim Fathers. The universalism of the Gospel was inherent in Free Church principles, but it was late in the eighteenth century before the Free Church denominations began officially to send their missionaries beyond the boundaries of the British Empire. The primary motive was to preach the Gospel to those who had never heard it—a task far from easy in India and China where religions older than Christianity had struck their roots so deeply, and had fashioned ancient civilizations. In Africa the natives were more approachable and teachable. Free Churchmen can take a legitimate pride in the history of their missionary work among non-Christian peoples. Missionaries have translated the Scriptures, founded schools and universities, taught children to read and practise the Christian virtues of truth, honour, self-control and love. Our medical missionaries, trained in British medical schools, have applied scientific methods of healing, surgery and sanitation, in lands where magic and witchcraft prevailed.

The vastness of Free Church Missionary activity makes it impossible for me to do more than indicate its nature and scope. It would seem that into every non-Christian land the Free Churches have sent their missionaries. And if I select two illustrations from the fields where Baptists have laboured it is because I know the Baptist work most intimately ; but such work is representative of the sacrificial service not only of British Free Church Missionary societies, but of societies in Canada, Australia, New Zealand and the United States.

William Carey is the father of the modern Free Church missionary movement. Consider him knocking at the gates of Asia as he arrived in India in 1793 with the Gospel. But in Carey's interpretation of the Gospel there was scholarship, there was humanism, there was science, and there was the message that every son of Asia had eternal value to God, and was as much an object of the divine love as any Englishman. The East India Company resented Carey's presence in India, but he acted with patience and faith and won the day. Lesser men would have lost the day and would have been expelled from India. Carey's battle was with one of the oldest philosophical systems in the world. For ages, Hindu religion had developed an inhuman caste system and had fortified it by all the devices and defences which philosophy could contrive. The present century has learned how deeply rooted the caste system still is ; but it was a much more dangerous task to attack it with the Gospel over 150 years ago. For seven years, Carey laboured for his first convert. He said how Hindus wished to accept Christ as their Lord and Saviour but wished at the same time to retain their caste—a matter on which Carey refused to compromise. He insisted that a profession of Christianity could not be reconciled with caste. Then Krishna and his sister were baptised and the caste system received its first blow. It happened on the night when these baptised Hindus sat down with English missionaries around the Lord's Table—surely one of the most historic occasions since the Apostolic Age. The converted Hindus had learned that the Gospel meant Universalism, a new value of human nature, of Christian brotherhood and of social relationship. But that night the rage of the Hindus was let loose. Inside the Mission House was the small group of baptised Hindu and English Christians ; outside, in the streets, the Hindu mobs were howling and threatening destruction of life and property. Carey and his fellow missionaries and the Hindu Christians would have been murdered unless the Governor of the district had heard of the plot and sent a guard to protect them.

Any civilization there is in Central Africa to-day is due to Christian Missionary work. The Gospel has effected the most extraordinary changes in the domestic and social life of the Congo area. It is some years since the Baptist Missionary Society produced a film which showed the results of fifty years of devotion and sacrifice on the part of its representatives. There were chiefs with sensual and brutal bodies, and their wives with frightened and degraded faces, living in their insanitary huts and under slave conditions. But after fifty years of Christian work polygamy had received its death blow. Instead, the Christian youth and girl were shown, giving themselves to each other in the beauty and tenderness of affection, establishing their home in loyalty to each other and to Christ. This spreading region in West Central Africa has learnt nobler conceptions of parenthood, of love and marriage, and the sanctity of family life. It was impressive to see the difference that fifty years of missionary

work had made to the human features : the change from animalism
to refinement, from vulgar habits to culture and tenderness—
wrought by the knowledge of the Word of God and the love of
Christ. The film showed the progress of medical science among
the natives. There was the scene of the witch doctor, dancing
and claiming to entice from evil spirits the secret causes of sickness, pestilence or death. No one knew when the witch in her
frenzy would point her finger at the culprit of the calamities which
had overtaken the community. These irrational or pre-rational
methods of explaining cause and effect terrorised the village.
But the film showed how medical missionaries, nurses, and
hospital methods had exposed such superstitions, and taught the
scientific principle of cause and effect which had driven fear away.
A new civilization has slowly emerged : tribal language has been
reduced to grammar and given literary form ; the natives can
read, work printing presses and publish their own books : they
have learnt to build decent houses, churches and social centres ;
to make bricks and boots and furniture. Whereas women were
the slaves of men, the men have now learnt the dignity of work,
and women have found emancipation for motherhood and home-
making. In non-Christian lands over the face of the earth,
Free Church missionaries have been evangelising, educating,
administrating and guiding the peoples along the high road
which goes on.

Carey in India ; Livingstone, Moffat, the Combers, Holman
Bentley in Africa ; Morrison, Timothy Richards, Gilmore in
China ; Williams and Chalmers in the South Seas ; explorers,
Christian Statesmen and martyrs—these are all makers of modern
history. It must have been early in the 1930's when a distinguished gathering met in London to honour Einstein ; an
occasion when Mr. George Bernard Shaw made a memorable
speech. He said great men were very rare ; at the most they
were a mixed lot, and in London their value was six a penny.
" Suppose I had to propose the toast, ' Napoleon ', I should
undoubtedly say many flattering things about him, but it would
not be possible to say the most important thing, and that would
be, that perhaps it would have been better for the human race if
he had never been born. Napoleon dreamed of making empires,
but there is an order of men who get beyond that. They are
not makers of empires but makers of universes. And when

they have made those universes, their hands are not stained with the blood of any human being on the earth ". Mr. Shaw added that Ptolemy, Isaac Newton and Einstein were the makers of universes.

We acknowledge gladly the genius of these physicists and mathematicians, for all truth concerning the Universe must serve God's purpose ; but there is an order of men whose motives achieve spiritual and moral progress ; they are men who have visions of bringing the kingdoms of this world to the feet of Christ. After all, the poor, the sinful, the oppressed, do not hear the word forgiveness or compassion as they try to learn what Einstein's theory of relativity can mean. But to reconcile East and West ; to break down barriers of caste and colour ; to live, to teach, to endure, and then to die at one's post for Christ, as Carey and his fellow missionaries have done—that is the greatest work a man can do for God and his fellow men.

CHAPTER XX

REGENERATION AND SOCIAL REFORM

I

REVOLUTION by military despotism is always a violent affair;
a political revolution may involve drastic changes for certain
sections of the population, but it takes a slower re-adjustment of
parties and powers in the State : a social revolution is slowest
of all ; it would be more accurate to speak of social evolution,
involving as it does the change of habits, customs and conditions
of human nature. Cromwell's revolution was military and
political ; but when the Levellers pressed on towards a social
revolution—that the rural and artisan section of the population
should no longer be excluded from the government of the country ; that land laws should be reformed ; that tithe should
be abolished ; that minorities should be tolerated—their programme was too far ahead of their contemporaries. It was
not until the eighteen forties, that a series of industrial reforms
began to ease the burdens of the workers. Since then the
urge of the social revolution has never lacked the voice of the
reformer.

Political and social revolution are closely linked with each
other ; but the lag in the social programme and the sense of the
frustration of the politically liberated are also often linked with
each other. When Free Churchmen were contending for religious and political liberty on the Statute Book, they found it
equally arduous labour to effect changes in social conditions.
To pass laws is one thing, to inspire or elevate human nature to
the standard of progressive legislation is another thing. Yet,
this was always the purpose of Free Church leaders ; they never
ignored—as much present-day social legislation does—the

human factor in reform. None knew better the cussedness and unreliability of human nature in the mass—a fact they had learned from every Biblical reformer, and most of all from the cunning Jewish rulers and the unmanageable mobs who demanded the crucifixion of Jesus. Hence the objective of Free Church preaching! Wesley had taught ministers to preach for conversions; he knew that apart from an inner spiritual change in human nature there would never be any enduring social progress. Numerous are the warnings of history on this matter. Reformers who neglect or underrate the human factor must not be surprised when human nature turns material gains into moral losses. Thus Free Churchmen related the inner spiritual life and motive to the creation of an environment in which men could fulfil the noblest ideals of community life. When we recall that outstanding Free Church leaders of the nineteenth century were mostly of humble origin, that they had known the cramping limitations of an industrial or rural environment, we possess the key to their power with the masses. If the iron had entered their own soul, the compassion and travail of their Lord had also entered it. Thus they preached the gospel and taught the Christian ethic, changing individual lives and training their generation in the principles of good citizenship. How this work affected social structures, or how the urge to social reform was due to, or encouraged by, Free Churchmen, can best be illustrated by different types of leadership in different social spheres.

II. FREE CHURCHES AND SLAVERY

" The initiation of the anti-slavery movement ", says G. M. Trevelyan, " is the greatest debt that the world owes to the Society of Friends ".[1] Slavery was an ancient institution, man's most inhuman treatment of man; it was mass cruelty on an inconceivable scale. It is found in the Old Testament, but is there much more humane than among other ancient peoples. The Hebrew slave was sure of emancipation, and against any brutality towards the Gentile slave the Law gave protection. In Greece and Rome slavery was common and often savage. Augustine said slavery was the reward of sin and the slave

[1] *British History in the Nineteenth Century and Afterwards*, p. 51.

suffered a just punishment. Aquinas thought slaves could be used as soldiers and on the grounds of expediency the Church and the State could hold as many as they needed. It was in 1562 that Sir John Hawkins began the slave trade between Africa and the West Indies, selling 300 slaves at £20 a head. By 1838 there were 800,000 negro slaves in the West Indies. The duty on each slave in 1713 was fixed at over £8 a head. Queen Elizabeth told Hawkins that his business would call down divine vengeance if Africans were sold into slavery without their own consent.

In 1761 the Quakers began their protest against the trade. In 1772 Granville Sharp contested in the courts the case of a slave in England : " The Lord Chief Justice presided ; notable barristers were briefed by both parties, and one of the greatest legal battles ever waged was fought out. The facts were these : James Somerset, a negro, had been brought to this country by his master, Charles Stewart. After a time the slave made his escape, but his freedom was short-lived. His master managed to lay hold upon him and put him on board a ship bound for Jamaica, where he could be sold as a slave ". Sharpe had instructed his counsel out of his own legal researches : " The court was thrilled by the eloquence of the rival lawyers, and the whole country waited for the result. The verdict announced by Lord Mansfield to the effect that no man who has put his foot on English soil can be a slave was one of the most memorable ever given in an English court of law and marked an important milestone in the emancipation struggle ".[1] Sharpe was a member of the " Clapham Sect " who formed themselves into a committee in 1787 to seek the abolition of slavery—all were evangelicals of the Church of England : William Wilberforce, Lord Teignmouth, Sharpe, Henry Thornton, James Stephen, Thomas Clarkson and Zachary Macaulay. Wilberforce led the crusade in Parliament ; between 1795 and 1799 several of his resolutions were rejected, but a bill for the abolition of the slave trade was passed in 1807. No longer could a Britisher buy or sell negroes. As Wilberforce became ill and aged, Thomas Fowell Buxton succeeded him as leader of the Parliamentary campaign ; not, however, until 1833 was slavery abolished in

[1] Patten, *These Remarkable Men*, p. 60 f.

the British Empire and £20,000,000 voted as compensation to the slave owners.

The "Clapham Sect" was "ready to co-operate not only with their fellow evangelicals, the Wesleyan and other Dissenters, but with free-thinkers and Utilitarians. Wilberforce confessed with chagrin that the 'high and dry' conservative party then prevalent among the church clergy obstructed the anti-slavery cause or were at best indifferent, while Nonconformists and godless reformers proved his staunchest allies ". Free Churchmen were mainly identified with the Liberal party in Parliament and supported Fox and his friends who were insisting on the end of the slave trade. But the men who roused the Free Churches and the British public to demand the end of slavery were the missionaries who had suffered persecution under the planters and who had first hand knowledge of the evils of slavery in the colonies. The speeches and resolutions in Parliament had awakened the hopes of the negroes, and when they thought the planters were delaying their freedom they revolted. John Smith, a missionary of the London Missionary Society, was accused in Jamaica of inciting such slaves, was tried by court-martial and condemned to be hanged. In the House of Commons Brougham spoke for four hours in his defence. Smith died in prison before the date fixed for his execution. Another serious riot occurred in 1831 ; again the slaves believed their masters were duping them, refusing "to let them go ". They organised passive resistance; later they became aggressive and burnt factories and the houses of the planters. Missionaries were arrested and Methodist and Baptist properties were destroyed by the slave owners. The soldiers killed four hundred negroes.

Eminent among those who came from Jamaica to England was William Knibb, a Baptist missionary. He was called to give evidence before committees of both Houses of Parliament. It was in the country, however, that his campaign for the abolition of slavery yielded amazing results. The committee of the Baptist Missionary Society regarded slavery as a political question and requested their missionaries to let it alone. When Knibb returned and met his committee he was advised to be prudent and temperate ; his answer was, " Myself, my wife, and my family are entirely dependent on the Baptist Mission ; we have landed without a shilling, and may at once be reduced to penury. But if it is necessary I will take them by the hand and walk barefoot through the kingdom, but I will make known to the Christians of England what their brethren in Jamaica are suffering ". At a public meeting at Spa Fields Chapel, Knibb revealed extraordinary powers of speech. " He began in a modest tone, soliciting a favourable and candid hearing, disclaiming all desire for revenge, but warmed as he proceeded to tell how the struggle was forced on them by the planters—how the prosperous work of the mission was interfered with, and their chapels rased to the ground by their infuriated rage ; how there were 20,000 Baptist without Sabbath or place of worship, and who were certain to be flogged, he believed, every time they were caught praying ; and closed with this touching and eloquent appeal : ' I plead on behalf of the widows and orphans of those whose innocent blood has been shed. I plead that the constancy of the negro may be rewarded. I plead on behalf of brethren in Jamaica whose hopes are fixed on this meeting. I plead on behalf of their wives and little ones. I call upon children by the cries of the infant slave whom I saw flogged on Macclesfield estate in Westmoreland. I call upon mothers by the tender sympathies of their natures. I call upon maidens by the blood-streaming back of Catherine Williams, who, with a heroism England has seldom known, preferred a dungeon to the surrender of her honour. . . . I call upon you all by the sympathies of Jesus. If I fail of arousing your sympathies, I will retire from this meeting and call upon Him Who has made of one blood all nations that dwell upon the face of the earth ; and if I die without beholding the amancipation of my brethren and sisters in Christ, then if prayer is permitted in heaven, I will fall at the feet of the Eternal, crying, Lord, open the eyes of Christians in England to see the evil of slavery and to banish it from the earth.

" If in the course of my address to the meeting I have said anything to offend, or divert their attention from the main objects before them, my subject must atone for it. If the society to which I have the honour to belong object to any opinions urged by me, I cannot help it. If I must speak at all, I must speak the real sentiments of my mind, and those sentiments must to my latest hour be uttered against slavery—slavery of any kind, but above all slavery of woman. For nearly fifty years has that friend of humanity, Wilberforce, advocated the claims of the oppressed African. Now that he is gathering his mantle around him, and preparing for his entrance into eternity, let the attending angel, as he descends to convey his ransomed spirit to the realms of felicity, whisper in the ears of the departing saint that AFRICA IS FREE " !

One of his greatest speeches was at Exeter Hall : " All I ask is that my African brethren may stand in the family of man ; that my African sister shall, while she claps her tender infant to her breast, be allowed to call it her own ; and that they both shall be allowed to bow their knees to that God Who has made of one blood all nations ".

To describe the effect of Knibb's speeches in the country is impossible. But it was this kind of oratory, full of compassion, pleading for the helpless slave, which moved the Free Churches to action, and in that very year the Abolition of Slavery Bill became law.

Unfortunately, a clause was inserted in the Bill of 1833 that there should be a six-year period of apprenticeship for the slaves, with a free Sunday. The system proved to be nearly as cruel as the old regime had been. Slaves were whipped as usual, others were tortured by the tread-mill and in the chain-gang. Again, Knibb used all his resources to end the brutality of the apprentice system ; he came over to England and enlisted the sympathy of Joseph Sturge of Birmingham, a Quaker, known for his devotion to total emancipation and all good work. Sturge and his friend Harvey visited Jamaica, and on their return to England gave evidence before a committee of the House of Commons. Petitions from all over the country poured into Parliament asking for the abolition of the apprenticeship system. Anti-slavery meetings were organised, but the Government measure, an Abolition Amendment Bill, was only passed by the small majority of three votes. The slave-owners were threatening defiance, but the Jamaican Assembly agreed to surrender, and to free 800,000 slaves on the 1st August, 1838. As you enter the Old Council Chamber at the Baptist Church House there is a striking bas-relief of the Jamaican scene on that day. In the centre of the bas-relief is an anvil with Freedom as its base ; on the left are shackled negroes and one is kneeling,

his chain across the anvil ; and there stands Knibb with his hammer
and chisel setting the slave free ; on the right are a liberated
man and wife and a negro with uplifted hands ; the memorial
of a noble missionary, who had burnt himself out at forty-two
to abolish slavery. " I know the Dissenters " said Lord John
Russell : " they carried the Reform Bill ; they carried the
abolition of slavery ".

III. MUNICIPAL REFORM

It is no part of my task to attempt any review of the history
of municipal reform. I wish to point out the motives and
methods of Free Churchmen when applied to local government.
If I select Dale of Birmingham as an illustration, it is because
his influence in his own city reads like one of the noblest triumphs
in municipal politics in the nineteenth century. Dale used to
urge Free Churchmen throughout the country to devote their
time and energy to municipal reform ; a frequent illustration
of his was that of Alderman White, a Quaker : " Two years
ago a friend of mine in Birmingham, who for very many years
has had a large Bible Class of young men on Sunday mornings—
if I say two hundred men I think I should fall short of the number
—stood for the Town Council when a vacancy occurred in one
of the worst wards of the borough. There were two or three
thousand voters in that ward ; they were a very rough set ; we
fought hard, and we carried him. Ten days ago he rose in the
council. He was able to say that he had visited every street,
every court in his ward. He told an appalling story of the
condition of the people in that ward and in some adjacent wards.
He spoke of the squalid homes in which they were living,
destructive to health and rendering all high moral Christian life
almost impossible. He submitted to the council an elaborate
scheme for sweeping all the wretched district away at a cost of
four and a half millions. The council accepted the proposal
unanimously. Now I believe that my friend was trying to get
the will of God done on earth as it is done in heaven just as
much when he was fighting St. Mary's Ward, just as much when

he was speaking in the Town Council, as when he was teaching his Bible Class on the Sunday morning ".[1]

Dale was foremost in helping to create this civic conscience. He says towards the end of the sixties a few Birmingham men made the " discovery " how much might be done to improve the conditions of life in the city. A few able men had served the council, but the standard was raised. It became the ambition of young men of culture and ability to serve their fellow citizens. The November ward meetings were enthusiastic on what a great and prosperous town like Birmingham might do for its people : " they spoke of sweeping away streets in which it was not possible to live a healthy and decent life ; of making the town cleaner, sweeter, brighter ; of providing gardens and parks and music ; of erecting baths and free libraries, an art gallery and a museum. They insisted that great monopolies like the gas and water supply should be in the hands of the corporation ; that good water should be supplied without stint at the lowest possible prices ; that the profits of the gas supply should relieve the pressure of the rates ".

Dale was deeply impressed as a student at Spring Hill by George Dawson, who had left the Baptists and was minister of the " Church of the Saviour ", built for him by his supporters. Dawson was the prophet of municipal regeneration, but its architect was Joseph Chamberlain, " who began to show proof of those great powers which have since been recognised by the nation. Mr. Chamberlain gave himself to the municipal work with a contagious enthusiasm. He did not merely enter the council, give a large amount of time and strength to its committees, make striking and eloquent speeches on the new municipal policy ; he used his social influence to add to the movement. He appealed in private to men of ability who cared nothing for public life, and he showed how much they might do ; he insisted that what they were able to do it was their duty to do. He dreamt dreams and saw visions of what Birmingham might become, and resolved that he, for his part, would do his utmost to fulfil them ". The *Birmingham Daily Post* supported the reformers, and urged upon its readers the new ideas of the municipal gospel. The new spirit made itself felt in many ways. " For instance, ward meetings were no longer held in

[1] *Life of Dale*, p. 400 ff.

public-houses. The councillors themselves found a new standard of dignity prescribed for them ".

But when Dale had paid his own tributes to Dawson and Chamberlain and others, the fact remains that he himself was the moral force of the movement. In the November elections he went into the wards where the contest was most challenging, addressing two or three meetings a night in support of the forward and welfare policy : " On the platform of the Town Hall the vigour with which he pulled off his overcoat as he rose to speak was a sure sign of what was coming ; and when the meeting was tempestuous, as often happened when both political parties were present in force, he ploughed along through the storm with the steady rush of an Atlantic liner as it shoulders its way through blustering seas. He would fight a campaign in the same persistent spirit until he felt it was done ". These Christian men were resolved to sweep away slums and carry through great municipal reforms for the community at a huge cost. For the most part Dale worked with the Liberal Party in the council, but he never hesitated to oppose them if they were satisfied with what was merely expedient rather than what was just.

It was after Gladstone's defeat in 1874, and as the Liberals were reforming their city, that Joseph Chamberlain was elected to represent Birmingham in Parliament. Better men could have been elected, said a Conservative London paper, but they were passed over because " Mr. R. W. Dale has nominated Mr. Chamberlain and the will of Mr. Dale is the will of Birmingham ". When thanking his constituents, Chamberlain referred to the newspaper's comments : " I have seen a statement that I go to Parliament as the representative of Mr. Dale. Well, if that be so, there is not a member of the House of Commons who will have a better, wiser, or nobler constituency. But you will at least remember this : that if Mr. Dale has any influence over the 50,000 electors of Birmingham, he owes it to his devotion to their highest interests, he owes it to his eloquent and outspoken advocacy of all that is good and great ". It was his power and prestige in Birmingham which tempted Matthew Arnold to escape from encounter by banter. Arnold had written an essay on " St. Paul and Protestantism," and had proved himself vulnerable on both St. Paul and Protestantism. Dale replied with an article in the *Contemporary Review* on " Mr. Matthew Arnold and the Nonconformists ".[1] " As he told us several months ago, he is no enemy of ours, though at times he rebukes us sharply ; what he aims at is our ' perfection '. But if his estimate of us is just, the errors into which we have fallen are so fatal, our faults are so grave, and our separation from the National Church is so serious an obstacle to the free development of our Christian thought and life, that he can hardly render us the service on which he has set his heart, unless he devotes himself to his kindly task a little more seriously ". Arnold was no match for Dale, whom he described in reply as a brilliant pugilist : " He has his arena down at Birmingham, where he does his practice with Mr. Chamberlain, and Mr. Jesse Collings, and the rest of his band ; and then from time to time he comes up to the metropolis, to London, and gives a public exhibition of his skill. And a very powerful exhibition it often is ". But Dale " had humour enough to relish Mr. Arnold's self-confidence as an exponent of the inner secret of the devout life ".

In ten years the municipal programme had transfigured the whole condition, and the very appearance of Birmingham. Noble schools were built, great schemes of educational reform were initiated, libraries were opened, and both the intellectual and the social activities of the community were raised to a loftier level. And if in older civic centres in England municipal progress was slower, Free Churchmen were nevertheless like Dale, applying their principles, and reforming social conditions.

IV.   FREE CHURCHMEN AND TEMPERANCE REFORM

Nonconformists have consistently contended for the extension of political and civil justice ; they have demanded a high moral standard of church membership and so have created a public conscience in relation to grave national evils. But it is curious how slow, and late, they were in measuring the social evils of which Drink was the main cause. Nor did well-known Free Church ministers and politicians initiate the attack on the Drink

[1] Dale, *Essays and Addresses*, p. 236.

Trade. Temperance reform began, as so many other reforms began, by a few consecrated individuals of the rank and file who grew, at length, their own leaders, men of vision and courage. Still, the pioneers of Temperance Reform in this country were Free Churchmen. It is well nigh impossible to imagine the abjectness, degradation and poverty of the masses during the eighteen thirties and forties in Britain. The Drink Trade knew how to exploit the victims of the Industrial Revolution. At the time when Science had done little to ease heavy manual labour in the pits, when hours of work were excessive, when the working population lived in insanitary hovels and the window tax kept their small rooms dull and dark—it was not surprising that they sought the warm, lighted, enticing gin-shops, where children as well as parents could forget their misery by getting " drunk for a penny and dead drunk for tuppence ", according to the advertisements.

The Drink Trade was then unfettered and its victims were legion. It is a sad reflection that the Christian Church should have been so silent and unmoved before this enormous iniquity. The majority of Free Churchmen belonged to the industrial classes ; even so, they never seem to have organised any attack on this shameless wickedness. The truth is that beer drinking was a national habit. Further, the toilers were starved by the Corn Laws, exploited because they were poor, and denied any right of combined action to protect themselves. When Lancashire and the West Riding were the workshop of the world, factory apprentices were working fourteen hours a day, often until they collapsed from exhaustion; half-naked children worked in the pits, pulling coal trucks along in the dark like beasts of burden. Under these conditions no attempts were made to control the brewing or the sale of liquor, the source of indescribable misery and crime. It was a dull world, lacking any competition against the monopoly of the drinking shops ; there were no outdoor national games ; outside their poor homes there were the Churches and the public-house and the majority chose the latter. Under these conditions, the beginnings of the Temperance Movement were as ethically significant as any social reform in the history of England.

It was in September, 1832, that Joseph Livesey and six other men of Preston signed the famous pledge : " We agree to abstain from all liquors of an intoxicating quality, whether ale, porter, wine or ardent spirits, except as medicine ". By this pledge they inaugurated a great social and ethical reform. The pledge has been varied, but the principle remains : it declared total abstinence as the one effective method of removing the evils of drink ; the words " except as medicine " have long been omitted from the pledge owing to the progress of medical science. Livesey was born in 1794 at Walton-le-Dale, near Preston. He was left an orphan and was taught as a child to weave at the loom in his grandfather's cellar. Every copper he saved was spent on pamphlets and books until he became a self-educated man. He left the loom and set up a cheese business and prospered. A kindly and generous nature, he was driven by the poverty and wretchedness of the people about him to political agitation. He was, however, eminently practical ; he saw that denunciation would never destroy the evil which wrecked the lives and homes of the people. Two methods must be adopted ; first, as many people as possible must be persuaded to pledge total abstinence : second, the poor must be educated and their energy directed to positive social improvements ; legislation must also be passed against a Trade which was destructive of manhood and all the nobler qualities of citizenship. Livesey and his wife opened a school in their home for adolescents and adults ; as the numbers increased they rented an empty factory during the evenings and on Sunday. This was an adaptation of the Adult School Movement. Livesey was a pioneer advocate of public parks, libraries, museums, cheap travel and all other counter-attractions to the gin-shop. Some of these he inaugurated in Preston. He opened the first Temperance Hotel in England. When the weavers of Preston were unemployed, and destitute through the cotton famine, Livesey proposed a new road on the bank of the Ribble, thus finding relief and work for forty thousand people ; when fever was raging in the slums he distributed free lime-wash, free soap, new clean chaff to all who would cleanse their homes and burn their infested straw mattresses. When the Preston bank stopped payment, Livesey was so trusted, he was elected as chairman and put its finances on a sound basis, preventing the ruin of small traders and the loss of the savings of the thrifty. For over fifty years Livesey waged unceasing warfare as a Temperance Reformer. He wrote and spoke in a robust, incisive style, and issued his articles and speeches from his own printing press. No personal or social aspect of the Temperance question escaped his attention. When he died in 1884 the statistics of Temperance organisations in the country were estimated at seven million abstainers. The seven men of Preston deserve the gratitude of all who care for the decencies of citizenship.

Another reformer was Jabez Tunnicliff, whose successful Temperance work among children led to the founding of the Band of Hope organisation. In 1847 the first Band of Hope Festival was held at South Parade Baptist Church, Leeds. Tea was given to four hundred children, mostly poor and without any schooling—as children were in the early days of the Band of Hope meetings throughout the country—but they were taught habits of cleanliness and self-control, were entertained and taught the facts of the destructive work of alcohol on the mind and body of youth. I know the value of such work among children, for my parents for upwards of fifty years were responsible for the Band of Hope meeting in the church where my youth was spent. In the weekly meetings, over so long a period, thousands of children up to thirteen years of age were taught the virtues of truth, honesty, self-control, and were fortified with facts of the devastating effects of drink on personal character and the home life of the nation.

Later in the nineteenth century, Dr. Dawson Burns, minister of Church Street Chapel, Edgware Road, was a national leader in the Temperance Movement. In 1883 he preached the forty-third annual Temperance sermon in his church. I am unable to record on how many annual occasions he preached on the subject, but from 1883–1895—the only discourses I know—his annual sermons on Temperance were masterpieces of sound Christian teaching on social and national ethics. These sermons are still readable and relevant. His literary style is never spoiled by fierce outbursts of denunciation : he presents a clear statement of facts and is as persuasive as clear. He appeals for personal abstinence from drink on the ground of loyalty to Christ, also because of the high value he set upon the quality and use of Christian influence. In 1883 the brewers began to agitate for legislation which would cheapen the sale and consumption of beer by a new system of multiplying ale-houses. Burns countered such a policy by demanding legislation which would give England Sunday closing, and local option by the inhabitants against the establishment of beer-houses anywhere and everywhere.

"We must have *legislation*. This is absolutely required, and of a kind altogether different from that which has hitherto prevailed. Nothing could have been more unfortunate than that the commencement of the temperance movement was attended by an attempt to cheapen the sale and consumption of beer by legalising a new system of free ale-houses. That one act of legislation has done more injury to the morals of the people of this country than any other that could well be named. In the years 1860 and 1861 other Acts were passed, attended with similarly, if not equally, disastrous results, affecting other classes. And, observe, that the amount of harm thus done continues. When you and I are sleeping, when you and I are doing nothing, or can do nothing for temperance, bad legislation will go on, and is always going on, to tempt, and to deprave, and to destroy the people. Now, I do think every person who has studied this question has come to a pretty strong conclusion that this sort of thing must be stopped; that this legislation must not only not go on, but be reversed entirely. This past legislation has been pernicious in the highest degree, because it was of the wrong kind, and we want legislation of another order, that other results may accrue. We claim that Englishmen may have a sober Sunday. The very least boon one would think the people could ask of a Christian Government is the power of intervening for their own protection, and that no district should be cursed by drink shops if the people want to be free from that curse. That is something at once so simple and so necessary that one need not utter many words about it. I have not, I am sure, to convince you that it is resquisite to be done—all I say is, do something towards bringing it about. . . . The present Government has no doubt been very much harassed since it came into office. It has a number of measures to bring forward, and is, no doubt, puzzled which to introduce first; but let us remember that there is no measure equal in importance to ours. There can be none. All the others are, probably, very good; but in regard to their effect upon the social condition of the people and the homes of England, they cannot compare for a moment with that great work of temperance reform which will follow wise legislation on this subject. . . . Therefore, we must do our best to influence members of Parliament. Do you know one ? Write to him. Tell him the country is looking out for legislation—especially that legislation which will give the people power to save themselves ".

In 1885, Burns describes the social evils of the time : " People sometimes tell us that former times were worse than our own. If so, they were very bad indeed, and that is poor consolation for ourselves. Besides, we must remember, when we compare past with present times, that the past times had not the advantages of these times. They had no teaching, they had no light such as we have—no great efforts for improvement such as we have now, and, therefore, bad as they were, even if they were worse than ours, our responsibility and our condemnation may be greater than theirs. At any rate, it is certain that strong drink is still the cause among us of evils of the very first magnitude. Still, strong drink taints and blights the physical, moral, and mental life of countless multitudes ; still darkens, impoverishes, and degrades the home-life of hundreds of thousands of families among us ; still penetrates the whole fabric of society, disturbing and disorganising wherever it proceeds, and whatever it touches; still wastes the food and the wealth of great kingdoms, not in satisfying any real necessity, but in creating a ravenous appetite and a raging vice ; still acts, producing greater devastations than volcanoes ever flaming, and pestilence for ever smiting ; acts as the prime minister of hell in opposing all influences of the Church, the school, and all evangelising and humanising institutions ; still bars to a large extent the advance of the nation to that degree of civilisation and morality to which all other influences tend to conduct it, and to which but for this malignant power it might have attained. Therefore, it is true, sadly true, that whatever else has been done, we still have to deplore that our own times are times of much evil from that cause which has been the cause of countless evils in the days that are gone. At the same time it is not well always, or chiefly, to dwell upon that which is deplorable. We have to take another view, and we have to say, with very much thankfulness ; that investigation, agitation and reformation results inspire hope for the future." Burns appeals for individual action, for the organisation of Leagues, Societies and Orders, with the objective of combined action in and on local areas.

In 1886, Burns arraigns the British Government for its home and colonial policy towards the Drink Trade. "Remember", he said, "this evil is national. It is no local evil. It is not something done in Cornwall and not done in Middlesex or in Cumberland. It is to be found in every part of the three countries constituting the United Kingdom. Not only so but it is an evil that has become chronic amongst us. It is not one whose commencement any of us can remember. It was here before we were born—before anybody we can remember was born. We go back age by age, century by century; we go through all the successions of dynasties away up beyond the Norman conquest; and so it is still. The drink evil has been among us for a thousand years performing its terrible work—a work of misleading, a work of undoing, a work destructive of human nature and dishonouring to God who has made that nature. Nor is this all, for, owing to the commercial and colonial enterprise of our country, we have not only suffered the evil to be amongst ourselves; we have not only gone on perpetuating it amongst ourselves, but we have conveyed it to those who, but for us, might have been happily ignorant of it—who were ignorant of it, some of them, before we introduced it among them. Is it not a very terrible reflection that there is hardly a native race in the world that has not an accusation to make against us in this particular—an accusation before high heaven as well as before man? The natives of the South Sea Islands, the natives of Australia, the Maories of New Zealand, the natives of India— millions of them—the Red Indians of North America, and the various tribes of Africa, have all cause to cry out against us, and do cry out against us, that we have introduced amongst them, in the most virulent form, the greatest evil by which they can be degraded and most rapidly destroyed. Then we build our houses of prayer, we circulate our Scriptures, and we call ourselves a civilised and a Christian nation. Perhaps the most shocking illustration of this iniquity is the most recent. Not later than October last a proclamation was issued by the authorities of Cape Colony, one of them being the Governor appointed by our own Queen, introducing free trade in spirits into the Transkeian district—a large district occupied by natives, and hitherto happily free from the drink evil. Those natives, as soon as they heard of the proclamation, assembled and denounced it as an outrage upon themselves, as simply a means of temptation and ruin to them to be put in their way by the British Government. The Gaikas, who inhabit that region, and who had been broken up once before through their drinking habits, look upon it as nothing else than a resolution to destroy them. They publicly declare that in their opinion it is a device of the English government to cause them to be the means of their own extirpation. Can anything be more revolting ? Can anything be more disgraceful to us as a people. Barbarians cry out against us and denounce us, and men to whom we offer the Word of Life throw it back, in our face, and say, ' Cease to tempt us—cease to destroy us '. And does not God observe it ? Is not God looking down from heaven to see it all ? And what does He think of it ? How does He regard our doings concerning the drink evil whether among ourselves, or in regard to outside populations ? Is God indifferent ? Does He not behold ? and beholding, does not He pass judgment against us ? Does not God say to us as to ancient Judah, ' your hands are full of blood '. ' Put away the evil of your doings from before mine eyes '. "

These Temperance Reformers were by no means supported by the churches as a whole. They encountered antagonism from the Anglican Church : and only by faith and patience did they find it possible to work with the Free Churches during the middle decades of the nineteenth century. They were mostly a small minority within the Free Churches.

In 1838, the Primitive Methodists in Hull decided to invite the Rev. John Stamp to become their minister and in the letter of invitation they stated that they required his promise not to allow the use of any chapel for total abstinence meetings, not to announce them from the pulpit and not to attend them himself, but to discontinue all connection with them. His answer was characteristic of a staunch teetotaler and gave great offence to some of the influential members of the Church. They reported him to the Primitive Methodist Conference and succeeded in getting him expelled by that body in 1841 without a hearing. John Stamp has been named the " first temperance martyr "—he was not the last![1]

---

[1] Clifford Carter, *Temperance and the Churches*; published by United Kingdom Alliance.

Livesey writes of the bitter hostility of ministers of the Gospel who denounced " the curse of total abstinence ". But the Reformers won their battles in the churches. " The first sign of a general awakening ", says Clifford Carter, was about 1880, although it should be mentioned that the Society of Friends started their Temperance Union in 1852 and that the " Rules of the people called Methodists, issued in 1743, prohibited drunkenness and spirit drinking ". Every denomination now has its Temperance organisation and is committed to the work of Temperance Reform. The Salvation Army demands total abstinence as a condition of membership. The Assembly of the Baptist Union of Great Britain and Ireland at its meeting in 1937 carried the following Resolution :

" That this Assembly urges upon all Church Officers and Members the personal duty of total abstinence ".

The Temperance Council of the Christian Churches of England and Wales, and the United Kingdom Alliance are powerful organisations which aim at influencing public opinion and legislation as no single denomination can do, though the work of the former is handicapped by the inclusion in its membership of organisations which do not advocate total abstinence.

Nevertheless there is a marked decline in the zeal for total abstinence amongst Church members. Far too often the influence of social custom invades Free Church life. Drink is provided at weddings and on other special and social occasions.

From his excellent survey of Temperance work in the Churches, published in 1937, Clifford Carter draws the following conclusions :

1. The leaders of every denomination are fully alive to the need for aggressive temperance work.
2. The organisation for effective propaganda is in a high state of efficiency.
3. Probably in most denominations the majority of Church members are total abstainers.
4. In many individual Churches, temperance sentiment is dormant and a great many members fail in their personal duty of propagating temperance principles.

5. There is an urgent necessity for (*a*) the appointment of a really active temperance secretary in every Church in every denomination, and (*b*) a new national campaign, with some definite object in view, which would call for the active co-operation of every Christian total abstainer.

An appraisement of the situation in 1948 is by no means so re-assuring; there has been a marked regression in the War years.

CHAPTER XXI

THE FREE CHURCH FEDERAL COUNCIL

THE achievement of religious and political freedom was resisted and long delayed by reason of the lack of Free Church unity and organisation. Nonconformist workmen could unite to defy the Combination Acts and organise themselves into trade unions ; but Nonconformist churches seemed unable and unwilling to unite their forces for spiritual, political and social ends. John Bright's oratory could thrill mass meetings and quicken the conscience of the multitudes, but to the end he was a great individualist ; the routine of Cabinet business and administration wearied him. If, after the repeal of the Corn Laws, he had created a political organisation during the middle decades of the nineteenth century, Free Churchmen would gladly have hailed him as their political leader and hero. The absence of Nonconformist unity and the betrayal of liberal ideas by Liberal majorities in Parliament arrested political and social progress.

It was in 1896 that Free Church leaders became convinced that unity and organisation were imperative ; and in the same year the National Free Church Council was constituted. Officially, the Free Church denominations had no relation to the Council. Individual leaders were Charles Berry, Hugh Price Hughes, John Clifford, Munro Gibson and many others, who understood that the evangelical faith and experience were the dynamic of Christian ethical progress. During the 1890's Free Churchmen were growing alarmed at the boldness of Anglo-Catholic propaganda and practice ; at the plans of Anglican leaders to over-throw the School-board system ; at Tory Imperialism which by 1899 had led the nation into the South African War. As these religious and political forces threatened the ideals and convictions of Free Churchmen they began to organise themselves for action. Local Free Church Councils were formed throughout the country and were affiliated with the National Council. By the end of the nineteenth century the Council had become a vigorous and potent force in the religious and political life of the nation. Its annual meetings gave Free Churchmen the opportunity of hearing their own eminent preachers and speakers. Among the younger men, J. H. Jowett, Campbell Morgan, Sylvester Horne, Arthur Guttery became national figures. Free Churchmen in Parliament were members of the National Council; Lloyd George was riding the storm, Arthur Henderson, Sir George White of Norwich, and others were exponents of Free Church principles in the House of Commons and in the country. The National Council contributed to the downfall of Balfour's Government and the Liberal revival of 1906. The South African War and the Education Act of 1902 were two decisive issues at the General Election. After 1906 the National Council inclined to rely on Parliamentary action rather than its own spiritual resources. This was the criticism of the Council in the volume of 1909 *Nonconformity and Politics* by a Nonconformist Minister. As in the past, the hopes of educational reform were frustrated when the House of Lords and the Bishops threw out Mr. Birrell's Bill; other progressive social measures were, however, placed on the Statute Book, making memorable the period from 1906 to 1914 as the advent of a new era in the moralisation of British political achievement.

It was during the war of 1914–18 that Dr. J. H. Shakespeare, the greatest ecclesiastical Free Church Statesman at that time, began to urge the necessity of closer co-operation between the official Free Church denominations. The National Council had worked independently of the official denominational machinery; it was a platform, not an official and consultative organisation speaking in the name of the Free Church denominations. Shakespeare thought many religious objectives could be reached as official representatives of the Free Churches conferred together, framed a united policy, and co-operated with Anglican and Parliamentary leaders. His aim was progress by negotiation rather than by public assemblies. " Parliament " he said to me on one occasion, " will grant every opportunity for religious work if Free Churchmen and Anglicans are united ". Pursuing this policy, in 1919, through Shakespeare's initiative, the Free Church Federal Council came into existence—an organisation constituted only of representatives officially appointed by the

Free Church denominations. This Council met annually in September, listened to important addresses, discussed at length and produced valuable documents on theological and ecclesiastical subjects, passed important resolutions, but as all such resolutions were referred to the separate denominations before any action could be taken, it often happened that business was delayed, and sometimes outdated a year later. Even so, the denominations were jealous of their autonomy and most reluctant to depute authority to the Federal Council. The annual meetings were constructive; they provided opportunities of fellowship and friendship between Free Church officials and representatives. The Federal Council did more than is widely known to change the relations of Anglicans and Free Churchmen; Carnegie Simpson's leadership of Free Church discussions and negotiations with Anglican leaders changed the religious atmosphere of the time and deserves honourable recognition. In retrospect it appears unfortunate that when Shakespeare was creating the Federal Council his book was published on *The Churches at the Cross Roads*, a book in which he urged the necessity of Free Church union, and further union with the Church of England, affirming his view that such union, " apart from episcopacy, was an idle dream ". The book stimulated controversy until Free Church unity was imperilled, nor was any union between the Anglican and the Free Churches brought nearer.

From 1919 there were now two Free Church organisations. They both served useful ends, one elected officially by the denominations, the other elected by the votes of the local councils and Assembly. But the existence of these two Councils confused Anglicans, the general public, and the Government. A question frequently asked was—which Council represents the Free Churches and can speak authoritatively in their name ? Did the President of the National Council, or the Moderator of the Federal Council, represent the Free Churches on national occasions? It was owing to these confusions that in 1939 the present writer moved that representatives should be appointed to explore the possibility of uniting the National and Federal Free Church Councils, thus creating one authoritative Free Church organisation which could speak for the Free Churches, having authority to conduct conversations with Anglican leaders on matters touching the religious life of the nation, also to represent the Free Churches in dealings with the Government, and to ensure publicity through the Press on Free Church life and work. The result of the deliberations was the present Free Church Federal Council, which held its first Annual Congress in 1941, the Rev. Walter H. Armstrong being its first Moderator.

The Constitution of the present Federal Council safeguards each federating denomination's " autonomy as regards faith and practice ". No decision can be enforced by the Council which subverts denominational " faith and practice ". Does this mean that the present Constitution of the Federal Council is the final word on Free Church unity ? Is federation the limit of denominational relationships ? Or is federation the practical step to one United Free Church of England and Wales ? The issue was raised at the first meeting of the Council in 1941. The work of uniting the two Free Church organisations was appreciated, but several speakers affirmed that Federation was a step to Free Church Union, and that union with the Anglicans was the final goal. To seek the closer co-operation of the Free Churches, a Commission was appointed in 1943 ; but it was clear that the denominations would not sacrifice their " autonomy as regards faith and practice ". The proposals of the Commission received careful consideration, but while confirming the desire for the closest co-operation, it was obvious that a United Free Church was beyond present achievement. The most promising procedure was to seek union between different denominations within the Federation. For several years the Baptists had a Commission considering the possibility of union with Congregationalists and Presbyterians ; and at the Baptist Union Assembly in 1937 the Commission reported :

" We are all agreed that, if this question of union with Congregationalists and Presbyterians were forced to an issue in England now, it would split our denomination. We are agreed that the majority of our people would probably decline to have anything to do with it and, if a scheme of union were attempted, would not come into it, but would retain a separate existence apart from it. We recognise that we ought honestly to face the question whether organic union with other Christian Churches is or is not desirable or necessary, but at the same time we are bound to have regard to the certainty of creating thereby a division amongst our own people, just as the Anglican representatives at the Lambeth Conference in 1923 (see *Documents on Christian Unity, 1920–4*", page 160) felt bound to insist on episcopal ordination for this (amongst other) reasons that, if they did not, there was a danger (to quote their own words) of creating pain and disturbance, or even possibility of schism, within our own communion ".

After the Report of the Federal Council on closer co-operation in 1944, conversations began between Congregationalists and Presbyterians with a view to union of the two churches in England. The debate in the Congregational Union Assembly in 1948 revealed acute differences on the proposals submitted, and the official communication to the Press was :

" That the Churches be informed that there is a difference of opinion in the Council as to the possibility and desirability of organic union, and that some Council members look to a policy of co-operation rather than to organic union ". " The truth is ", said the *Christian World*, " that, as soon as the talks began, both Presbyterians and Congregationalists seem to have had a reawakening as to the value of the ' specific witness ' to which each of the two Churches is committed. Each party perceived virtues in its own Order which perhaps, before the talks started, it had tended to undervalue. This may be, possibly, a sign of spiritual and intellectual vitality. It is perhaps well that men should not lightly surrender any part of a heritage consecrated by generations of conviction and devoted service. Yet the need for visible Christian unity remains as urgent as ever, and there yet remains the problem of forwarding visible Christian unity without, at the same time, surrendering all that is truly in the ' specific witness ' of a denomination ".

The Commissions which have examined every avenue towards One United Free Church, or towards union between two or three federating denominations, have been unable to arrive at organic union. The failure of such efforts does not reduce the value of Federation, but rather emphasises that it is at present the most practicable solution of Free Church Co-operation. It provides the best workable instrument of Free Church life and witness. Moreover, there is deeper evangelical and spiritual unity between the Federated Free Churches than between the groups within the Church of England. The time has passed when we were competing sects : to-day we co-operate and " keep the unity of the spirit in the bond of peace ". And as we pursue the objective ends for which the Church of Christ exists, it may be that barriers will break and a new Church arise, more worthy of our Lord and Saviour Jesus Christ.

INDEX

INDEX

INDEX